A Survey of
DAR ES SALAAM

J. A. K. LESLIE

Published on behalf of
East African Institute of Social Research
by
OXFORD UNIVERSITY PRESS
LONDON   NEW YORK   NAIROBI
1963

Oxford University Press, Amen House, London E.C.4

GLASGOW NEW YORK TORONTO MELBOURNE WELLINGTON
BOMBAY CALCUTTA MADRAS KARACHI LAHORE DACCA
CAPE TOWN SALISBURY NAIROBI IBADAN ACCRA
KUALA LUMPUR HONG KONG

*Printed in Great Britain
by Western Printing Services Ltd
Bristol*

AUTHOR'S NOTE

I have not included a list of acknowledgements: no survey of this sort can be made without the time and aid of many busy and well-informed people. Professor A. W. Southall of the East African Institute of Social Research and the Statistical Branch in Dar es Salaam gave me invaluable technical advice; many others have been most helpful, not least the very many Africans-in-the-street who put up so cheerfully with so many questions.

Much of the survey, written in 1957, has been overtaken by events. It describes a Dar es Salaam which has since changed in many respects and a situation which has become radically altered since the achievement of independence.

CONTENTS

LIST OF ILLUSTRATIONS

We are grateful to the Information Department of the
Tanganyika Government for permission to use the photographs
reproduced in this book.

SUMMARY OF TEXT

OBJECTS

The objects of this survey were various: for the Dar es
Salaam administration it was hoped to provide some factual
details not so far available; for those responsible for policy
to give a less diagrammatic picture of life in town; for other
readers, some basis for comparison elsewhere.

It is incomplete both in the areas of town surveyed (the
mainly African areas) and in the aspects of life selected for
study: even in its chosen field it makes no claim to scientific
standards of accuracy or completeness.

METHODS

The methods used were based, for statistical purposes, on a
systematic random sample of 5 per cent. taken in August 1956:
all figures, therefore, relate to this date. Interviews, discussions
and competitions over the whole period of the survey (February
1956 to mid-December 1957, with gaps) served to check and
supplement this material.

HISTORY

Dar es Salaam did not exist as a town until founded by
Seiyid Majid, a Sultan of Zanzibar; the first urban inhabitants
were slaves and soldiers: thereafter, and particularly in German
times, it gained what its more ancient neighbour Bagamoyo
lost, the influx of population from all the traditional routes to the
coast. It gained immensely in size and population after the last
war and nearly doubled in African population between 1948
and 1957. As a result the African inhabitants are to a large
extent separate in newly laid-out suburbs designed especially
for them. The rate of increase has fallen sharply in more
recent years.

WHY AFRICANS COME TO DAR ES SALAAM

Despite the rigours of town life more Africans continue to
pour in and to stay longer than, economically, they should:
they are drawn by the success stories (not necessarily always
true) of those who have gone before; the sight of goods brought

B

home by those who have done well; and their polish; a dis-
belief in such stories as they hear of unemployment, and a
converse belief in stories of available jobs; a mistaken confidence
in an inadequate education; the discontent with country life of
the boy who has been to school; a dislike of irksome duties and
discipline at home and in the village and tribal society; the
search for an uncontributing anonymity in town; and by the
glamour of the town's reputation; all come basically because
it is in the town that they can get on to a cash basis of living:
thinking of what money can buy, and disregarding the necessity
of paying for everything one gets.

PROBLEMS: LONELINESS

The problems of life in town are part active tensions and
strains, part the absence of something that should be there.
Among the former may be classed the uprooting of a man from
the communal life of the country and his setting adrift as an
individual; this is discussed under the title of 'loneliness'. To what
extent is he in fact cut adrift?

GROUP OF TRIBES

He is still a member of various groupings: a group of related
tribes, those of his route to town and those which have with his
an *utani* relationship; and while this does not give the protection
or satisfaction which it used to do, it relieves to some small
extent the feeling of being among aliens.

TRIBE

There is his tribe, more important to those whose tribal
groups in Dar es Salaam are small and compact and less to the
big tribal communities which have by reason of their size lost
their cohesion. The influence of tribal elders and tribal
associations is waning and is not now important to the younger
generation.

AREA GROUP

Of groups who come from a single area or village, some
retain a marked fellow-feeling, based usually on actual kinship.
These groups have more cohesion than most tribes, but can
have only if the area they come from is compact.

KIN, EXTENDED FAMILY

The basic unit in town is the kinship group of cousins, uncles and nephews; it is on relatives of this degree of nearness that a stranger to town depends until he can fend for himself. Very few come to Dar es Salaam without a relative to go to, and most, particularly of the more numerous communities, have a positive web of kinship ties criss-crossing the town.

STRICT FAMILY

Even to those who bring wives to town the extended family remains often more important; it is considerably more important than the 'free marriages' which make up the bulk of marital arrangements.

SUBURB

The built-up, town-planned suburbs have hardly any cohesion at all; what little cohesion there is, is to be found in the more 'rural' areas within the town, and also in the old villages and even in the remains of the shanty slums. Here village communities have been able to evolve in such a way, based on priority of settlement, that the community has a certain 'structure', an order in society, into which the new-comer can fit himself in the appropriate place.

HOUSE

The Swahili house, sheltering on the average some twelve souls in six or more rooms, does not form a social unit; it does combine both richer and poorer on the same plot, so that there is less of a West End and East End than there would otherwise be. The bungalows, flats and terraces built by the Government for renting form even less of a social unit, and each block of 'Quarters' is as disparate a collection of individual households as is a commuters' suburb in a Western city. Again it is in the rural and village areas, where most houses shelter a single family, with relations, that the house is a place where friendships and alliances are formed.

OTHER GROUPS

Most people find their reliable support in the extended family, and their friends at their work and in 'gambling' schools, football clubs, or jazz bands according to taste. Mosques do not form a cohesive 'congregation'.

FRUSTRATION

The second of the strains to which an African in town is subjected is that of frustration: his aim in coming to town has been to get cash; yet he finds that he is poor (whereas in the country, with far less money, he was not): yet being poor he is surrounded by tempting things which can be had only for money; all the glamour which helped draw him to town— dances, women, drink, clothes, cinemas, taxis, require money before he can enjoy them; they are so near yet out of his reach.

Then he is poor, but surrounded by the apparently rich; there is always somebody to be seen enjoying the things he cannot get. Even when he is most flush there is always somebody going one better.

To get cash he needs work, yet the Government, whose duty he believes it is to provide work for all, does not give him work: sometimes he feels it actively wants him out of it. The necessity of 'buying' jobs (by a bribe to the foreman, etc.) is an additional irritant.

HUNGER

Most Africans believe that they go hungry at least some time in the month, and a great many in fact do. This is due (given the present ratio of pay to opportunities of spending it) to the inexperience of most Africans of the management of money. Details of expenditure on food were not studied since the report of the East African Statistical Department's domestic budget survey was expected very shortly. One solid meal in the evening is customary and general, regardless of income, with a smaller snack at midday.

Closely related to the problem of spreading income over the period between paydays, preferences as to the number of paydays a month were studied, from which it appeared that most people were being paid the way they liked, but that there was a bias in favour of fortnightly pay, which is interpreted as a monthly rate with the right to an advance at mid-month sufficient for necessaries, leaving as much as possible for capital expenditure at the end of the month.

NO JOB

Employment and unemployment are both in Dar es Salaam relative terms: for a substantial proportion of those who work do not do so for all the working days of the month; while a substantial number of those who seem to be unemployed do odd jobs of porterage, or have small trades; many combine a few days of paid work with an equal or greater number of days of small trade or rest. It was not found possible to measure the extent of these variations. The ease with which a man can live in Dar es Salaam without working a full month has diluted labour to a significant extent; this ease is due partly to the income derivable from small trade and partly to the willingness of any man to support a relative when he has no income, sometimes for several months. When the number of jobs falls, therefore, it does not follow, at least for a period, that the surplus labour leaves town. A crude figure of those who said they had a job (including small trade) during July 1956, gave an overall figure of 19 per cent. of men aged between 16 and 45 as being without work. There was a concentration of such people in the areas of low rent such as Buguruni, and in Kinondoni and Msasani. There was no evidence that 'unemployed' used subsistence cultivation to keep going. The effect of the minimum wage in raising wages in the lower levels, particularly among the employees of Asians and Africans, is so far small, though there is evidence of a reduction in staffs to avoid a higher wage-bill—two-thirds of the sample of those who had been getting less than the minimum wage, mainly domestic servants to Asians and Africans, and some unskilled labourers, had disappeared by the time the check was made.

Wage-rates are enhanced by substantial amounts earned by overtime and by secondary employment, as well as by net borrowing. Figures confirming this are available from the East African Statistical Department's domestic budget survey.

NO PROSPECTS

Most of the population has little prospect of advancement to a better-paid job, because most of the population is entirely uneducated. Those educated to such a standard that the progressive firms are picking them out with a view to managerial jobs in the future are very few; those educated, but below that standard, are able to get good steady jobs with normal prospects, but they too are a tiny proportion of the population. Those with Standard 8[1] or below are lucky if they land more than an artisan or 'office boy' job, where very many are not on an incremental scale and wages move upwards only in time of scarcity; the only class which has noticeably improved its position is that of the dockers, who through a strong trade union, and favourable tactical position, have attained to more than twice the normal unskilled wage: a study of the mode of life of the docker compared with the unskilled shows that this difference in wage has not resulted in a higher standard in the necessities of life.

Constant changes of job make advancement through training unlikely. A habit of the coastal peoples of paying a more or less annual visit home is partly responsible for these recurring changes of job.

So long as there is an abundance of low-quality labour at low rates of pay, the labourer has no incentive to improve output, nor the employer to improve the quality of his staff. The introduction of the minimum wage at least made a start on breaking this vicious circle.

Shopkeeping in Dar es Salaam is almost impossible for the African with relations, for a businesslike hard-heartedness has still to be learned, and understood. But many of the small trades, in which Africans are dominant, are lucrative enough to have enabled some to climb right out of the rut.

DEBT

The domestic budget survey of the East African Statistical Department shows a significant proportion of income in the wage-groups studied to be from net borrowing, which appears never to be repaid. There must presumably be groups, among the higher paid, of net lenders. There is also a substantial amount of debt at any time outstanding to employers and to landlords; credit from shops is mostly only on a monthly basis, and then only to steady customers. Capital windfalls are often deposited with shopkeepers and gradually consumed. Conversely many houses are improved with Arab capital on the

[1] Each standard represents one year of schooling.

security of the rent, and some have eventually passed into the Arab tenant's hands. Pawning is widespread but of smaller importance than net borrowing. Using data from pawnshops a violent monthly cycle of debt and repayment is shown; this is confirmed by the takings of dance halls and bars, and of the buses, which all show the same cycle of high consumption at payday followed by little or none. Unlike borrowing between Africans, much of which is never repaid, pledges pawned are nearly all redeemed.

The agricultural seasons are important even in town, and indebtedness is relieved for many by a capital sum accruing from the rice harvest in June/July, mainly from fields in their home districts.

OVERCROWDING

There was grave shortage of accommodation in the period of expansion after the war. This has been relieved to a certain extent by the building by the Government of single-family housing in bungalows, terraces and semi-detached villas, at rents which are economic except for the writing-off of the cost of the land, a main access road and water kiosks; these rents are well below market rates; and to a much greater extent by the provision of building plots whereon Africans can build their own houses, which are invariably built to the big 'Swahili' pattern.

Accommodation for the now slowing annual increase of population should in the future be provided by the Swahili house; by allowing economic laws to operate it avoids the friction inseparable from 'controlled' housing; its owners form a large stable class with roots in the town; it is infinitely flexible in design and has been adapted to every taste and pocket. Provided that conditions of grave shortage, leading to the building of shanties, are avoided, the historical tendency of uncontrolled building in Dar es Salaam has been to improve, not to deteriorate into slums.

The end of the shortage and the probable consequent lowering of rents will come at a time when there are too many large houses built for renting, and not enough for single-family occupation; there is little sign yet of the use of more than one room per family, except by the most highly paid who are being enabled by Government loans to build permanent-material houses.

The cost of building a typical Swahili house is roughly three times what it was in 1939. Rents, therefore, now bear in the case of the older houses no relation to historical cost. They are high even by the criterion of replacement cost. They are also high in relation to the income of the tenants: a fifth appear to be paying more than a quarter of their monthly basic wage-rate in rent. The rent of 11 Shs. to 15 Shs. per month is the most common, not only in the lower wage-groups, but in every wage-group including the highest, displaying the low priority which accommodation takes in most people's list of desirables.

The capital for the large private building programme which has been going on comes partly from compensation resulting from slum clearance; and partly from the savings of clerks and small traders, helped by the proceeds of cultivation; no less than a third of new builders at Magomeni[1] also owned another house already, so that some of the building is a ploughing back of profits into the business. Building by women is a significant proportion, many being enabled to build by compensation for old houses pulled down, and others by the profits of small trades.

The density of occupation of rented and other rooms is very generally about two souls a room throughout the town; in Kariakoo at least the density has decreased over the past five years. Asians[2] were more crowded than Africans.

The type of person who wants a plot to build a Swahili house, and the type who wants to rent a Quarter, are studied: it is particularly the Christian and the educated who prefer the latter; they show that there is a general demand for a two-room flat provided it is still as cheap as the present single room in a Swahili house.

There are long waiting lists for both Quarters and plots to build Swahili houses: but both contain a large number of 'dead men'. The demand for Quarters is inflated by their being rented at well below the market rate.

---

[1] Magomeni is the first suburb to have been re-surveyed, in 1959, as part of the continuing survey of Dar es Salaam. Comparative figures are given in Appendix C.

[2] The term Asian as used in East Africa refers mainly to Indians and Pakistanis. Other Asiatics are referred to specifically.

Some more Quarters are required for the tiny minority who rate good building standards and privacy high in their list of priorities; for the great majority the building of Quarters cannot solve the housing question; for them what is required is sufficient building plots to ensure that there is room for all and that, therefore, rents fall to a more normal level. The best reason for concentrating on the provision of building plots is the desirability of having as many Africans as possible owning houses in the town.

LACK OF COMMUNICATIONS

As the administration of Dar es Salaam has been authoritatively studied recently in the Molohan[1] report this survey touches only on a few points of interest in this respect.

The basic difficulty is that the more urban a capital town in East Africa becomes, the more it must be overweighed by the almost entirely un-African interests of large trade, business, and in this case the port.

Since the evolution of the Municipality a gap has opened in administration between the power to accept or reject proposals, and the African public which has proposals to make; this gap has not yet been successfully bridged, and the District Commissioner is uncomfortably straddled endeavouring to do so.

The recent strengthening of the Administration was necessary: it is not a common enough sight to see officers of Government in the back areas; the placing of officers resident in each suburb is particularly important, since only after office hours can most citizens be met.

A link is required between Ward Councils and the Municipal Council; no reason is seen why the African members of Municipal Council should not be indirectly elected[2] through the Ward Councils and if necessary the Liwali's Council.

The difficulty of the lack of Native Authority powers (but not of a Native Authority) is mentioned.

The Ward Councils have not yet caught on, mainly because they have had no money to dispose of, and nothing appears to them to come of the views they put forward. There are signs

[1] *Detribalisation* by M. J. B. Molohan, C.M.G., M.B.E., Government Printer, Dar es Salaam, 1957.

[2] This and numerous other suggestions, made when this survey was written in 1957, have since been overtaken by events.

in places, however, of factions competing for election, showing
a real interest.

The authority of elders in general is declining, and in
particular that of the 'headman-class' and the tribal elders.
In the rural and village parts they still hold very considerable
authority, but in the town-planned areas this is on the wane.
Though conservative they reflect accurately changing opinions
of the populace.

News is transferred in Dar es Salaam slowly: mainly by the
mutual visiting of relatives, but also through clubs, tea-shops
and hotels. Radio is mainly in the hands of Arabs and reaches
only a minority. Newspapers, though read avidly, however dull,
also reach only the literate minority. The Government papers
and the radio are much distrusted, and the anti-Government
papers conversely sought after. There is a great need for Dar
es Salaam parochial news, simple, direct and undiluted by the
need to reach a territorial audience: there is scope for a Dar es
Salaam Public Relations Officer. Interest in world news is
confined to the spectacular.

IDLE HANDS

There is a large, but so far unmeasured, degree of under-
employment; any petty incident quickly gathers a crowd. It is
so easy to live in town without a regular job, or even without
a job at all—with the help of relatives—that many stay on
longer than they should, and fall into the temptation to pilfer
or get into similar forms of trouble. Cases coming before the
Resident Magistrates' and Local Courts and thus through the
Probation Service are studied, a comparison being made
between the merely foolish (those who had drifted into petty
crime but were considered good probation risks) and the bad
(recidivists and others not considered fair probation risks);
the differences in the circumstances of the two groups were
small. In both the proportion of Muslims was rather higher
than usual; Dar es Salaam produced less than its fair share,
while Kiserawe, Rufiji and Morogoro produced more; short
residents, single men, and those whose parents were away all
produced more than their fair share. There was no concentration of them in any one area, though a fair number had
their own, rural, huts. Fewer than normal paid rent, and a

large number were housed free by relatives. No reliable comparison could be made about duration of job, but long service seemed to be no guarantee of good conduct, nor did the high pay of dockers: in general, as one might expect, most of those who fell to temptation were those most exposed to it—dockers, porters, watchmen, drivers, turnboys[1] and houseboys. But the unemployed also had their fair share and more.

RELIGION

A man's ethics being founded partly on religion, partly on his upbringing, and partly on fear of the law, the state of religion in the town is discussed: the vast majority of the population are Muslims, but many of these are really pagans in Muslim clothes (for only a very small minority are prepared to admit to being pagan in town); in any case the observances of Islam are strikingly absent here; this is not confined to town, but is true, to a large extent, of the whole coast, though in town the rules of religion, like all rules, are more than usually evaded. Most take only to the social aspects of Islam, cleaving still to the ancestral religion of their tribal areas. Many can observe the ancestral religious rites at home, making journeys or sending remittances from town: such rites, for e.g. sickness, are a significant item of expenditure. Some have adopted Zaramo[2] spirits for medicinal purposes. There is a lot of tolerated 'Islamic' magic, in the form of divinations, charms and talismans. Muslim and pagan are inextricably mixed in town, but some at least of the Christians like to keep apart: particularly those who have retained touch with their Missions (a supervision which Muslims do not have—and this is another of the attractions of Islam). Some tribes, particularly the coastal, are almost exclusively Muslim, and only a few of the minor tribes are predominantly Christian.

The attraction of Islam in Dar es Salaam is that it is the religion of the majority, and the donning of a *kanzu*[3] is a simple but effective membership card enabling the country bumpkin to be accepted as a civilized man; it is also in sympathy with

---

[1] A turnboy is a driver's assistant, in fact his apprentice; he is the youth who cranks the starting-handle.

[2] Zaramo are the tribe in whose area Dar es Salaam lies: they form about one-third of the population.

[3] A *kanzu* (literally, 'little house') is an overall nightdress-like garment, usually of white calico.

Bantu conservatism and reliance on elders, tradition and continuity, its accent on the community rather than on the individual; it has enabled its adherents to laugh off the material success of the 'new man' and to retain their own self-respect though lacking in wealth, education and hustle. It is undemanding, and has no unwelcome organization for the supervision of its adherents' private life.

These attractions must be weakening now, since new currents of thought are directly opposed to the spirit of Islam: the new leaders are almost exclusively Christian, and many are educated; they attack the power of the elders and advocate the equality of young and old.

PUBLIC OPINION

Public opinion, normally the circle of one's neighbours, has little force in town, where one's closest—one's relatives—are scattered over town, and one's friends are mostly people met at work or at clubs; one's private life is one's own business, except as food for gossip.

SCHOOL TEACHING

There is little or no teaching of ethical behaviour in town; children learn more from the streets. Only a minority go to Koranic school, and the teaching there is of a very automatic and uninspired type. At the same time the recent difficulty in sending one's children to both Koranic and modern school was a real deterrent to sending children to modern school.

PARENTAL TEACHING

Parental reinforcement of religion and the ethics deriving from religion is in many cases absent in town, where many children come without their true parents, or even on their own.

THE LAW

The better chances in town of 'getting away with it' mean that the fear of the law is a smaller deterrent to wrong-doing than it is up-country.

MARITAL RELATIONS

Amorality is apparent also in marital relations: strict marriages complete with bride-price are not easy to arrange in Dar es Salaam, if only because so often the senior parties are not there.

MIXED MARRIAGES

Mixed marriages between tribes are not common, and occur mostly between old residents; between related tribes they are more common, and do not give rise to friction due to different customs and taboos.

'FREE MARRIAGE'

More casual relations are believed to be the rule. No measurement was found possible. Types of 'marriage' are distinguished: the full marriage with parents present and bride-price paid; the permitted remarriage of a divorcée without parents or bride-price; and the formal marriage without bride-price; the living-together of two persons for the length of an infatuation, sometimes growing into a semi-permanent liaison on a basis of mutual liking and convenience, but without formal bonds; the regular but not exclusive visits of a call-girl, and purely casual visits to a prostitute.

Instability of marriage is a coastal phenomenon even in the country.

DIVORCE

The longer-established tribes in Dar es Salaam show a higher rate of divorce; and this applies also to those who have been, individually, longer resident.

LEGAL POSITION

All cases of marriage and divorce are heard in the Liwali's court by strict Muslim law, irrespective of the tribal custom of those concerned: if both parties wish their dispute to be heard by tribal custom they do not go to court, but to an elder of their tribe. This is an immense simplification, and has so far proved reasonably acceptable, although it bears heavily on women. Muslim law takes no account (officially) of dowry.

PLURAL WIVES

There is a surprisingly large minority (6 per cent.) with more than one wife, despite the uneconomic nature of such a marriage in town.

GRASS WIDOWERS

A very great number of marriages take place in the home village, and coastal tribes very often leave the wife behind, cultivating, while the man goes to earn money in town. Others do not marry in their first 'tour' in town. Wives are left behind partly to avoid losing their affections to the smooth operators of town, partly to avoid their getting expensive tastes, and partly because whereas at home they are an economic asset, in town they are in most cases a liability.

ECONOMICS OF WIVES

A wife in town is a hostage to financial misfortune and is not prepared to put up with as much in bad times as a single man. There are, however, many small but lucrative trades open to women; the proceeds of these are not necessarily passed on to the husband any more than his whole wage goes into the family coffer; there is almost universal distrust between man and wife (and more particularly man and mistress) on financial matters.

'MWALI' CUSTOM

The *mwali* custom of the seclusion of unmarried girls until the time of their marriage is to be found even in town; more often the girls are sent to the country; so also are growing boys.

INDEPENDENCE OF WOMEN

An independent woman has many advantages in town, both financial and otherwise, and many are loath to give up this independence for a formal marriage. This independence has raised the status—or at least the bargaining position—of women in town. It cannot be attributed wholly to a disparity between the sexes, for the women are in fact 42 per cent. of the whole. But it may be an echo of a formerly greater disparity.

PROSTITUTION

Prostitution is not a problem. It is a necessary safety-valve, is not over-abundant, obtrusive, or likely to corrupt the young. As carriers of disease its practitioners are less likely to be dangerous than the far greater number of amateurs.

STRICT FAMILY

Not enough is known on which to base a firm policy of making the strict family the basic unit.

CRIME

Amorality in the criminal sector expresses itself in neutralism, a refusal to take the side of law and order; this has its roots deep in Bantu magic beliefs, and neutrality or even hostility towards anyone outside the clan.

CHILDREN

Amorality stems also from lack of discipline in up-bringing: many children come to Dar es Salaam to avoid this discipline; often once in town a child frees himself from it.

URBANIZATION: GROWTH SLOWING

The growth of the population is slowing down and may now be no more than 2–3,000 additional Africans a year. The employment of a large part of the 35,000 Africans reckoned by the Labour Department to be in regular employment depends, not on current business, but on active expansion, in that so many are employed directly or indirectly on construction. When present construction slows down there may, therefore, be an actual decrease in African employment.

URBAN NUCLEUS

If, however, there is some growth, at however reduced a rate, the nucleus of more settled people will grow—even if it does not grow in proportion to the whole.

TYPES OF 'SETTLEDNESS'

People are 'settled' in varying degrees: some like the Nubi have no other home; nor any links outside (e.g. some Manyema); others, though born and bred in Dar es Salaam, have strong links with their place of origin; others, not born here, have made it their home and expect to die here; others, called here 'border-men', are really part of Uzaramo but happen to be inside the Municipality border; they retain much of the rural life and are unlikely to move elsewhere. These classes are considered as 'settled'. But the last class, of border-men, cannot be thought of as urbanized.

Then there is a class called here 'career-men', come for their working life, but with spells of leave at home, and an intention to go home on retirement.

One of the largest classes is here called 'spenders', coastal men come to get on to a cash way of living, but returning home almost annually and with no intention of settling permanently, though they may come back again and again.

There is another sub-class of 'spenders' which comes for one or two 'tours' but eventually tires and does not come again.

A small class of 'target-men' come for a specific sum of money, or as apprentices to learn a trade. They dislike the life and return home as soon as they may.

To measure statistically the proportions of the population falling into each class was not attempted. Instead certain indications were taken: birth in town, length of residence, visits of a month, and of a year away; houses owned, and the age distribution, particularly of older people; and having one's wife and children in town. These are discussed and the deductions which may and may not be drawn from them.

It is concluded that a statistical formula for measuring 'settledness', or 'urbanization', must await a more precise definition of terms and also comparisons at intervals of time, based on the same definitions and methods of measurement. It is this which the proposed continuous survey is intended to supply.[1]

---

[1] The proposal for a continuous survey has since been approved, and the first suburb, Magomeni, was re-surveyed in 1959, the comparison with 1956 being summarized at Appendix C.

I. INTRODUCTION

Object of the survey

THE object of this survey of Dar es Salaam, commissioned by the then Colonial Government in 1956, was to obtain sufficient factual information and sufficient insight into its significance, to enable all those with an interest in improving the life of the town to see the best ways of doing so, the factors leading to tension or anarchy, and the factors tending to an easing of strain.

A great deal is known about Dar es Salaam, but much of it is locked either in the heads of officials who will not remain for ever at their posts, or in official records which are unlikely ever again to see the light of day. The survey which follows does no more than confirm in more detail what was locally known already, and to those whose daily life it is to administer the town it will contribute little more than a few interesting new minor facts and figures.

To those who do not know Dar es Salaam but are interested in its problems this survey may be of some use as putting together in one place a picture which gives some idea of African life in this town. To them the fact that the survey has discovered nothing new may perhaps be evidence of credibility.

The survey does not, however, pretend to give a full picture of the whole community of Dar es Salaam: with the time, staff and experience at my disposal it was clear that to attempt such a complete survey would be absurd; the community chosen for study was, therefore, that which lives in certain quarters of the town, which are in fact mainly occupied by Africans; this had the advantage that it is the African element in the community which suffers most from the unfamiliarity and complexity of town life, which has most need of the help of the Municipality and Government in dealing with the difficulties of such a life, and about which there is most ignorance. Such members of the other races as live in the areas chosen were included in the survey, but it is mainly on the

C

Africans of Dar es Salaam that attention is fixed. Even of the Africans it is not by any means a full picture: it omits for instance the 1,500-odd who live in the Oyster Bay area and a few hundreds living in the Commercial Area and elsewhere.

Furthermore, in the areas selected and the aspects of life which were examined much of the information is unavoidably superficial, and where a more thorough study has been attempted there yawns between it and the next many gaps which I can only hope somebody will have the time and opportunity to fill.

Summary of methods

The basis of the report is the tabulated answers to a set of questions asked in August 1956 of some 5,000 persons. The persons to be asked these questions were selected by a systematic random sample, by listing all the houses in the area and then taking every twentieth, and all those living therein. This method gave a good geographical spread and still seems to be the most satisfactory way of setting about it in Dar es Salaam.

Before the questions were put, six months were spent, not only listing the houses (not all of which were on the town registers), but discussing life with officials, elders and young people until it became clear what facts were required and, therefore, what questions should be asked. Some questions which departments wished us to ask had to be dropped because a true—or any—answer could not be expected (an example of this was questions on stillbirths). Some which were in fact asked proved a waste of time (an example is the questions directed to measure the extent of 'free marriage').

When the set of questions was ready a month was spent in training enumerators, 115 of whom were used. Teachers, Labour Inspectors, medical students and others helped out with evening work. Perforce a number of unemployed yet literate persons were used, and among these the standard of education, honesty and ability was not of the highest, with the result that no less than nine months had to be spent in checking their results, some of which were entirely bogus, others (the more dangerous) partially so. More detailed inquiries on particular subjects followed and helped to act as a further check, so that a great deal of the fabrication and inaccuracies was discovered and removed. But when dealing with a virtually uneducated and highly suspicious community such as this it would be a foolish man who supposed that fabrication and inaccuracy have been eliminated. My claim is only that my figures are the least inaccurate yet obtained for Dar es Salaam.[1]

The data on which this report is based are being renewed by an annual factual re-survey of one quarter of the area, thus not only keeping the data sufficiently up to date to be usable, but providing a series of four-year comparisons which should be of great value for estimating trends. The first such comparisons are summarized at Appendix C.

History of Dar es Salaam

It is logical to begin at the beginning, and in this case it helps to understand the modern town to see its origins and how it grew up. The history of modern Dar es Salaam[2] begins, for all practical purposes, with the decision of Seiyid Majid, Arab Sultan of Zanzibar, to found a new settlement. In doing this he had the agreement of those few fenced villages of the Zaramo, a chiefless, matrilineal tribe living in family groups, which were found in the neighbourhood of the present harbour. These villages, each with a nucleus of related families and an accretion of travellers, clients and settlers, were each under a head, who took the honorary title of *Pazi*, and were governed, each independently, by a balance of personality and power which was constantly changing. The Madenge family near modern Mtoni, and the Mwinyigogo family at Gerezani were those most directly affected by the Seiyid's coming. They welcomed his protection and did not demur when he took land —till then thicket and scrub—whereon to plant coconuts. They in fact took from the Seiyid presents of cloth and money which he understood in the sense of a sale of the land. He brought in slaves from Kilwa to clear the bush, and these slaves, many later freed on the spot, must count as the first urban inhabitants of the town of Dar es Salaam.

---

[1] The methods used are described in greater detail as an appendix to the statistical tables, which are not published in this volume, but which may be examined by arrangement with the Chairman, East African Institute of Social Research.

[2] The name, an Arabic one, means 'House of salvation'.

The Zaramo, so tradition has it, owe their origin to a war with a marauding band of Kamba from Kenya, who fought and raided their way down the coast and attacked the part-Arab Shomvi of Upanga and the other settlements; these called in the Kutu from Morogoro—where was the nearest tribe with a centralized organization powerful enough to stand up to the raiders: the Kutu and the Doe made war successfully on the Kamba, who were driven back (a remnant is supposed to have settled in the village now known as Mkamba); some of the Kutu families which came down for these skirmishes found the coast to their liking and settled and so formed the Zaramo; from this time, tradition says, they had no overlord and lived each family by itself in its fenced village, owing allegiance only to its chief elder.

Besides the Zaramo in their villages there were at that time also small settlements of Shomvi or Shirazi, all on the foreshore, one at the Ocean Road hospital site, one in Upanga on the Msimbazi creek and others across the harbour mouth. These, originally a mixture of Arab and African, had by then already intermarried with the Zaramo to such an extent that their rights and customs were to a great extent inextricable.

When the Seiyid began in 1865 to develop the town he brought also a garrison of *viroboto*—fleas—who in the case of Dar es Salaam were Hadhrami Arabs, called Shihiri.[1] Other Shihiris were brought in as dockers and porters in the town. Both these nuclei quickly seized the opportunities observed by their innate eye for financial gain and launched into the pedlar and small-shop trade in which they hold a dominant position to this day.

On the death of Seiyid Majid in 1870 his policies died with him, an occurrence not unknown in later stages of the town's history; the coconut plantations continued, but by 1873 only two houses were habitable and land was valueless; when the Germans took over they found little left of the settlement. But with their placing there the temporary capital of Tanganyika, growth was rapid. The population is estimated to have risen from a few dozen before Seiyid Majid, to 5,000 by

[1] Called Shihiri from the town of Shihr on the Eastern Aden Protectorate coast. It is now a somewhat opprobrious term since the Omani Arabs (called Manga) affect to despise them as of lower social class.

Colonel, (later Field-Marshal Earl) Kitchener's estimate in 1886, including 107 Indians, 100 Arabs and 600–700 Zanzibar royal slaves. Thenceforward growth was slow but steady until the last war:

1886	5,000	(Kitchener's estimate)
1894	9,000	(Deutsche Kolonial Blatt estimate)
1900	18,000	(Deutsche Kolonial Blatt estimate)
1913	19,000	(Deutsche Kolonial Blatt estimate)
1921	20,000	(Census)
1931	24,000	(Census)
1943	37,000	(Estimate based on hut count)
1948	51,000	(Census)
1951	72,000	(Census)
1957	92,330	(Census)

The presence of shops, modern wonders and employment drew in the Zaramo then as it does today, and they soon formed the bulk of the population, the remainder drawn from almost every tribe with access to the outside world: those from the coast road from Kilwa (whence came not only slaves but the leaders of Islam) and from the Songea highlands (whence came fighting men for the German forces): those on the slave and ivory route from the Congo (whence came porters, soldiers and slaves). All these tribes had in the days before European rule had to run the gauntlet of the hostility of strangers, and had in the course of time evolved a system of blood-relationships, an early form of passport, which can be traced to this day in burial customs in Dar es Salaam.

Before the Seiyid the fenced villages of the Zaramo lived, as did the rest of the tribe of which they were the fringe, by cultivation: some of the Shomvi villages lived by fishing from dugout canoes (they had no cloth to make sails and the outrigger sailing canoe came, according to tradition, with Hindu traders from Kaure, Bagamoyo and Zanzibar).

After the Seiyid the new, slave, population lived by employment, and worked on clearing the thickets and planting and tending the coconut plantations. As trade with the hinterland gradually transferred from Bagamoyo to Dar es Salaam, so did employment, and an employed population. When the Central Railway Line was building, employment increased, and its completion meant the final victory of Dar es Salaam over its rival Bagamoyo, which had been the main port in the days of the first explorers.

The British took over the German buildings, but finding their housing over-Spartan put in hand a large building programme in what is now the Burton Street area; a bad fire in the low hutments where many of the demobilized askaris had settled led to the clearing of Mnazi Mmoja and their resettlement mainly at Chang'ombe kwa Wanubi: it also, deliberately or not, led to the division which can still be traced today, into African town and Commercial Area. The British took up the German plan for the former and laid out what is now Kariakoo,[1] which for years was, together with Kisutu, the beginning and end of the African part of Dar es Salaam.

The Commercial Area grew slowly but steadily, and its dependency, the other side of Mnazi Mmoja, grew too, as employment drew in more temporary and permanent settlers. Ilala[2] was laid out next. Beyond these two there were only scattered hamlets and single huts, but these formed the nuclei round which others settled whenever a boom in Dar es Salaam or a crisis up-country brought in a new influx.

It was immediately after the last war that Dar es Salaam began its period of spectacular growth. The pent-up demand for consumer goods, for exports, for outlets for capital, all conspired to force a headlong pace. Building could not keep pace. Slums and shanty-villages sprang up and were out of control by 1947. Any land not developed grew overnight a mushroom cover of huts; Government land in particular at Makaburi, Gerezani, Keko, filled with what promised to be a series of slums dangerous to health and order.

By 1948 the population was 51,000. By 1952 it was 72,300. But by 1952 the worst of the slum conditions and the overcrowding that went with them were under control. This was due to the use of the British Colonial Development and Welfare Fund, spent on buying up land and settling those moved from the slums on to building plots for African houses. Crowding persists in places, but there are now empty houses as well, and

---

[1] *Kariakoo*: a phonetic spelling of Carrier Corps, the porters of the 1914–18 war.
[2] Ilala named after Ilala in Nyasaland, the homeland of many Yao soldiers of the Germans and British.

although the African population in the August 1957 census was some 92,000 the housing situation is better in all areas than it was in 1950.

The future of the town can only be guessed; the waves of the post-war surge, duplicated all over the world, have not behind them the tide of any particular local advantages, and have in recent years been blown on by little more than confidence. Much of the business relates to the building boom and depends on its continuance. It is even money whether Dar es Salaam's next ten years will resemble more the recent boom decade, or the inter-war uneasy progress, but growth of a kind continues.

How Africans come to be in the town

A stranger to African conditions, seeing the contrast between the new concrete buildings and comparative modernity of the Commercial Area and the mud and wattle of Kariakoo; hearing the complaints of inadequate income and food, the indebtedness, the queues at the pawnshops; the poor standard of housing, lack of privacy, and unemployment, might well wonder why Africans come to Dar es Salaam, or why, having come, they do not return the few miles home again—for the most part within a day's bus ride. If the average African is lonely in the big town away from his kin and the closed circle of his hamlet, at a loose end with no paternal organization to keep his days turning, a prey to the tricksters and moral dangers inherent in any town, unprotected by the discipline and inhibitions of tribal and family life, adrift with little prospect of improvement, why does he continue to come in year after year, in ever greater numbers? Why do some always stay on?

I put this question to a number of Africans, and one of them composed the following reply, which I have translated from the Swahili but otherwise left untouched.

'It is not everyone who finds hardship in town; many of its inhabitants do well and live very comfortably, and they too have come in from up-country. Many of them are fortunate enough to be well educated or have some skill and qualifications which enable them on coming to town to get a good job easily, with good pay sufficient for their needs and comforts. As these have no hardships they proudly write to tell their parents all about it, lest they worry about their living in town; they write home and describe the pleasures of town life and the wonders of the town. Their parents naturally, getting these letters, lose no time in broadcasting the news of their sons' success to their neighbours in the village, and the details are passed from one to another by word of mouth till almost everyone knows about it.

'These letters are not the end of it: every now and then there will be presents and cash to the parents, and finally the young townsman will come to the end of his tour of duty and be due for, say, fourteen days' leave. So, as he has bought himself good clothes, a bicycle, a gramophone and so on, he is bound to take these with him on leave to prove what he has been saying in his letters.

'Now the other young men who stayed behind up-country: when they hear how well he is doing in town they are able to console themselves (although they are in fact very envious), firstly because they have up to now no visible proof and secondly because they can disbelieve his stories. But now here he is on his way, and actually arrived, burdened down with the world's goods: everyone, elders and youngsters, comes to welcome the conquering hero, men and women together; a cock is killed, they can smell the Lux on him, see his stockings girt about him, a watch on his wrist to tell him the time, rhumba records rend the air, a cycle carries him, small change jingles in his pockets, coppers are tossed out as worthless; what, you live in a village without electricity? No cinema? No dance hall? No bands? What a dump!

'His stay-at-home contemporaries listen with barely concealed envy; before he rises in the morning they already fill the courtyard waiting for Milord to wake and speak the golden words. Till he wakes every youngster speaks in whispers "the big man is sleeping"—like a District Commissioner. So on until nine in the morning, then he rises, a fine *khanga* at his waist, a vest proudly flying at the mast, towel over his shoulder, a toothbrush in his mouth, hot water ready in a ewer in the lavatory: he washes for a full hour and a half, while scented soap stings the nostrils of the young men waiting outside and those waiting to greet him in the courtyard. One of his female relations has already gone in and made his bed, quickly swept the place and carefully tidied it before he should finish his bath. Out of the bath my lord combs his hair and the mirror testifies to his handsomeness—cor! his parting shows up like Kichwele Street.

'He is ready, and so is tea, that you could cut with an axe, ranged along the table: "help yourselves" is said, the young men waved to partake: my lord, the sophisticate, does not take sugar. "This is for children." He shows them how to pour the tea, milk and sugar; the connoisseur asks each, "I say, is the sugar enough?" "Quite thanks"—before he has tasted it—once tasted "Ughh! it's bitter" he says to himself, but he hasn't the face to ask for more sugar, but drinks it up fast hoping for a chance at the second cup: he gets his second, the same, and a third, and still he goes on, dying by inches like an officer and a gentleman, unable to confess defeat until six cups have gone down. The young men drink many cups, but my lord—half a cup is his rule.

'Soon he is called outside to greet his aunts and his married sisters, and they are so much all over him they wash his shining feet (pale from the use of shoes) in a *chimbundi*, and pass the water round to drink. This is done outside in the courtyard, where there is a press of folk, and the mothers of those other young men are all muttering to themselves, "Ah, if only this was my Johnny what wouldn't I do—anyway what's my Johnny waiting for, I'll tell him this very day and he can go to town and be like this fine fellow!"

'Meanwhile those young men in the room have taken the opportunity to clean out the sugar basin: they know nothing of the dark days to come, but counsel each other, "This is too much, I *must* go to town"; they are all saying this from the bottom of their hearts, "Just look at his room, the headman is poor compared to this; look at his food, he picks at a single slice of bread and drinks half a cup of tea." Another cuts in: "Do you imagine there in town they hog their food like us gulping down great hunks fit to choke? No, these people are as finicky as anything, dainty, that's what they are; didn't you see how he bathed this morning, cold as it was: you couldn't!" Another: "These townsfolk mix so with Europeans they live like them too, only their skin's a bit darker." The first says "Whatever happens, when he goes back I have just got to go with

him: here in the country we live, but what a life! It is nothing
but work."

'Let us call these three Ali, Juma and Joseph; each of them
has his special reasons for leaving the countryside, and a fourth
is called Lucas and is the one who has been to town. Let us
take these four to represent their fellows and let each explain
himself. After these ceremonies outside Lucas wanted to talk to
his friends, so they went to the bachelors' hut and knocked,
and all the young men inside welcomed him in, dropping what
they were doing, leaving the sugar bowl and wiping their hands
on their garments.

'The scene is now set in the courtyard, and Ali takes up the
running:

'*Ali*: Well, Lucas, we have been longing to speak to you
since yesterday right from the moment you arrived, but what
with you being tired from the journey and then all these people
wanting to see you we didn't like to force ourselves on you.
But having heard about your letters and now seen for ourselves
the sort of person you have become, we hope you will tell us all
about the town, for often we hear that life is hard there, one
hasn't enough to eat, or place to sleep, and getting a job is a
headache, but here you are and look at you!

'*Lucas*: It is true what you say, but think a bit: if everyone
had such a hard time of it in town, wouldn't I be the same?
If somebody says it is all hardship don't listen to him; here in
the country have you never gone to bed hungry? Here in the
country do you work for yourself? Have visitors of your parents
never arrived and you been winkled out of your room and
made to sleep in the passage? It is true it is not easy to get a
job, especially for the lower orders, but for people of good
family like yourselves to have difficulty in getting a job I don't
believe, because all jobs there are "care-of-so-and-so" and those
they are care-of are people like myself (here Lucas puts himself
forward as an important person able to help his friends who
are out of work).

'*Ali*: Yes—yes, absolutely Lucas, you're dead right. Lucas,
as you know I am highly educated. (He breaks into English)
I finish there Standard 6 kuspeak English I do (I'm fluent
and can tumble out the lingo so that an Englishman will
say bravo). Just now this is practice tu, match bado till

I go see this European of English nitamtell I want job to you I am finish Standard 6 there about my home. My year is now 20.

'As far as I can see there's not the slightest doubt but that I'll get the job, today I'll tell my sweetheart that I'm going to be a clerk in town and then I'll have the money to marry her without delay; oh, she'll be thrilled to bits, as she knows that if I go to town I'll be a real guy, a head clerk, and then all that'll be left for the parents will be to sign on the dotted.

'*Lucas*: Thank you very much, Ali. I am a houseboy to a European, and as the Memsahib only knows English I know more of it than you think, but if what you have been speaking is real English, then certainly you will be a success, more than I. Clerks in town get as much as 700 Shs. or 800 Shs. a month. But I am forget, you see Mista this my true I speak. You not forgot because yes I am see.

'*Juma breaks in*: Hey there, let us into this conversation; what's the use of our having ears if we can't understand? Say it so that we can all get it. Joseph, are you there?

'*Ali*: Forgive me, all this English makes me stutter; the tip of my tongue has more English than saliva. But look, Lucas, my father is a poor man, now what about the fare? Let me think . . . yes, I'll enlist at the labour recruiter's with some others, and when I have succeeded in getting as far as the town and before they can send me to Zanzibar I'll melt away.

'So Ali goes off to enlist in manamba,[1] and finds the work too much for him; he has no return fare, no clothes, no money for bride-price; his sweetheart can't understand why he still hasn't got a clerk's job; here he still is, without a bean. He has given up hope of getting back home.

'When will we see Ali again?

'*Juma*: Lucas, old boy, we have a very hard life here in the country; the authorities—I don't know if it is the chief or his assistants—have their knives into us. And as for Father and even Mother . . .! Listen, it was only the other day, you've seen the maize, cucumbers, and vegetables, all ripe? Well, this day hunger followed me around all day, I ran away from it but my feet wouldn't get me away, so I thought it best to go

---

[1] *Manamba*: derived from 'numbers', means recruited labour, in this case clove-picking on Arab plantations in Zanzibar.

to our field and help myself to some cucumber. I admit I took one and swallowed it down without chewing. Then I got a mad desire to eat some maize and broke off three and went home to roast them. Presto, as the first was ready I began to eat it, and then the second, when in come my parents from visiting. They see me and start straight in to abuse me, tell me never to darken their door again. That evening there was a big storm with lightning, one bolt of which struck a tree in that field and it fell and ruined a stretch of the crops: then in the morning everyone said: Ah, yes, Juma ate unblessed food before we had sacrificed, that's why their field was destroyed. So the news spread and they sent me to expiate it, and when I got there the omens were against me and I was an outcast to the whole village. My father is an old man but he has no gratitude; since he was exempted tax he has been to work for the chief only five times, every time it is his turn it's me that goes, and as you know these old boys do this freely just to please the chiefs and show their gratitude for having been taken before the D.C., for the D.C. doesn't know how old they are, and the chief is relied on to certify that he is old enough to be exempted, so one must show one's gratitude by cultivating in his field, building his hut, cutting the grass on his paths and so on, without a cent in payment.

'Then I hate it here, better get a change of air—town air— even if it kills me. I am lucky enough to have borrowed the fare down, though I haven't enough to come back. But every day they sit on me, and now there is nothing for it but to disappear and give myself a break; in the town there are many people and many jobs, but here what job can a chap get? It's just the messenger coming in the morning, early, with a little bit of paper summoning me to the court; you get there and they tell you, you are charged by the agricultural inspector for not having a cassava field; if you ask who the inspector himself is you're told, "That child over there". If you ask who is prosecuting and where he is they'll say: "So you are one of these bush lawyers, are you? Do you suppose a full agricultural inspector will tell lies?"

'Elders like this are not to be borne, in the end you may be had up for murder, better go to town where nobody knows me, and nobody will say what's that you're eating, what's that you're wearing, every man for himself and mind his own business: but here! You've only to cough and somebody ticks you off for getting your feet wet.

'Last week I returned from safari with the dresser, carrying his loads, and only a little later they volunteered me again to carry the D.C.'s loads, nothing but work, any time there's loads to be carried it's always me; I think you know that young clerk at the ferry, well now, the rains are starting and lorries won't pass, off I go again, soon I'll develop wheels and be a public service vehicle. Go to town any day.

'*Joseph*: What happened to Kibeku will happen to you. What is said to be is, and if it isn't it soon will be. The same troubles as my friends here have me too by the throat. I'm up to the neck in almost everything. When Juma asked if I was here, I certainly was. This countryside of ours is awful. Every year you hear "tax tickets, tax tickets". Who are you anyway to collect tax off me? Aren't you an African like myself? If I give you this money what will you do for me? If the game just consists of giving me a bit of paper, well, I don't understand it. You, Bakari, do you get this money for yourself? These Europeans who use it don't see what's going on, they don't say anything, or go following people round saying "tax, tax". Since you put on that uniform you have turned into a European yourself. This place is getting too small, I'll go off to town. In town they don't know who is who, which came today and which left yesterday. Here everyone knows everyone else, and however we twist and turn these tax clerks follow, oh, the son of so-and-so hasn't paid yet, and that young chap over the hill by the big tree. Tax, tax—but where's the job to earn the money? Lucas, is it like that in town?

'*Lucas*: Well, it is, but tax in town goes by seasons, and also it goes by areas or villages, but we who live in the European parts aren't afraid of it because they don't come into the European parts; it's only when you go into town or go visiting in the built-up areas or for other business and happen to go in when they are having a tax raid, then you may get caught, but many slip through even so. Often people help each other: if one man has got through without being caught he passes the word on and it doesn't matter if you are his tribe or not, he'll stop you and say, "Brother, there's a raid in such and such a

place, if you have paid fair enough but if not have a care."
Those who have paid can most easily pass the word on in this
way as they don't reason that as they have paid why shouldn't
the others. So the word gets around quickly and it is not
difficult to escape the net.

'*Joseph*: Thanks, that's the land for me. Then look, on
Thursday night I was with my girl-friend Sofia in my hut and
imagine my face when it appears that she is going to have a
child. Her parents find out it was me that done her wrong and
had these appointments with her each night, and in the
morning they surprised us and hauled me off to court, and
there I saw three more, all odd shapes, and their parents
behind ready to charge me with the same offence: wow! It
looked as if it would be a quadruple wedding, each one at penal
rates of bride-price. Before I knew where I was, I was down for
4,000 Shs. for four brides and two weeks to pay. Where could
I find such a sum? And if I don't pay by then I'll be up for
enticing the young, not a civil but a criminal case: the jail door
yawns for me, brother. There's no way out but to run for it.

'So Joseph ran away to town to avoid his case. Once there
he's not Joseph but Yusufu.

'When shall we see Joseph again?

'Our three young men have had their say; let us complete
the tale with a word or two:

'Often there are strikes, and a short notice is given, so that
the worker has not time to lay anything aside for the period
when he will have no pay, and has not enough to pay his
fare home. Many go on strike, and when it is over not all go
back; some find their jobs have ceased to exist, and with no
work and no money they wander the streets not knowing what
to do.

'Our friends up-country hear of a strike in town, well, all
the drivers and boys in the world flood into town hoping to
take their place. Far more come than there are vacancies for,
and the remainder wander about the streets. Many jobs have
lapsed or been reorganized and many employers try to rid
themselves of the necessity of employing anyone.

'Lucas returned to town, his leave up; now he is a success
and it remains to show his wealth. He tries every pleasure,
catches the eye of every girl, thieves and not-quite-thieves

surround him, he is penniless. He can't go back; in no time the
cycle is sold, the gramophone follows, now he is a real townsman, a big thrash today, penniless tomorrow, the watch is
gone, anything of value is in pawn; the salary is pledged long
before it comes; he borrows; on payday his balance is 5 Shs.,
the next day he begins again to borrow some from the next
month's pay. Lucas has nothing, but he can't go back. Tell me
now: will he ever go on leave home again? No, it was only
yesterday I saw him—broke again.'

What does this all add up to? People come to Dar es Salaam
not to eat well, or to live in comfort without overcrowding—
for they come from the countryside where, whatever else is
left to be desired, food is free, money being required, in normal
times, only to exchange a surplus of one kind for a deficiency
of another, or to get greater variety; room to stretch out again
is no trouble at all up-country, where a day's work without
a penny changing hands will produce another room. It is not
food or housing that draws, but the hope of acquiring money
to get the world's goods (both eyes on the high wages, and a
fine disregard for the equally high cost of living), the desire
for a brighter life and to a large extent a tradition among
many coastal tribes that one must have seen Dar es Salaam
to have lived; an escape from the discipline of family, tribe
and government into the uncontributing anonymity of town,
where one takes what one can get and puts nothing into the
kitty, and with any luck gets away with it. At the same time
the young man lives, while remaining invisible to the authorities, to shine among his fellows, as it were to jump the long
queue of promotion in the esteem of the community.

It is against these aims of the city migrant that their difficulties and frustrations must be judged: the lack of food and
crowded accommodation are irritants but not sufficiently
irritating to persuade the migrant, without the intervention
of other factors, to leave the town and return to ample food
and ample room at home a short bus-ride away.

II. THE SURVEY

Alone in the big city

IT is a commonplace of the countryman come to town, the world over, that he is overcome at first by the strangeness of the life, so different from the one he led. In the West the countryman may well be entirely alone in a city, knowing no one. Is this so here?

It is not. It would be difficult to find a single African who arrived in Dar es Salaam knowing not a soul. There are a few such, drifted by the accident of war service or transfer far from their homes, people from South Africa or the Sudan, but they are very few indeed and usually the circumstances which brought them give them also some protection and provide an organization to guide them. The vast majority come not as single units but as a part of a stream extending not only in breadth over large numbers of their fellow-townsmen but in depth back through decades to the first inhabitants of Dar es Salaam or beyond to the slave and ivory caravans. Almost every African who decides to come to Dar es Salaam comes to a known address, where lives a known relation; this relation will meet him, take him in and feed him and show him the ropes, help him to seek a job, for months if necessary until he considers himself able to launch out for himself and take a room of his own. Even then if he falls on evil days he can count on a meal and a loan, given not grudgingly but as a normal obligation, in the same category as the obligation of a man to feed his children.

This applies to a man of almost any tribe, though some tribes are of course here in larger numbers than others. Of the 113 tribes of Tanganyika recognized for the purposes of the census, 67 were found by this survey in Dar es Salaam, and including Kenya, Uganda, Rhodesia, Mozambique and Congo tribes, members were found of 100 different tribes. So no man need be alone with nobody of his own background and language to consort with; and the smaller the group of representatives of a tribe in Dar es Salaam the more do they tend to cling together and keep a spirit of community.

When Dar es Salaam was a very small town, and most of the immigrants came by foot, the earliest entrants naturally set down their loads at the first opportunity, on the side of town nearest to the direction of their coming. As others followed them, and went to the addresses of those already there, and then 'hived off' and built themselves houses nearby, there was a perceptible polarization of tribes, each group tending to inhabit the quarter nearest their place of origin. As the town grew bigger and more desirable areas crystallized out, drawing the more successful of all tribes together, this grouping was much blurred. But even today it is still discernible in geographical groups. Still more is it discernible in groups of people with similar characteristics and similar ways of living.

Thus the largest community to which an immigrant African belongs is that of his 'route', the tribes which follow, and have for decades followed, the same road to town. In the days before the coming of the European and law and order, these tribes, with the necessity of travelling through alien territory, had developed out of the wars and raids a relationship called *utani* by which the tribes of a single route gave each other mutual recognition as allies. If a member of one of these tribes died *en route*, in the territory of a tribe which had bonds of *utani*, he would be buried by them as though he had been a member of that tribe. To a certain extent he could also depend on their help if he fell sick or otherwise became a legitimate claimant on the community: the tribe in whose territory he found himself took the place in his life which his own tribe would have done had he been at home.

The Zaramo tribe which surrounds Dar es Salaam was of course a party to all these pacts, as all tribes had to pass through their territory. They in their turn had specially close ties with the tribes of Morogoro from which they sprang, and with their neighbours of Utete and Bagamoyo. Beyond these tribes which had the town on their doorstep, so easily accessible that at all times they have provided the great bulk of the inhabitants, the earliest and still the biggest stream of migrants is that along the coast from the south. These have much in common, the Swahili language and coastal culture, Islam, and a diet

D

including rice, coconuts and fish. The common background
is less marked as one gets further south down the coast, until
those from Portuguese East Africa are an alien people, though
with a long tradition of travel to Dar es Salaam for work—in
their case the most common objective of going on to the cash
economy being a gun and dogs for hunting, at least in the old
days.

The closeness of the tie may be judged from the fact that
Wakili Saidi Chaurembo was recognized as the representative
not only of the Zaramo but of Ndengereko and Rufiji as well
while the late Saidi Litewa represented the Ngindo, Nyasa,
Makonde and Makua as well as the local Shirazi.

After the southern coastal stream next in importance
comes the 'central line' stream, following the route of the old
slave and ivory caravans, the outlet to the sea now diverted
from Bagamoyo to Dar es Salaam. The strongest part of this
contingent is the tribes of Mwanza, Tabora, Nzega and
Kahama; and still there are some of these who were slaves,
guides, soldiers or middlemen on the caravans, who have their
homes all along the route from the coast of Kigoma and beyond,
who continue to find their way down to Dar es Salaam to stay
with others of the Manyema community. The Nyamwezi,
Sukuma and Sumbwa had a single representative in Dar es
Salaam, Juma Sultani, while the more far-flung, Gogo, Haya,
Rundi, Ganda and Bembe, joined the Manyema in being
represented by the late Fundi Wakati.

After these two big streams come two smaller, that from the
south by the inland route, the descendants and imitators of
the mercenaries from Ulanga and Songea, and the Yao from
beyond. Many of these are permanently settled in very old
communities, often in pockets where they predominate, and
the Yao in particular have built up for themselves almost a
privileged position as a community of long standing deserving
of a say in affairs. The Yao and Matumbi shared a representative, Jumbe Msimu. The Ngoni, Nyakyusa, Fipa, Wemba and
part of the Ngindo were represented by the late Hamisi
Faranyaki of Ngoni.

The other smaller stream is also from the coastal peoples,
this time from the north and from Zanzibar. Like those from
the southern coast they share with the Zaramo and with each

other a preponderance of Islam, the Swahili traditions and culture, and diet. They are joined by those tribes which live in and around Morogoro: the Kutu, Zigua, Bondei, Kwere, Nyika, Doe and Luguru all shared a single representative, the late Asmani Kumra.

These are the main traditional streams of migrants into Dar es Salaam. Smaller numbers are provided, particularly in these days, by the South-West route, from the Southern Highlands and, beyond, from Rhodesia, whence come many of the young artisans.

In addition to these traditional routes are the more modern, of people using the new modes of transport, often brought here on transfer in Government service or in that of firms, educated and secure, career men coming to spend a working life in Dar es Salaam and then retire home. These come mainly from the West and the North. Such few Chagga, Luo and Luhya as used previously to come to Dar es Salaam allied themselves with the Luguru and were represented by the late Asmani Kumra.

These are the migrants seeking a money wage, the unskilled; and those seeking a career, the skilled; there remain groups of those whose trade demands an urban population for its practice: the Indians, the Arabs, and in a different sense the ladies from the North-West.

Today's immigrant on one of the traditional routes has, therefore, a larger community ranged to his support, beyond that of his tribe. At no time were the practical benefits of this support very positive, rather the *utani* relationship implied an absence of hostility, except in adversity when assistance might be claimed.

Most of the forms of this *utani* relationship encountered in Dar es Salaam are of the 'passport' type, through generations of travellers passing through each other's territories; some, however, like those with the Ngoni are of the 'conquered vassal' type, the result of old wars, whereafter the victor had the right to indulge in the *utani* abuse of the defeated, to organize his burials, for a *quid pro quo*, and to help himself uninvited to food. In time of need he could also claim the defeated as allies. Finally many are of the true blood-relationship of cousins, but these are not here relevant. The following table gives the tribes with which each of Dar es Salaam's main tribes is said to have *utani* relationship. This table is put in with some reluctance, as it has not been verified, and should be regarded only as a basis for more careful inquiries.

Utani and Language Relationships

The following tribes have *utani* relationships and understand languages as indicated:

Tribe	Watani	Language understood
Zaramo	Nyamwezi, Nyagatwa, Ndengereko, Digo, Doe	Kutu, Kwere, Kami, Nyagatwa, Luguru
Luguru	Sagara, Vidunda, Zigua, Doe, Digo, Sambaa, Bondei, Ngoni, Mbunga, Pogoro, Segeju	Vidunda, Sagara, Zigua, Kwere, Doe, Kutu, Zaramo, Kaguru, Kami
Rufiji Ndengereko	Ndengereko, Nyagatwa, Matumbi, Ngindo, Makonde	Matumbi, Ngindo
Ngindo	Makonde, Mwera, Rufiji, Ndengereko	Matumbi, Ndengereko, Rufiji
Nyamwezi	Zaramo, Ngindo, Sukuma	Sukuma
Yao	Mwera, Ngoni	Mwera, Makua
Matumbi	Ngindo, Makonde, Ndengereko	Ngindo, Ndengereko
Mwera	Ngoni, Yao, Ngindo, Makonde	Yao
Ngoni	Hehe, Yao, Mwera, Makonde, Ngindo, Pogoro, Nyamwezi, Sukuma, Pangwa, Bena, Ndendeule, Matengo, Nyasa, Safwa, Sokile	Ndendeule, Matengo, Nyasa, Bena, Pangwa
Pogoro	Ngoni, Hehe, Ngindo, Sagara, Mbunga	Mbunga, Safwa

Tribe	Watani	Language understood
Makonde	Mwera, Ngindo, Ngoni, Matumbi, Ndengereko	Matumbi, Ndengereko
Makua	Ngoni, Ngindo, Makonde, Yao	Bena
Hehe	Ngoni, Pogoro, Gogo, Bena	Bena
Bondei	Luguru, Zigua, Sambaa	Zigua, Sambaa

Tribe

A more compact community from which the immigrant is never completely divorced is his tribe. Apart from the Manyema and the 'Sudanese' (the remnants of the British and German Askaris) none were found in the survey who had lost their tribal names; these two exceptions have lost the individual names of their Congo and Sudan or other northern tribes, but have re-formed into a closer community of persons with similar background and interests by forming as it were new 'tribes'. In so doing they have in fact knitted themselves closer together than most of the larger tribes, which, simply because they are too large to operate as a unit, each member known to all the others, have got out of focus and lost much of the loyalty they once inspired.

When Dar es Salaam was smaller, and each tribal community was in its turn smaller, the leaders of the tribes had considerable influence. In most cases one of the earliest immigrants became the acknowledged spokesman before Government, and this was given recognition when the Germans insisted that each tribe buried its dead from the hospital, and appointed recognized leaders of each tribe to see to it, and report deaths, for the purposes of a death register. Several tribal associations date their origin from this. There were then the 'presidents' of the main tribes, with assistants, some of them the leaders of geographical pockets of the tribe; lower down in the scale there were messengers who passed round the news of a death in the tribe and invited people to the ceremonies; seldom were there any formal meetings of all members of the tribe, but they met together in strength at funerals and at periodic dances, where old and young both attended; and several of the elders known for their sagacity were used as arbitrators by those of the tribe who trusted them and wished their disputes settled by the law of the tribe, rather than by the universal law of Islam which the courts enforced. It is doubtful if tribal lore and the education in tribal ways of the growing boys was ever undertaken in any organized way by these associations in the town, and such tribal education as boys and girls did obtain was found by going home, back into the orbit of the tribe proper in its essential rural setting.

The fellow-feeling of tribe has not had the effect of separating the members of different tribes out into distinct suburbs or even pockets of a single tribe. The tendency to settle on the side of town nearest one's home can be discerned now only statistically. For instance it is roughly true that Ilala is a Zaramo area, in that they, who form a third of all Dar es Salaam, there form 60 per cent.; and that Magomeni is a Nyamwezi favourite, in that they, who form 3 per cent. of Dar es Salaam as a whole, there form 6·5 per cent. But with a few exceptions such as the small hamlets of Ngoni at Kiwalani, and of Nyamwezi at the back of Kinondoni, there are no areas where a tribe has a village or a hamlet to itself. This of course has had its effect in reducing the influence of tribe on the lives of the immigrants, of diluting the feeling of being surrounded by one's own, and increasing the interest in those of others.

Many factors have tended to weaken the hold of the tribe on the urban African: perhaps the most effective has already been mentioned, that of size, making it impossible for all members to know each other even by sight or repute. The same influence has been at work in the other communities: Oyster Bay[1] has become as much a disparate dormitory suburb as Temeke or Ilala Quarters, as devoid of any community of interests or desire to get together or know one's neighbour.

Size of the tribal community is one factor; another is its being mixed inextricably with other tribes, within all areas, streets, houses, occupations and even families. This has meant that a man's friends, once he has ceased to live with the relative he first went to, are found not in his own closed community, but

[1] A mainly European area.

at his work, where there may be men of a dozen or more tribes working together, at the coffee shop or football club or gambling school or street corner, where if a man met is of the same tribe it is purely accidental.

Another is that one of the aims of the young man coming to town is to escape from the bonds of tribal and family discipline (hence the preference for living with strangers) and he, therefore, does not seek out his tribal leaders, or actively register himself at his association. As the associations have no organization for seeking him out he remains unknown to the leaders; in modern days he has nothing material to gain from the protection of a tribal association, and a steady drain on his purse on the debit side if he does take part in their activities, attending funerals and collections for repatriation or the payment of fines. So most young men keep away from tribal associations, and they are carried on by the original elders, whose reward is the prestige of being a recognized spokesman and a pillar of the funeral ceremonies.

An exception to this is the case of the small up-country tribe, whose members in Dar es Salaam are mainly educated, and Christian, and who form their association because they genuinely feel the need for 'someone of their own kind' in a mainly uneducated, Muslim and coastal town. Such tribes as Pare, Chagga, Luo, have flourishing associations which more resemble the clubs of other immigrants; at the regular meetings of these associations there assemble a fairly high proportion of the small total of members, often bringing their wives, talking the same language—in both senses—and reinforcing the sense of community which exiles have.

Education has been another factor working against the tribe in town, for the reason that the leaders of the associations have almost by definition been elders, who were either completely uneducated, or were educated in the Arab manner by learning by rote passages from the Koran together with *Qasidas*; this type of education in its day gave them much of their prestige, but today the call is all for Western education, and those who grew up too long ago find themselves with diminished prestige, their status questioned by the young, to whom the elders, and the association they stand for, seem out of date and irrelevant. Again this is only generally true, for in some tribal communities the young, in addition to revolting against the old, have formed a new, equally tribally based, association, relying on the younger and more educated members of the tribe in Dar es Salaam: an example of this is the Pogoro Association.

Thus the largest tribal community of all, the Zaramo, who form nearly two-fifths of the population, have no tribal association at all; to them this seems entirely logical: as they say, 'we are the original inhabitants'; to most the necessity for a tribal organization in Dar es Salaam is solely to bury the dead, lest his goods become forfeit and his spirit be not given its due deference; and to this way of thinking those who are the original inhabitants have no need for help in this, for are not their relatives all around them?

Similarly the Rufiji, the second biggest tribe, with 9 per cent. of the population, are so numerous that nobody could lack a relative to bury him; it might be equally argued that they are so numerous that nobody need feel alone: they too have no association, though both tribes have at one time or another had political associations.

The Luguru, the next biggest, have the remnants of an association, though it was again primarily a political one, started by a chief, Kingaro of Kinyori near Morogoro. The Luguru, from whom the Zaramo sprang, claim a sort of ancient authority—if a very tenuous one—over most of the tribes of the province on the ground that only they had a Sultan, and that, therefore, all those who had no ruler of their own (and the Zaramo never achieved a single overlord) owe in a sense allegiance to them. Be that as it may the Luguru have close ties with many of the tribes of Dar es Salaam, particularly the Zaramo, the Vidunda of Kilosa, the Sagara, Zigua, Kwere, Doe and Kutu of the near north and west, whose languages are mutually intelligible; they have an *utani* relationship with a number of tribes: a war relationship, born of fighting, with the Doe of Bagamoyo, who appear to have been the fighting troops of the days of the Kamba war; and with the Ngoni, Mbunga and Pogoro of the south-west with whom there were of old constant clashes. In addition to these relationships born of old defeats and victories there are the 'passport' types of *utani* with the Sagara, Vidunda, Zigua, Digo, Sambaa,

Bondei and Segeju, all of whom had occasion to pass through Luguru territory or through whose territory they themselves had to pass to reach the old first port of Bagamoyo, or on journeys further to the north, to Pangani and Tanga.

Their tribal association is called the Ukami Union (the Kami are the lowlanders, the Luguru proper the men of the Uluguru mountains).

This union which modestly claims twelve members (who are in fact a committee or executive, their numbers thinned by the years) was founded in 1938, and covers the following tribes: the Kwere, Luguru, Kutu, Zigua and Kami, all of whom are said by them to acknowledge one chief Kingaro of Kinyori near Morogoro. Their languages, though different, are related and mutually intelligible. The union was founded during the visit of Kingaro to Dar es Salaam in 1938, when he personally chose its head. Under the head is a committee, a total now of eight, the other four having died. Only the head is chosen by the Sultan, and he then chooses the further members. There is no attempt to have a reporting system, nor is a list kept of members of the tribes here in Dar es Salaam. The members of the union number about 40, but there is no subscription and no regular meetings.

Their main object is to act as a mutual burial society; every time one of their number dies there is an *ad hoc* collection; members are asked for a set amount, which varies, and nonmembers throw their contributions on to a cloth spread on the ground. If the next of kin is inexperienced in buying what is necessary they will help him, but really it is the job of the next of kin, and any surplus left over is his. One member of each of the tribes with whom they have an *utani* relationship must also be present, and will hinder and abuse the procession until paid the customary fee. They retain a sheikh who officiates at their funerals. He is paid a fee of 2 Shs. but then distributes it to the poor.

Their method of keeping in touch and of finding any given person (for instance the addressee of a letter) is typical of the organization of many of these associations: there is no list of all members of the tribe, a method which would these days be quite impracticable, with the swollen numbers and the lack of any enthusiasm on the part of the younger generation for coming into any kind of control or supervision by their elders; instead the simple and effective method used is that the head of the association, an elder of very long standing, knows the leading elders of each subdivision of the tribe in Dar es Salaam: these subdivisions are based on geographical villages or areas in the home country; thus on the affairs of a man from Matombo the head will ask the leading elder (resident in Dar es Salaam) from Matombo to call, and if it is a letter he has to deliver the elder from Matombo will either know the addressee, or will have his own circle of friends and leading men from the smaller subdivisions, the hamlets, of Matombo, who will be consulted, until the man himself is tracked down. Thus on the full tribal level there is no close track kept of the whole population in Dar es Salaam of that tribe, but the ability is there to split the whole population up into progressively smaller communities, until the stage is reached where the ties of kinship, the constant visitings between cousins and second cousins, can be brought into play and used as a medium of communication.

Members of the committee are supposed to give traditional teaching to young boys, but in fact this has more or less died out; the teachings took eight days, and girls had their teachings given by women. Mostly nowadays any such teaching is done up-country, and many children are sent there for this purpose. In Dar es Salaam such things are almost forgotten.

Among the Luguru, even more than among the other close neighbours of Dar es Salaam, the Zaramo, it is customary to return home for the more important events of life: birth, marriage and death; although Luguru do die in town, it is a generally recognized preference to die at home with due rites and among the elders of one's generation, so that in the case of extreme old age or a long and wasting illness, the result of which seems assured, most Luguru make arrangements to return to their home village to die. Similarly with marriage; in the old days, when slavery was still an actuality or a recent memory, it is said to have been very difficult to obtain a local girl in marriage, for fear that she would be sold to the slavers; and in more modern times marriages with town girls are somewhat frowned on for the converse reason that their morals are suspect by the more old-fashioned elders in the home country, and they are believed to be infertile, inconstant and expensive to keep. So young men from the Luguru—as from most other up-country tribes—prefer to take a bride from among their own people, chosen with the knowledge and approval of the parents on both sides (a thing not easy to arrange in Dar es Salaam itself, where resident parents are in a minority). But it is at the time of birth that the Luguru are particularly anxious to go home, to have the baby surrounded by the women of the family, and again with due traditional rites. This preference for bearing children in the home country results in only 5 per cent. of Luguru males having been born in Dar es Salaam, compared to 26 per cent. of all Africans surveyed.

At the time of initiation of boys and girls, it is also customary for the Luguru to go home: so much so that there is no organization in Dar es Salaam for the teaching, or the dances customary at this time.

With the most important occasions in life requiring a return home, where the full organization of tribal life and tradition can be applied in a form undiluted by town ways and unmarked by the influence of alien tribes, the Luguru are able to retain their tribal feeling of oneness more strongly, and to live the alien life of town as a temporary sojourn, their traditional beliefs and ties with the home village constantly renewed.

Small family disputes, or matters which require to be decided on a basis of tribal custom, are settled within the community by the elders of each family rather than by the central organization. There is in fact no set organization for this purpose, and a dispute is taken to the elder at the lowest level at which there is to be found a man whom both sides to the dispute will accept—perhaps an uncle, or a cousin; a few elders have established a reputation for sagacity, but there is nothing to force anyone to go to them or prevent them consulting another elder who is in that particular case preferred.

The Nyamwezi, another of the larger tribal communities in Dar es Salaam from the earliest days when they were the porters on the caravans, had at one time a strong leadership, which they shared with the Sukuma—to whom they are related; there are Sukuma and Nyamwezi scattered all over town, with a preponderance in the rural areas both within and without the Municipality, as far as Kawe, Ukonga and Ubungo;

in the earlier days, when recruitment for clove-picking in Zanzibar and other traditional forms of employment were less organized, the immigrant Nyamwezi had greater need of help from his tribal representatives in Dar es Salaam: today little remains of this but a small 'doss-house' run by the tribal head for those who cannot be bothered to look themselves out a relative, or perhaps wish to keep together as a band while waiting for their ship. Some scandals over common funds broke this association as they have broken so many, and now most are reluctant to join in any such organization which requires subscriptions.

None the less, the head of the Nyamwezi tribe in Dar es Salaam, Juma Sultani, retains very considerable personal prestige, as his reputation stretches back to the home country, and this prestige does to some extent give the tribal community in Dar es Salaam a sense of unity.

In 1952 there was an attempt to form a new association, called the Sukuma Association; this was partly a revolt against the traditional elders, and was organized by younger men as a branch of the home union; like many associations of this type it depended on the passing enthusiasm of a few men, usually educated and, therefore, almost by definition subject to transfer. The association was born, and remains on the books, but a short talk with today's leaders of it is enough to show that it exists only on paper.

What community of feeling there is among the Nyamwezi is in the rural pockets where they form, in a limited area, a majority, and can hold their traditional dances at week-ends and talk their own language as though at home. For the lonely man who retains strong memories and ties with home this is a' congenial atmosphere, and explains why so many of the Nyamwezi are to be found in the rural areas, cultivating while waiting for a job, or the next clove season, or simply because the market prices are higher than at home, and keeping together more perhaps than any other of the major tribes of Dar es Salaam.

Often found in company with the Nyamwezi, in rural pockets, are the Ngoni, a tribe of raiders turned mercenaries. Through their constant wars they formed an *utani* relationship with a very large number of tribes; through their service with the German forces they became constant visitors to and settlers in Dar es Salaam. They, like the Nyamwezi, had a strong organization among themselves, and like that of the Nyamwezi it has withered away, though not to quite the same extent.

One reason for the Ngoni tribal organization retaining some of its strength is that they tend, more than any other tribe, to settle in pockets: their 'capital' in Dar es Salaam is Keko, where their most prominent elder, Ali Magurumbasi, was the first squatter on this Government land. He is still there, and this continuity and longevity undoubtedly contribute, as they do in the case of Juma Sultani of the Nyamwezi, to his continued influence. Outlying pockets, whose chief elders consult Ali Magurumbasi and, as it were, owe him allegiance as their senior (though he does not issue instructions to them or control them in any way) are to be found at Kijito Nyama (the furthest part of Msasani, a purely rural area) where the chief elder is Juma Ngahokara; at Kiwalani (in Kipawa, another rural area) whose chief elder is Usangire Putile; at Upanga where was Hamisi Faranyaki; and at Kinondoni where is Mohamed Linikuta. There are also links with pockets in Mbagala and Bagamoyo. In these areas the Ngoni though not unmixed are in a local majority, and are able like the Nyamwezi in similar areas to have their own dances and speak their own language, although in Dar es Salaam as a whole they are only a small fraction of the population, the tenth biggest tribe. In Keko, although they are quite outnumbered by the numerous other tribes which have settled there, they have retained their pre-eminence through Ali Magurumbasi who as first settler is the 'squire' of the place, whose permission succeeding settlers sought to build and cultivate in the creek, until in the post-war rush new immigrants became too numerous and too urgently in need of a place to live to bother with such things. Near him in Keko lives also Salehe Kilema who was at one time recognized by Government as the Ngoni spokesman.

As with the Luguru the chief elders made contact with any given person through the elders in Dar es Salaam of the area of the home country from which they came; to be sure Ali Magurumbasi claims that every new immigrant is registered in a book and pays a subscription, but the book is not to be seen and is in fact unlikely ever to have existed. He claims, too, that a new immigrant who has presented himself before the elders (and nowadays very many of the younger men do not) may be referred, if he does not know already, to the chief elder in Dar es Salaam of his part of the home country, and that elder will probably ask him who he is staying with, who his father and relatives are, so that for a time at least he can be traced; after a few weeks he himself will have visited any relatives he knows scattered over Dar es Salaam, and thereafter, however often he may move house, he will not be difficult for his own people to trace. But being introduced in this way to the elder in Dar es Salaam of his home village does not necessarily mean that he goes to live near that elder: in the old days this probably happened more, but now when it is so easy to move from end to end of town to visit friends, a man will go where it is convenient for his work or where rent is at his level, rather than to be physically near to his own folk.

When a chief elder of one of the Ngoni pockets dies, the Ngoni of that pocket decide his successor, and inform Ali Magurumbasi: he has no power to appoint, or conversely to depose, for the position of chief elder, though it is an office to the extent that such an elder has functions: as spokesman before Government, as the medium through whom Ali Magurumbasi or the local Jumbe would consult the people of the pocket, as adviser in parochial and family affairs, organizer of burials, arbitrator in little disputes, particularly those which require to be decided by the tribal custom; yet it is an office in the structure of the little community, the pocket of that tribe, not primarily that of the tribe at large, or of Government; it is one which has grown from the ground up. It is, therefore, of the most valuable and satisfactory kind.

In common with other tribal associations, whose functions now are limited, at the full tribal level, to burials of their dead, the Ngoni Association has below the chief elder another elder who is a kind of messenger or secretary; it is his function to know the subsidiary elders and when one of their community has died to take the news round to these and see that as many as possible of the community attend, and thus spread among themselves the cost of the shroud and other necessaries of a funeral. These messengers are not paid but they have considerable prestige and must in time find themselves in a favourable position to succeed the chief elder, since they know and are known by all the more important elders of the tribe, and as the chief elder becomes more aged take over gradually much of his duties.

In theory most of these associations have meetings, but it is very seldom nowadays that in fact they take place, only when 'there is something to discuss which concerns all'. Few matters in town now concern all the members of a single tribe and nobody else, unless it be a cemetery for the Manyema (who have their own), or the death of a very eminent elder. So in practice there are partial meetings at funerals and at weddings, and even to some extent after *jando* (circumcision ceremonies held on an all-Muslim, not tribal basis) when the boys of the tribe and their parents may celebrate together.

Of a different type are the associations of the Manyema and 'Sudanese'. Neither of course is a true tribe, and the Sudanese do not even come all from the Sudan. The Manyema are partly the descendants of the slaves from the Congo, the name itself being taken from an area in the Congo, and partly of a company of mutineers who fled in Belgian times from the Congo, many to join later the German forces; and the Sudanese, or Nubi, are the remains of the askaris demobilized after the first war. The two groups have some things in common, a predominance of old people, and of old women in particular, among their number; close association with a government which has passed away; long residence in Dar es Salaam, dating back to a time when they each had their own village: the Manyema lived in the area now covered by the New Africa Hotel, to the Askari Statue, and back to the Splendid Hotel, whence they were town-planned in 1906 or thereabouts and moved to Bagamoyo Street; meanwhile the Sudanese village was established in Gerezani, where is now the open space at the south-west end of Kariakoo, and along the Arab Street section of Pugu Road; the Sudanese were cleared from there after the big fire of 1921, and moved to Chang'ombe kwa Wanubi. With a fairly exclusive locality of residence, both these groups had by recent years at least become 'tribes' in the sense of having a common feeling of loyalty to each other in the face of a world outside that was 'different': both groups considered themselves, and still do, rather superior to the other tribes of the town; neither has any ties of *utani* with any of the Tanganyika tribes—naturally enough as they never fought or travelled as tribal people but under the protection of Arabs or Germans.

The formal association of the Sudanese was formed in 1921, and at first they had annual elections, by open discussion and agreement, but they so seldom wished to change their officers that there have not been elections for some time now and the present officers in fact hold their positions for life. The association claims 350 members, which must include all women and children, as there are hardly a hundred adult male Nubi left now, only half a dozen or so being from the original soldiers. They cover many tribes, Dinka, Shilluk and so on, with different languages and chiefs, but their isolation from the other tribes has by now thrown them so much together that they have formed a 'Sudanese' tribe whose language is Swahili, and only a few old people retain any of the original languages. Most of the children know only Swahili and Arabic (the latter language was a *lingua franca* to the educated of the South Sudan). The Dar es Salaam association is also the headquarters for some small branches elsewhere in the territory. Head of them all is a woman, Mama Kidimara, the oldest left alive. There used to be a male head, one Jabiri, who lived at Chang'ombe, but since his death there has been no active head. Being so few they can all meet together should there be anything to discuss, and they have no sub-branches in Dar es Salaam: the last occasion for such a meeting was when in 1956 scholarships to Egypt were being offered. They have otherwise no regular meetings, only the now more frequent funerals, which they can all attend, and at which all contribute to the cost of the shroud. They still have their own dances, the Daluka for weddings, the Tumbura, Bori and Gundu for driving out evil spirits; but they have no set place for dancing them, nor are they exclusive to the 'tribe'. Their children have no formal teaching in the lore of their ancestors, and they follow more and more the Muslim ceremonies of puberty. 'We are so few now, and the rest are so many, that we cannot keep these things up.' Their old position as the Government's favourite askaris is lost, though the Traffic Lines, their old barracks, which they still call 'the Boma', stands, though much altered now. Many of the

German Askaris were allowed to rent accommodation outside, and both Nubi and Manyema availed themselves of this to settle in the surrounding countryside.

Their private disputes they say they would take to one of their own elders, but they are so few and so old that such disputes are very few indeed. Unlike the Manyema, who are the citizens of Dar es Salaam *par excellence*, they have between them all not a single Ward Councillor.

Perhaps just *because* they are so firmly entrenched in Dar es Salaam, the Manyema have no real association in Dar es Salaam; they feel, as do the Zaramo, that they are the 'original people' of Dar es Salaam and, therefore, they have no need of a special organization to protect them. From the earliest days they have had a form of association, which like those of other major tribes has become disused except for the one purpose of burying their dead. The Manyema, alone of all the tribes in Dar es Salaam, have their own freehold cemetery. Theirs was the first mosque to be built, and its successor is still one of the best: it is true that the first three Imams were Zaramo, but later the Manyema were sufficiently in control of it to replace the Zaramo with four unpaid alternates of their own, of whom one Bakari Salum continues to take the services. A young man who has two houses in Dar es Salaam, and has lived here in some affluence all his life, was able to say with confidence—if over-simplifying—that there is no Manyema association in Dar es Salaam. What he means is that for him and his generation it has no force or usefulness; indeed most of these associations whose sole function now is the organization and financing of funerals are confined mainly to the older men, the younger ones thinking there is time enough to worry about such things later. This particular young man attends no special mosque, his friends are scattered all over town, not confined to any one locality as the Manyema used to be, and of all tribes; he has no recollection or tradition of where his family came from, or even whether his father came from Tanganyika or the Congo. But he does hold sufficiently to his tribe to have married a Manyema girl, quite uneducated, rather than a stranger of like education to himself—he completed the middle school course and is literate in English. But most of his friends belong to his own generation and ideas, being found mainly in his

E

football club. Thus the Manyema, so like the Nubi in some ways, have managed to fit themselves into the changed ways without losing their feeling of exclusive solidarity, backed by their strong tactical position as house-owners who got in on the ground floor.

An example of another kind of tribe is the Pare, which like the Chagga has few members in Dar es Salaam, but those few mainly Christian, educated and well-off, with better-paid jobs. Many of the wives are also educated, often teachers, and this is reflected in the kind of tribal meetings which are held, more like those of a European club, where men and their wives meet to exchange news of home and of their life in town; meetings are regular and organized, there is a constitution and officers, regularly elected, and the members of the association tend to be young to middle-aged rather than elders.

The Pare are one of the smaller communities: in the 1952 census there were less than 100 of all ages and both sexes, and they themselves claim some 30–40 adults. They are thus able to be a closely knit society, feeling themselves somewhat apart from the general run of Dar es Salaam people by reason of their better education and standards of living. This is reflected in the fact that four of their six leading officers live in Quarters (a term used to denote Government- or company-built rented housing of permanent construction). All are elected annually by secret ballot. There is a register of members, and a monthly subscription of 1 Sh. There is no pressure put on a newcomer to join, but the advantages of the society of his fellows are usually enough to induce him to do so. They do organize funerals like other older types of association, but in the nature of things this young community is not often called upon to do so. They have no dances here in Dar es Salaam, or traditional teachings, the children being brought up in Christian rites. The question of disputes being settled by members of the association has not arisen. Finally they do not use the association as a postal distribution centre, but each has his letters addressed to him direct through his firm or department.

This type of association reflects a tribal group in Dar es Salaam which has a real cohesion in modern conditions; the members of the group gain a real advantage, of mutual sympathy and understanding, from each other's regular company; and the reason for this cohesion, as for that—of a very different kind—of the Manyema, is that they are an exclusive group, apart from the bulk of the population. They are the strangers and the exiles: for the bulk of the population, the uneducated, Muslim, coastal common denominator, there is not the incentive to band closely together, for they are strong in numbers and the atmosphere of the townsfolk is familiar and sympathetic to them; they can rely on the number of their own kin for the mutual comfort and understanding which the few from the distant tribes have to get from a society of the whole tribe.

Although the Chagga are very largely a community of the educated, there are, in addition to some young boys down to see the world and working in hotels, some elders of long standing: for instance the Chagga Association claims to have been among the first, having fairly regular meetings from 1919 on, when there were only a very few; those early settlers, now older men, are still acknowledged as the prominent men of the community, but the life of the association now derives from the great majority of young, educated, career-workers, who come here in a job, go home on leave, and return. They are the officers of the association, though they are careful to keep the older men on the committee and pay them due deference; nevertheless these older men feel that the atmosphere has changed, and they do not have much to do with the affairs of the association.

Even these comparatively young leaders of the association find it difficult to keep the interest and allegiance of the still younger, many of whom are not members; it is not until something practical is done, beyond mere meeting for meeting's sake, such as the organization of a tea-party on Chagga Day, that such people are attracted to join. Even the feeling of apartness of an educated, Christian community in the midst of an uneducated Muslim population is not so strong as it used to be, as the numbers of similar persons increase with the years with the centralization of government and business in Dar es Salaam, and it is more possible to find friends from among people 'of one's kind' outside one's own tribe.

Somewhat similar to that of the Pare is the association of the Nyakyusa, a young man's association: this was recently formed, from an educated minority, and although it is open to all Nyakyusa it was used mainly by this minority; it has remained sufficiently alive to hold elections and actually change some of its officers, and they would like to have official backing in order to run a sort of employment advice bureau and if necessary a repatriation organization; on their own, however, they have not the cohesion to do so, and in fact the association is more a club of a few like-minded members of the tribe in Dar es Salaam, which would perhaps have passed away like so many products of a temporary enthusiasm were it not that the necessity for registration of the association periodically reminds them of its existence.

Another of the same kind is that of the Fipa, who on their formation in 1953 claimed 80 members out of the 250 Fipa of all ages and both sexes in Dar es Salaam; this association ran into trouble when its president joined the United Tanganyika Party and was, therefore, ostracized by all; the officers of the association, once chosen, put themselves forward for re-election annually, at any rate in theory; but in practice with the entry of politics it has become too hot for most to handle and has fallen into abeyance.

One tribe where the changing needs of the tribal members in town are reflected is the Pogoro, a fairly large community (some 1,600) mainly Christian and educated but with a minority of the labouring class; they began in 1912 with one of the old type of associations; it had a president and secretary, but also an ancient without portfolio, repository of their lore and history, who was the real organizer of burials; the secretary is a young, educated man, who would more normally form a breakaway association in opposition to that of the elders, but in this case has chosen to bring new life to the old one. Although they have a constitution which enjoins annual elections, they forget to have them, and the ancient is of course a permanent institution; it is admitted that the majority of members of the tribe do not join or take any part in the association; burials are in practice conducted, through the ancient and his messenger, by the old men of the tribe, since it is only the older men of long standing who are known to the messenger and traceable by him when the time comes; the association organizes no dances—this dates from a time when dances led to fighting, for which the officers of an association were held responsible:

so now in the accepted tradition of all organizations they take no responsibility for the acts of their wilder elements; letters are often addressed to their 'accredited agent', who used to be a houseboy in Government House and was, therefore, in a position of eminence.

The place of this association in organizing dances has been taken by another, the Ulanga Mahenge Drum Study Society, which was formed in opposition to the main association; this, having something practical to offer, is a flourishing society; a less successful one is yet another breakaway called the Ulanga Young Boys, which has very few members and is quite cut off from the older association.

Of all the tribal associations most fall into a middle group, less clannish than the Nyamwezi or Ngoni, a little more coherent than the too numerous Zaramo, Rufiji or Luguru, not so exclusive as the old communities of Manyema or Sudanese, or the small new communities of Pare and Chagga: such a tribal community is that of the Mbisa, who live in Northern Rhodesia, neighbours to the Rungu, who are here in far greater numbers. They number some 30 to 50 persons, mainly young men who came here as houseboys and clerks, not for manual labour—for which the normal market is south, in the mines. Most are pagan in their own country, though there are blocks of Christians and Muslims: on arrival in Dar es Salaam the pagans quickly choose themselves one of the two main religions.

Although the members are so few, and in education rather above the average, the Mbisa has not become one of the young men's associations such as those of other similar tribes like the Chagga; their association goes back to 1919, and is still led by those older men who came in at that time; there are no regular meetings, and if an officer of the association has to be replaced, which is very seldom, as they are appointed for life, there is a friendly, informal meeting of the elders. There is no registration or in fact any organization except the usual one for the burial of one of their number: even for this there is no 'messenger' to spread the news, but it spreads by their mutual visiting, the elder of the bereaved family taking the initiative. Two elders of the bereaved family will make a collection and take the proceeds to buy a shroud and planks for the grave, and make arrangements for a Sheikh to take the service, while two younger men of the tribe will dig the grave; they take no part in settling the inheritance, except as expert witnesses before the Liwali's court, where the law is that of Islam.

At one time they had an official flag, like many of the older associations, and an official number (No. 20) given to a list of Government-approved dances; it is symptomatic of the decline of these old associations that the flag was accidentally burned and has not been replaced. Now they do not have their own dances and for puberty rites join in with other Muslims for the non-tribal *jando* rites.

This typical association shows how what was once a compact community has lost its sense of unity and exclusiveness; the older men remember but do little about their old association, except for funerals; while the younger men find little need for one, relying on their closer kin, and, to a large extent now, on themselves.

Another example is the Nyiramba Association, whose head was at one time the spokesman for all the tribes of that direction: the Nyaturu, Nyiramba, Rangi and Gogo. When the Government ceased to use the system of tribal Jumbes his influence became confined to members of his own tribe, the Nyiramba; he has a stall in the central market, where he is easily met by any of his tribe who wish to see him or inquire about another; but the activities of this association also do not go beyond burials, and the delivery of some letters, and the putting up for a fee (20 cents a night) of any who cannot find a room; recently a rival association, of the young man's kind, was formed; it conforms closely to the type, having been started by a group of young and educated men, in a flush of enthusiasm which was not sustained, and now exists in little more than name: for such associations have nothing practical to offer, and the companionship of persons of their own tribe is not any longer so valuable a thing to tribes with many independent links in town, who do not think of themselves as a people apart, and are prepared to find friends, not very unlike themselves in education, background and religion, from among the people they meet, of any tribe, at their work or in the houses where they rent a room.

There remains one further type of tribal association, which

is half-way to an association based on kinship, in that it covers, not the whole tribe but only those who come from a certain area: such are the Mbaha Union and the Marui Association.

The former is a union of the emigrants from the Mbaha area of the Nyanja tribe of Songea District; the Nyanja are a section of the Nyasa, and the union itself estimates that there are about thirty emigrants from Mbaha here, about half of whom are members; they are also members of the wider Ngonyama Union (a name made up from the initial letters of the three neighbouring tribes, Ngoni, Nyasa and Matengo) which has sufficient vitality to run a football team. The members of the tribe who come up here are mainly the more educated who seek clerical or artisan jobs which, they say, are difficult to get on the Rand, the market for their labouring classes.

As they are all from the same village, and to some degree related, they do in fact receive from each other practical help, in loans to tide over a period of unemployment, or to enable a member to visit home: not only is security for such loans good with people whose families are neighbours back home, but even without such security they feel a real obligation to help, which is not nearly so strong when the other is only a member of a large tribe. Particularly they help each other by keeping track of any suitable vacancies for jobs, and informing early those of their number who have not yet landed one. They tend to live in groups of two or three, particularly bachelors, and if they can they get three adjoining rooms in a Swahili house, thus forming a small homogeneous enclave in an alien community. With this mutual support they are able to organize a Sunday entertainment, usually the dance *mnganda* in one of several different styles, where one or more teams of dancers will perform, for the enjoyment of themselves and of by-standers of other tribes—for this very modern-looking dance, danced in modern clothes by obviously educated young men, has not the disadvantage of seeming old-fashioned and 'backwoods', as other traditional dances have. The picture of a clannish band of exiles is completed by their habit of doing a three-year 'tour', as bachelors, then returning with their wives and children (from home) to form a complete family, talking their own language among themselves—many hardly succeed in learning Swahili in a three-year tour—and losing none of the traditions of home, thinking always of the time when their career will be finished and they can 'retire home'. Even sanctions can be applied in so compact a community, for if a man refuses to accept advice, or the verdict of the elders in a dispute, a letter can be sent reporting him to his parents or elders, who can bring further pressure to bear.

They run the football team begun under the name of 'Navy', referred to above, while another joint effort is that of the 'Radio Players', all Mbaha people (who have made many records, plays, concerts and recordings of dances and tribal songs); they are considering letting the Ngoni and Matengo in on this. Unlike the Nyasa they are not interested in jazz, but are specialists in their traditional dancing and songs, fortified by much listening to Lusaka radio.

Their ties with home are strengthened by their custom of sending children home to school: they say that standards at home are higher, as there is more competition, but that if a child has failed to get into a middle school at home he may be brought to Dar es Salaam where it is comparatively easy to get in: a corollary of this is that there is a steady stream of remittances home from the exiles in Dar es Salaam, to pay for the school fees.

A contrast to this tight-knit association is the Marui Association, formed from those Zaramo who come from the Marui area, about three hours' journey from Dar es Salaam by car, and also those from Samvula, Tete, Ngazire, Kisangire, Vikumburu, Kihare and Yombo. This association has little more practical result to show for its existence than the older type of tribal association; it has three officers, or elders, of long standing, who are permanent leaders, but apart from performing a few funerals appear to do nothing; even funerals seem to be slipping out of their hands, and it was admitted that a man of their area might well die in hospital in Dar es Salaam without their coming to hear of it. Except for the fact that its leaders are elders it bears a close resemblance to the type of association formed by a few enthusiastic young men who are transferred or lose interest shortly after. It suffers from the same inhibitions as other associations of the main tribes, that the public have been bitten so often by such unions whose subscriptions fly off into the pockets of their treasurers, who sooner or later abscond;

they are now careful, they say, not to have any subscription: it is more likely that nobody is willing to subscribe.

INTERLUDE

Kinondoni Rural

The municipal boundary runs the far side of Mwananyamara kwa Ali Maua (the village this side being called Mwananyamara kwa Ali Nyanza). On the side is the pump which extracts water for the Tanganyika Packers; the Lake is said to be deep and the water never to have dried up; there is a hippo in it.

Here where the population is mostly Nyamwezi but with a mixture of Zaramo and a few of other tribes, there is great variety in the windows; some are merely holes blocked with plaited coconut fronds, some have wooden shutters, some are picked out with paint, or blackened around; some have a pane of glass, or a sheet of mosquito netting, or expanded metal, or bars; a few have curtains; and one had the coil springs of an easy chair.

There are a comparatively large number of mosques in these rural areas, each kept up by a single man, not by general sub-scription; most are mud and wattle, but in Kinondoni (as opposed to Temeke) they are on the whole of better materials and in better repair than the surrounding houses, several being well whitewashed; perhaps this is because they are the responsibility of a rich man rather than of a Sheikh (as in the town) who relies on contributions, most of which must go towards his own keep.

A clothes-line is full of pink pillow cases (over the top only, held on by tapes round the back), and a pink sheet; nearby a launderer is ironing, over a mile from the nearest village.

Throughout Kinondoni one finds signs of the proximity of the sea (nearly two miles away) with nets hanging up to dry, floats being made, fish being dried, and the little matting weights, filled with stones, which hold the nets down. People from here fish both at Msasani and at Gerezani, at the far end of the harbour, and even as far as Ununio.

Along the sandy paths comes the Municipal health lorry, as ubiquitous as the mosquito sprayers.

People here are more polite (to each other) than elsewhere in Dar es Salaam, '*shikamuus*' being bandied about like '*jambos*';[1] any older woman gets it, or older man, and quite a lot of middle-aged men, though both my guides were men of substance (one an over-seer of many years' standing, the other a Ward Councillor).

---

[1] *Shikamuu*: literally 'I grasp your feet', the old slave greeting. *Jambo*: the normal greeting, equivalent to 'how do you do?'

'*Sabulkheri*'[1] is rather putting on airs here, among the Wanyamwezi.

A fruitful source of racial aversion must be the way African children when little are frightened by the '*Mzungu*'[2] bogyman; if one is naughty he or she is told, 'you be good or the Mzungu will eat you up'; many a time I am greeted by a terrified and howling child held fast by a smiling mother or elder sister while this threat is applied; they seem, surprisingly, to get over it quickly enough when a little bigger, and most children are not shy to approach a European, but something of the early terror must remain and become fixed in a general attitude.

To withhold one's own name, or even more the name of another, is instinctive; a neighbour will never divulge the name of the owner of a house if the owner is anywhere about: for one thing there is the fear of giving the wrong name, most people having more than one, to make tracing more difficult if one is being sought by authority for failure to pay tax, desertion from a contract, a crime, or anything else. It would be a great psychological advantage if this survey could dispense with names.

Brummy jewellery has come to stay; many of the women even out in the coconut plantations are now wearing the gold-coloured earrings (*heleni*[3]) and necklets as worn by their European sisters nearer the sea-front.

A police askari is on patrol, alone, in the backwoods behind Kinondoni; at night their patrols are confined to the built-up areas. A sergeant is also around on his motor-cycle.

Some of the older houses are built in a hollow square, one having as many as 22 rooms, each about 8 ft. by 8 ft. and 5 ft. or so high, neatly plastered, with good doors, many with slogans painted on them: 'gone to Kahama' and so on. At least two of these hollow squares are used for up-country dances every Saturday night, going through to Sunday. Nowadays many dances are danced, the various tribes dancing in the same place and watching each other's. A house nearby has a stack of *ingata*, the coronets of banana leaf which are used for carrying loads on the head: but these were stained red and are used as anklets and armlets for dances. If these Nyamwezi have a dispute they take it to the owner of the compound group of huts, the head of the family as it were, and if he is defeated by it they then go, not to the tribal head but to the Headman.

An old man passes with the long-handled brushes used for sweeping the cobwebs from the high ceilings of Swahili houses; the

---

[1] *Sabulkheri*: an Arabic greeting, 'good morning'.
[2] *Mzungu*: European.
[3] *Heleni*: a phonetic spelling of ear-ring, *l* and *r* being interchangeable.

poles are of mangrove, the brush part of sisal, and several people have this as their main trade; in the coconut plantation country there are of course many making thatch, also mats, plaited, and sewn together on little boxes which stretch the material tight.

There seem to be an inordinate number of Triang tricycles in the bush: almost any house of pretensions has one; today I saw a child's car, apparently in running order; sets of milk tins of different sizes make a set of drums on which they play tunes, while others strung on axles make a sort of hobby-wheel; everywhere there are Dieldrin tins (for palm-wine tapping, and others use oil or paint tins), baby powder, tennis ball and insecticide tins, which have found their way inland from Oyster Bay and the Kinondoni European houses. The child which had the car had also gum boots on. All the paths bear the tracks of cycles.

Many houses have fancy numbers on the doors, such as 1765, or Post Office Box numbers; one man (at present in jail) had some six notices round his house, with arrows pointed in all directions giving his name, address, and instructions to visitors; another had his name and address and the suffix: 'a fine boxer'; many of these signs are well painted on proper boards, some with rain-guards.[1]

Extended family

Of course it is not the tribe as a whole, even in his home country, which makes a man feel at home. The tribe, or even a section of it, rarely convenes except in emergency; it makes itself felt for the most part through its traditional officers, the clan heads, the subchiefs and headmen. In town none of the leaders of the tribes are traditional, in the sense that they come from 'royal' families; they owe their position as leaders mainly to prior arrival, and then (as between early settlers) to personality. They have none of the backing of the old tribal religion, with its associations of particular groves, annual ceremonies, and initiation and the teaching of tribal lore. In no tribal association in Dar es Salaam have such functions been taken over by the town leaders; where the tribal territory is within reach those who wish to attend such ceremonies attend them at home; among the more distant tribes they are simply omitted, and a tribe without the tribal religion, with its secular duties performed by police, courts, hospitals and so on, must in time lose its reason for cohesion. The tribesman then

[1] Note: this and some other Interludes have previously appeared in *Tanganyika Notes and Records*, to the Editor of which acknowledgement is made.

falls back on the core of the tribal structure, the extended family.

The web of kinship

When an African is asked, hypothetically, 'if you could rescue from drowning either your wife or your brother, which would you save?' the odds are heavily in favour of his leaving his wife to go under. The family in the Western sense of a man, his wife and his children, though important to him, and to his confidence and sense of well-being, is not the most important; his more binding tie is with his brothers, uncles, cousins. Hence the paradox that when the up-country African steams into Dar es Salaam station to make his fortune, he does not come as a stranger, though his wife, if he has one, is left behind: he comes, quickly contacts a close relative, and is at once enmeshed again in the web of kinship. Very few indeed come to Dar es Salaam without knowing the name and address of at least one such relative, to whom he goes on arrival, if he is not met at the station, and with whom he lives and feeds until he has sorted himself out. So the loneliness of great cities cannot afflict the African in the way it can afflict the European or American who is flung, alone, into the vortex of strange faces.

This web of kinship may be of great assistance on arrival, first in breaking the first shock of strangeness, and tiding him over the first few days (though financially most bring enough to keep them for the first week or two), and later in helping him to get a job. Jobs now are hard to come by, with a shrinking market for the normal unskilled labourer, and without a sweetener few foremen will take on a man unless he happens to be related, or unless his relatives can pull some strings. Thereafter he will spend much of his time out of hours in visiting other relatives and being introduced, until he has a criss-cross of places where he is welcome and can claim help in time of trouble, a place to hide from the tax-clerks or his creditors, a free meal, free room or share of it, or a small loan; thenceforward, however much he may be bewildered by the strangeness of life in town he is never alone, nor is he dependent on his own strength and confidence to anything like the same extent as the man who has only the support of his wife;

particularly as so very many of the wives in Dar es Salaam are uneducated and even less sophisticated than their newly arrived husbands.

Soon he acquires friends at his work, or picks up acquaintances at *hotelis*[1] or gambling clubs, and these may in time become his closest friends, but the web of kinship remains, and the help which he sought in his first and hard days is sought in turn from him, the circle of cousins, uncles and nephews continuing to practise in the town the family communism which was the law and practice in the up-country village, levying from the harder-working and more successful a continuous toll which goes to support the weak, the unlucky, the thriftless or the idle.

Of the many who claimed, in answer to a question, to be 'married', it is believed that the majority have marriages which are either shortlived, though a minority are formally entered into, or are temporary unions for so long as the infatuation or the convenience lasts. The nature of these unions is discussed later in this report. Where so many are of comparatively short duration, and based on such frail foundations, it is to a man's kin, his extended family, that he turns when in need, rather than to a companion, whom he calls *mpishi* (cook); who, if she knows that he is hard up, may leave him, and on whose loyalty he cannot for a moment depend.

Suburbs

We have examined some human groupings: the groups of 'related' tribes; the tribes themselves, and sections of them and the extended family; there are also geographical groupings, which up-country tend also to bind men together and give each that feeling that he is not alone, which is necessary to support his confidence. In his home country the human and the geographical groupings are inseparable: the tribe inhabits mainly the tribal territory, the section of the tribe its own particular section of that territory; the individual ridge or valley is the territory of an even smaller subdivision. Geographical nearness, particularly if the area is cut off, or compact, reinforces near relationship.

Here in town also there are recognizable geographical

[1] *Hoteli*: eating-house.

divisions: there are the main wards, Kariakoo, Ilala, Magomeni, Temeke, and Kinondoni/Msasani; each ward has its
known boundaries, its executive head and his assistants; its
council; all have a certain degree of self-sufficiency, with their
own mosques, schools, markets, bars and shops, some their
own dance halls. In the large new suburbs which were created,
to a town plan, from 1951 onwards, it was a fundamental
object of the plan that each suburb should be so self-sufficient
as to develop a corporate spirit of its own. This may in time
become so: at present it is not; a man may live in Temeke but
he looks to the centre of town, using his own suburb merely as
a place to sleep; facilities and amenities such as schools,
hospitals and markets do not make a community, though their
absence may help to destroy one; nor do institutions which
have had to be manufactured, such as the ward councils (had
there been a community spirit there, something like these
councils would in the course of time have grown up). Such a
spirit manifests itself in many ways: where a man finds his
friends, where he goes for his stroll in the evenings (and here
the pattern is twisted by the very newness of most of the
suburbs, for a man's old friends are by these large-scale shifts
of population scattered all over town, some in the old parts
and some in the new, and his evening visitings are similarly
scattered); there would be clubs, perhaps football matches,
on a ward basis, were there any feeling of ward solidarity,
but there are not; it would be too much to expect, in an
illiterate and uneducated population, ward newspapers, but
even ward branches of political societies lack any parochial
warmth; interest in ward council elections, meetings, requirements of the ward, all would be developments to be expected
were the wards units, but all are lacking. Even shopping is to a
very large extent done in the central market rather than in the
ward markets.

These wards are of course, with the exception of Kariakoo,
artificial groupings for administrative convenience; their subdivisions have a much better chance of evoking a 'parochial'
loyalty.

Particularly is this so of the groups of houses which grew up
naturally, without planning. These are in Dar es Salaam of
two kinds, the slices of rural Africa which by an accident of

boundary are included in the town but were incorporated with their administrative and social organization intact; and the more urban areas (classed as village for the purpose of this survey) which, though often composed mainly of immigrant Africans, have built up an administrative and social organization very similar to that of a rural area.

To take an example of a Rural area: the area called in this survey Kipawa (more or less coterminous with the Health Department's Mwale area) includes the village of Kipawa itself, just within the Municipal boundary; it was once part of the Kiserawe District, coming under the Mtoni area which contained Mbagala, Buguruni, Msasani, Mabibo, Segerea, Kinyerezi, Mtoni and Tabata; as such it came under the usual District hierarchy, except that since the Zaramo had never had a traditional chief, but only a series of fenced villages (*pongono*) each under a sort of 'chief elder', there was for some time no apex to the pyramid of headman, until shortly after the war there was created the artificial post of *Jumbe Mkuu* to be the senior 'chief' of the District; the *Mndewa* or headman of Mtoni then came under him, and under the headman of Mtoni was an unpaid head of Kipawa; this, confined to the village of Kipawa, was the only original part of the large area now known as Kipawa; the other parts were later settlements, or were pieces excised from Kiserawe District by later movements of the Municipal boundary, and tacked loosely on to Kipawa as being too small to be on their own; such are Minazi Mirefu, a comparatively new village, previously bare ground, whose inhabitants were asked by Government to choose themselves a head, as they had no traditional head: they chose one Ramadhani Mwinyi Bahari, a Zigua, not because he had any traditional rights there, but because he was a man of character and personality and nobody else could claim longer residence; another hamlet is Kiwalani: this was Government land deriving from the plantations of the Sultan of Zanzibar, and after the first war demobilized soldiers, mostly Nyamwezi, and later some Ngoni, were allowed to settle there; the Nyamwezi died off and the headman is now an Ngoni, Usangire Putile, who is in close touch with the Ngoni 'representative', Ali Magurumbasi who lives in Keko, though he is not in any practical sense his subordinate. Mwale similarly is a settlement of newcomers, and its head is Salehe Asmani, a Rufiji, whose father was the first settler. Yombo on the other hand is an example of an area snipped off like a cutting by the boundary makers from its parent Yombo in Kiserawe District: it has its own head, the son of the headman of Yombo on the other side. This whole area known as Kipawa, containing as well as these hamlets, and the village of Kipawa, a long strip of rice-growing country parallel to the railway and merging into Vigunguti (part of Buguruni), has been gradually squeezed in recent times by encroachment from two sides, the Veterinary plot on one side—from which several families were evicted—and the aerodrome on the other, whose boundary marks lie deep in the village itself.

Over the whole area the representative in the affairs of Government is Mzee Kitambaa, who is unpaid except in respect of his attendance at the Temeke court as an assessor: for he is one of those redundant headmen who were 'laid off' when their numbers were reduced to get rid of the least effective and concentrate the available funds on the more effective; being thus declared redundant does not affect his position except financially, and he remains the head of the Kipawa community (in the other hamlets, each with its head, he would not presume to interfere without consulting the individual head). His position, which is subject to the acquiescence of the people, derives from his being the grandson of Kirakara, who was the authority in both Kipawa and Yombo when both were part of the Kiserawe District; Kirakara had two sons, Mwarabu who was father to Kitambaa, and Mwinshehe who was the father of Shukuru, who is now the Mndewa of the Mbagala area of Kiserawe District. When Kirakara died Mwinshehe was appointed in his stead; he had an unpaid helper, who 'came to his house frequently, and was often seen there, and often sent on his errands, and chose out his own sons to run messages and tell people to pay tax and so on'; in the course of time this helper, called Tweka Mnyamwezi, became understood as the almost official clerk of Mwinshehe, and when Mwinshehe went he was made headman; there arose a dispute over the 'succession', which came to a head when the Municipal boundary was extended and Kipawa excised from the Kiserawe District: there were two parties, one of

1. Part of a planned 'neighbourhood', including a church, some Swahili-type houses, shops, flats and open space.

Nyamwezi and Ngoni (based on Kiwalani) backing Tweka, the other, the Zaramo (based on Kipawa), backing the traditional Zaramo succession through Kitambaa. Both sides were summoned to Ilala to state their cases. On the side opposed to Kitambaa was one Asmani Singasinga, a Mwera, who had come to Dar es Salaam first as a houseboy to a European. He argued that all the inhabitants of Kipawa were strangers, as they had all moved there from the Government Veterinary reserve; but Kitambaa maintained that Kipawa had been the domain of the Zaramo in general and his family in particular since the beginning, and that if any newcomer settled he required one of the Kirakara family to come and show him the wells to use and the land to cultivate. So the issue was settled in favour of the Zaramo faction and Kitambaa.

From these details it may be inferred that there are two rules for leadership in a Rural area inside a town: if there was a community there before the town—as in Kipawa village and Yombo—it retains its traditional leaders; even if the old community is cut in half by the boundary, as in Yombo, the large half lying outside, then the next in line is chosen as leader, in this case a son of the headman on the other side. In the choice Government plays, normally at least, no active part; if there is any interference in the purely parochial methods of choosing a successor on the death of a headman, it comes from the Wakili,[1] who is himself the senior Zaramo in town, as well as the apex of the Government system, so that he wields great influence in Zaramo affairs; but he too would normally merely accept the local choice.

The second rule is that where all are strangers in a previously empty piece of land, the first settler is, as they say, the *mwenyeji*, the original or owner.

This rule can be seen more clearly in the Village type of community where the village itself has grown up naturally (although greatly affected by the proximity of the town) without planning or control: such a village is Buguruni.

The first man ever to settle in Buguruni was one Momba, a Zaramo who had previously lived on the foreshore where there is now the Sewa Haji Hospital. Buguruni was then scrub and thicket, uninhabited. Momba put up some huts (in ki-Zaramo

---

[1] Wakili: a Government-appointed senior headman.

F

vibuguru) and this hamlet of himself and his family became known as 'at the huts' or Buguruni. The next arrival was Kirumbi, also a Zaramo, who married into Momba's family and settled with him (it was common practice in those days in a matrilineal society for the son-in-law to be given land by his father-in-law and to settle with his bride: the loss of this land on divorce was an added incentive to him to stay with her, while its use made it unnecessary for a stranger-suitor to take his bride away, a thing which in those days of slaving no father would agree to); later still there came non-Zaramo, such as Feruzi Ambari, a Pogoro slave, whom Momba granted room to cultivate; and Farhani, also a Pogoro slave, who not only was granted a plot but married into Momba's family; as time went on the settlement grew, each new entrant obtaining permission to cultivate from the first settler, some of them then sub-allocating their plots to others.

It is from this history that the position of all the important persons of Buguruni today derives: pride of place goes to Binti Madenge, although she is a woman, because she is in the direct line of descent from Momba himself (Madenge having married Momba's sister); she has also other attributes of leadership, being aged, of long residence and the owner of coconut trees (giving her a high economic station).

After her people usually mention Sim Saleh, grandson of Kirumbi, who is also aged, Buguruni-born, and the owner of coconut trees.

Then there is Zaidi Khamsini, an Mbisa, who was, for a consideration, given part of his shamba by Kirumbi: he is now aged, owns coconuts, and has built a mosque (thus achieving the respect due to a religious man).

Selemani Farhani, son of Farhani the Pogoro, is young, but he is recognized as a man to be consulted, as he is of the family, by marriage, of Momba.

Finally, there is Mwinjuma Salum, whose father married the uterine sister of Momba; he was elected Mndewa (paid headman) on the death of his predecessor, Mwinjuma Bakari, but was deposed by Government a year later, and succeeded by the present headman, Asmani Salehe; he is middle-aged, owns coconuts, and is still an important man.

Many of these leaders of the community, deriving their

authority from their connexion with the first settler, are too old for day-to-day problems, and would not themselves serve, for instance, as Ward Councillors.

That does not mean, any more than it does in the tribal society up-country, that their influence is diminished, but that they exert that influence through their nominees; thus it happened that in the elections for Ward Councillors in Buguruni (and in similar communities of Dar es Salaam) the men elected were not these prominent men themselves, but the candidates whom they put forward to be chosen by acclamation.

The foregoing comments have referred almost exclusively to the administrative systems which these rural and village communities have evolved; but where such systems have evolved without outside interference they reflect also a social system, for the two are scarcely separable: a man's place in the affairs of his village is the same as his place in the esteem of the community; the man the Jumbe consults is also the man who settles the quarrel between man and wife. A stage further, the community which has a recognizable administrative structure, self-evolved, is also a social community, and one which has to have its leaders appointed has no social cohesion either. If a man comes fresh to town to a village where the community has its superiors and inferiors, its first-comers and its later arrivals, the latter owing deference to the former and each finding his own level, if in short the community has an administrative 'structure', then it has also a social structure which enables a newcomer to be accepted into society. But if he comes and settles in a collection of Quarters, as at Temeke or Ilala, or in the great hive of Kariakoo, and finds no such administrative structure, no chain, link by link from first to last, then he is as much alone as a newcomer to London, and must rely either on his own relative, or on those he meets casually and at his work.

INTERLUDE

A wide boy

'I had a big quarrel with my aunt last night: as you know I have been meaning to go home to Kilwa for some time, but had no money to get my things out of pawn and buy suitable presents for my parents and brothers and sisters. After a year in town they would expect quite a lot, or else assume that I had been a failure and wasting my time. Anyway I didn't seem to be getting anywhere so eventually I had to write and ask them to send me money. They did, but not in quite the way I wanted; they sent a quantity of cashew nuts from the new harvest from our estates, and got me to sell it, but the proceeds were not handed over to me but to my aunt, and she won't give me anything until it is time to go to Kilwa, lest I spend it all first. Well, yesterday was the day I had fixed to go home, but some of the clothes I had been having made for myself and as presents—I had two good suits made—were not quite ready, so in fact I had decided to put off going for a few days. Anyway I went along to my aunt in Temeke and asked her for the 500 Shs. which she held for me, but she said "until I see your bundles all packed up and you on the bus with them you don't get a penny." I was furious, and we shouted at each other all night so that the neighbours came to separate us. But she wouldn't budge. So here I am, I have run through all the rest of the money and have nothing to go on with, until I actually go home.'

.   .   .   .   .

'Some of these drivers are difficult people: I live as you know out at Temeke, which is a long way if you haven't much in your pocket. Anyway I don't want to spend money on bus fares. So I usually catch the Goan school bus when it is returning empty, and the driver lets me on for a few cents. Yesterday I signalled to him and told him that just at the moment I hadn't a cent, and do you know, he refused to take me! I told him, "I have been on this bus ever so many times, and paid you each time, I will bring the money tomorrow", but he said, "no money—no ride." I was livid. So I went to the Goan school and said to the headmaster, "how much do you charge for going on the bus?" "Oh no," he says, "this is a school bus, and the children go free." "You're mistaken surely," I say, "lots of people pay fares on it, and not children either; in fact I myself often go on it, and pay the driver." He goes off in a rage, and sure enough I hear that the driver has lost his job. I see him later that day and he gives me hell. "Well," I said, "you wouldn't take me and let me pay tomorrow. You know I'm a chap to be reckoned with."'

Houses

Below the tribal group, the tribe, the emigrants from a single village area, the extended family, the inhabitants of a suburb in town, and a hamlet at the extremities of town, we come to the next social unit, the 'Swahili' house.

The Swahili house

The Swahili type of house which shelters nearly three-quarters of the African population of Dar es Salaam is built very much to a single design.[1] There is the main house itself, divided by a central corridor off which are three rooms each side. There is thus a single front door, opened and shut first and last thing by the landlord (if he lives in the house) or his agent. Once inside one looks straight through to the courtyard, half as big as the house, where all the laundering, dishwashing and general chores go on. At the back of the courtyard are usually three rooms, which are latrine, kitchen and store when the house is comparatively empty (or when the house is of the better-than-average type), or all three may be used for sleeping and rented out, the latrine and kitchen being set at one side instead.

The rooms in the main house are large and airy, not from open windows, as almost all have shutters (which are kept closed except when it is day and there is somebody in the room), but from access to the airspace under the roof, since the ceiling does not often cut the room off from above. The size is very generally about 12 ft by 12 ft. The rooms in the court-yard are smaller, and a good deal lower, the floor space being about 8 ft. by 10 ft. as a rule. In the courtyard rooms one can usually just stand up inside but not very much more whereas in the main rooms the ceiling, if there is one, is a good nine feet up. The window shutters in the courtyard rooms are also usually smaller. Altogether accommodation in the courtyard is poorer, and the rent correspondingly lower, usually by five shillings a month.

Once inside one's own room there is a fair amount of privacy, though the sounds of a good big quarrel will reverberate throughout. But low voices will not carry through the mud-packed wall unless the place is quiet. Each room has a door, on which one fits one's own padlock, and a sack or curtain is hung across the doorway when the door is open during the day, so that passers-by do not see in.

The passage varies as a living space; in some houses it is much in use, two or three persons sitting there polishing stoves or pans; in others it is empty, all these activities going on in the courtyard. Sometimes there is a bed in the passage, which means that somebody's young son has grown too old to sleep

[1] See plan on following page, Fig. 1.

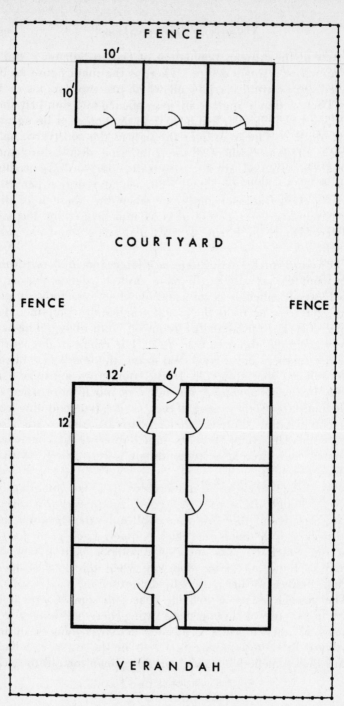

Fig. 1. The traditional Swahili house

with his parents but has not got a room of his own elsewhere.

Most of the men go off during the day, usually quite early, as they have to walk to their place of work and still get there by seven or half past. The women stay behind, and by half past eight or nine one may usually see several of them having a breakfast of tea together. They talk together as they do their chores. Very often they have a roster for sweeping (bachelors and grass widowers will pay a shilling a month extra on their rent to have it done for them, unless they can prevail on some relative to do it free). At midday they may have a communally cooked meal, eaten together. But when in the evening the men come home, each one goes back to his own room. There may be six or more fires or stoves going separately, and each dish of food is carried off to a separate room and the man and wife, and children if they have any, eat it together independently of the rest of the house. After the meal the men may foregather in the courtyard, or on the *baraza*[1] in the front of the house, to talk together and to passers-by, or more often they go out to friends elsewhere.

Up-country an *mji*, a collection of huts of persons of the same family with their wives and relatives, forms a close social entity; when one is in need he or she can rely automatically on the rest; in most places all are of the same tribe, have the same background, even though there may be some variety of experience and of occupation. They talk the same language, both literally and metaphorically. They bear many common obligations; the conduct of one will affect the others: a divorce of one will affect the property of others in the *mji*. Many of their outside friends will be the same; there will probably be only one mosque or church for all to go to, or if pagans they will be closely bound to the same ancestors.

Does the Swahili house form any sort of entity which would compensate an up-country tribesman for the loss of his *mji*?

Before trying to answer this let us see what two such housefuls look like. Take first a particularly full houseful, in Ilala close to the centre of town. This house, built soon after the war, is of the old style, which is still in the majority though rapidly losing ground to a better type which offers cement floors, corrugated iron roof and so on in return for a slightly higher rent (not much

---

[1] *Baraza*: front veranda, often with mud-brick bench.

higher, as a fall in rents seems to be disguised by a general rise in amenities offered). This old-style house is in the same general pattern already described, all walls being of rough mud rammed in between double frames of poles and laced sticks, but with no final clay dressing to make a smooth finish or take a white-wash. All floors are of trodden earth, rather lowered by constant use and sweeping and falling away from the walls' original level. The roof is still mainly coconut thatch, but there are some sheets of corrugated iron inserted to stop leaks where they have occurred. Besides the danger of fire, such a roof is expensive to maintain as it should be replaced about every third year, and nowadays costs a good £15 or more to replace, and thatchers' fees are rising all the time.

This house has the usual six main rooms, three on each side of the central corridor, each with its one door opening out into the corridor, and a shuttered window opening into the narrow passage between houses. In addition it has no less than five sleeping rooms in the courtyard. The kitchen has an iron roof, as the roof is low and thatch would easily catch alight.

In these eleven rooms live a total of thirty-three souls; this is a record number—I know of no house in Dar es Salaam having more, and technically it is overcrowded. Yet even here it is not overcrowded throughout. For the rooms are divided thus: the owner has one in which he lives with his wife and three small children, five in all in one room. This may be rather a scrum, but not an unhealthy scrum. There are two more families like that, man, wife and three small children, each in one room. Another family has two children, making four in all, and three more families have one child each. Then there are two young brothers sharing a room and its rent (a thing landlords do not like unless, as in this case, they are people from his part of the country whom he knows well, otherwise single men are un-welcome as there is always the risk of their getting involved with the wives of the house, particularly if their working hours do not coincide with those of the husbands). Finally there are three men each living alone in a room to himself. One is the son of the wife in one of the other rooms, and another is a grass widower whose wife is away at home for a time; the third is the nephew of the husband in that same family.

There is no evidence that people choose their rooms by

seeing who the other tenants are. They look only at the type of accommodation and the rent; except that they have often heard of the vacant room from one of the tenants, so that they will at least know him before they go there. Certainly there is no rule that persons of one tribe drift together. This houseful is in fact perhaps more homogeneous than most: the owner is an Mbunga, his wife a Pogoro; next, a Zaramo couple; then, a Kutu man with a Zaramo wife; then a Zigua with a Luguru wife; a Haya with a Zaramo wife; a Pogoro couple; a Tonga with an Ngoni wife; a lone Rufiji, a lone Luguru, the two Pogoro brothers, and a lone Zigua. This is certainly quite a collection, ten tribes in eleven rooms, but when one looks more closely it is not as diverse as all that: for instance, the languages of Mbunga, Pogoro and Ngoni are more or less mutually intelligible; the Zaramo and Luguru tribes, though they cannot understand each other's languages, both speak Swahili fluently from boyhood and are in fact closely related tribes. The Tonga and Ngoni are also related. And through constant intercourse through the centuries there is little difference between a Zaramo and a Rufiji, both are Swahili in culture and language. In addition, as described above several of the tenants are related to other tenants: the fourth family, the Zigua with a Luguru wife, has a nephew of the husband in the lone Luguru, each in separate rooms.

It did seem to me that the owner of this house had, whether by selection of his tenants or by his own example, managed to impress his own character and ways on the whole house. He was connected with the King's African Rifles all his life, as a tailor, was honourably retired and built this house with his gratuity; he is the type of man one would expect with such a history, quiet, courteous, and contented. Several of the tenants have clearly come to the house and stayed there because they liked him; unlike most landlords he really is almost the head of the *mji*, helping them out when they are short, and taking an interest in their family news.

What else have they in common? Not education, for the 19 adults in the house are a pretty fair reflection of the town as a whole, having 8 who had no education of any sort, 2 who went to a Koranic school only, 3 who started but failed to complete the primary course, 5 who completed it, and 1 who completed the middle school course. The result of this education was that 9 of the 19 claim to read and write Swahili in Roman characters, and three Swahili in Arabic characters. The eight illiterates were the wife of the owner, the Zaramo couple, the Kutu and his Zaramo wife, the Haya and his Zaramo wife, and one of the two Pogoro brothers. Education or the lack of it certainly ran in families, all the educated wives having educated husbands, and as ever the Zaramo were conspicuously less educated than up-country tribes, but as something held by the occupants of the house in common education must be counted out.

How about a job? Do people with the same sort of job tend to drift together in one house?

Here, apart from the owner who is retired, there is again a pretty fair reflection of the town at large: there are three dockers (one casual, two monthly), two labourers, two house-boys, a welder, a driver, a plumber and a mason. Their incomes vary equally: one (the plumber) gets 60 Shs. flat a month, two get 75, one 90, one 60 plus food (worth perhaps 100 or so), two get 120, and one 7 a day (which generally means that he works enough days to get about 120 in the month); the owner is getting 138 monthly by his rents (none of which are in arrears), one is getting 150, one 165 and one (the mason) 225.

Are they all long-term residents, or wanderers? No, whatever may be the verdict on each of their histories when they are complete, they are now at different stages, some being people of long standing, others comparatively new arrivals. Taking the menfolk only, one had less than a year, one 1 year, one 2 years, two 4 years, one 7 years, and six more than 7 years. This is close to the average for the town at large, as far at any rate as the relation between long residence and short residence is concerned. Certainly length of residence is not a thing these tenants have in common.

What happens in the evenings when work is done and people are free to sit and talk with their friends? Do these people gravitate naturally together, to talk to each other as being the people they know best, with whom they can most easily relax, the people who 'talk the same language' and are interested in the same things? The answer seems to be about half and half.

The owner rather naturally tends to stick around, and to some of the tenants, particularly those who have been with him in the house for some years, he is also their best friend; of those who gave a definite answer to this rather difficult question, four excluding the owner usually sat and talked in the house (either in the courtyard or on the baraza) and four others usually went to places outside. Some had special reason to do so: one was an Ngoni and he had gone on first arrival to live in Keko, where lives the head of his tribe, and he still likes to check in there now and then. It has to be remembered that none of the tenants has been always in this house, and some have had as many as six moves since first arrival in Dar es Salaam. A good deal of shifting from house to house goes on, usually for personal reasons. Sometimes it is the landlord they don't get on with (perhaps he is too insistent on getting the rent on time), sometimes there is a quarrel with other tenants, and often that quarrel is to do with women: with most of the men away all day, but some still around after doing a night shift, or being unemployed, and the combination of a communal court-yard where all may talk without offence and the private rooms giving opportunity to the tempted, is often too much to resist. That of course is why most landlords refuse to give room to a bachelor and bachelors find it very difficult to get a room unless they can disguise their status by acquiring a 'wife' at the time of application—she can 'visit relations' soon after and not return.

Leaving this teeming Ilala house, full of families with children, reigned over by a well-liked landlord, a houseful that has a pleasant atmosphere, let us turn to one in Kariakoo.

This house was once a very good address, abutting as it does on Mnazi Mmoja and, therefore, as near as one can get to the Commercial area and the jobs to be found there. But for some years now it has been marked on the planners' maps as scheduled for demolition, which in practice means that if you can keep the house standing by repairs it will not be demolished, but if it once collapses then you have lost all but the value of the materials. This has affected various landlords in various ways: some are busy improving their houses just like landlords all over town; others, like this one, have decided to waste as little money as possible on the house and just get what income they can while it lasts. This house has a corrugated iron roof put on some years ago, walls of mud and wattle and mud floors. The latrine is in poor repair, and there are just the six main rooms in the house itself for sleeping in. No repairs or improvements have been made for at least six years (during the tenancy of the oldest tenant).

The house contains in its six rooms twenty souls, again well above the town average, which is twelve. Again the reason is that this house has more children than usual, three of the six families having two children each, and a fourth one child. One family also contains the wife's sister, who sleeps in the same room with the husband, wife and two children. Rent for each of the rooms is 20 Shs. per month (more than the Ilala one, partly because of the house's central position, partly because of the iron roof). The owner is an absentee, living at Bagamoyo, and he gets £6 per month or £72 per annum in rents due. I say rents due advisedly, as every member of the household is behind with the rent. This is because the landlord has once or twice failed to make the journey from Bagamoyo to collect the rents promptly at the end of the month, and of course all the tenants then spent the ready money and are having to pay it back by instalments. They have not any expectation of getting away with it in the end, but meanwhile his income is behind schedule.

What have these tenants in common? In tribe they are not so mixed as those of the Ilala example; there is a Nyamwezi couple; a Nyagatwa with a Rufiji wife; a Luguru couple; a Zaramo couple; a Rufiji couple; and a Sukuma from Shinyanga who was brought up in Dar es Salaam, with his Zaramo wife. Although at first glance there seems to be a lot of mixture, seven different tribes in six rooms, there are really only two strains, the coastal (Nyagatwa, Rufiji) and the ivory route (Nyamwezi, Luguru) which both have strong and long-standing ties with the Zaramo who form the central block. Both Nyamwezi and Luguru tribes have ties of blood brotherhood with the Zaramo and will see to burials of each other's people.

In length of residence in Dar es Salaam they are a mixed bag: three of them have lived here all their lives, and of the other three one has been here seven years, one three and one one year.

Their education, or lack of it, is typical of the coastal peoples: of the six men, four have had no education whatever, one started but failed to complete the primary course, and one did complete it; all five wives were entirely uneducated and illiterate; the men were slightly better on literacy: one had some English, three had Swahili in Roman script, two Swahili in Arabic script, and only two were quite illiterate.

Their jobs were all different: there were a mason; a houseboy to an Indian; a hotel cook; a railway labourer; a dresser at the Sewa Haji Hospital; and a driver on long-distance transport. Their wages varied from the 60 Shs. of the railway labourer (which means that he did not work all month, as the minimum wage was then 3 Shs. per day), through the 75 Shs. of the houseboy and the hotel cook, both no doubt with quite considerable pickings to be had, to the dresser at 150 Shs. with a free uniform, and the driver at 120 Shs. plus 5 Shs. per day while on safari, which is pretty often (without considering the passengers he takes on, on his own account).

Asked where they met the friends they now know best, the Nyamwezi and the Luguru both found them among people of their own tribe (in the latter case they were people at the same work too, as the New Palace Hotel bakery section is a monopoly of the Luguru). All the others found their friends at their work. Not a single one had his best friend in the house.

To describe each of the 400-odd Swahili houses surveyed in this way would disclose endless variety, so many are the combinations of tribe, education, background and economic status which gather in these Swahili houses. It will suffice to quote one or two more examples, such as the house, owned and partly occupied by an Arab, in old Magomeni (Mzimni).

The owner is one of the Sumeith *Sada* (descendants of the Prophet), a family who live mostly in Shibam, a merchant city in the north of the Eastern Aden Protectorate. He has been here for many years, never very prosperous, too easygoing to do very well. It took him three years to complete this house, which is one of the older ones in Magomeni, and he is continuing to improve it now. It is in a good position, a corner shop in one of the few navigable streets in the sand sea of Magomeni.

The original six-room house has been converted so that one

side remains as before except that its bit of courtyard, including
kitchen and latrine, is fully cut off from the rest, with its own
front and back entrance. The rooms on the other side, where
the Africans live, have been made to face sideways, so that
each of the three rooms has its own door opening not into the
middle passage (which is now incorporated into the Arabs'
half) but into the remainder of the courtyard. In this there is
one kitchen and latrine common to the three rooms used by
the African tenants.

The reason why several of the African tenants are behind with
the rent is that the owner has so easygoing a temperament.
He has also allowed another Arab to use one room as a shop,
without rent, and has put up the other Arabs free to give them
a start in life.

He has an African wife, from Dodoma, but she is at present
in Arabia, where apparently she is content (Shibam has quite a
lot of black and mixed blood, though the slaves come not from
here but from the 'Sudan'). To marry thus into the country is
not common among the modern Shihiris, and indicates that
he dates from an earlier wave of immigrants.

This house is fairly typical of the way in which Arabs (and
in Kariakoo many Indians) live in houses partly occupied by
Africans: they cut themselves off into a semi-detached half-
house, and never see the Africans except on business. One would
say that the two races had come to a pretty good *modus vivendi*,
in this house perhaps more than most as the owner was so
accommodating over rent, although the Arabs claim to work
all day and keep watch all night, as (they say) every African is
just waiting for the chance to rob them. The Africans on their
side have a very healthy respect for the quick temper and
dagger-happiness of the Arab. There are many opportunities
for quarrelling in day-to-day shopping, where the Arabs have
a reputation for overcharging and underweighing, and in the
patronage by the bachelor or grass-widower Arabs of African
light ladies. But on the whole there is a fairly peaceful co-
existence, fortified by mutual economic interests, such as the
Arab provision of capital for improvements to an African's
house, the higher rent he is prepared to pay, and his willingness
to give credit (at a price which the African usually does not
calculate).

Another way in which this house is typical of a certain pattern of living here is that there is in it, of 14 souls, all adult, only one woman, and she has since moved. I was assured by one of the Arabs that none of these young men lacked for female company, so the coming and going must be complicated, particularly as all the rooms except one are shared between two or three men; most landlords are said to look very askance at room sharing, and even at bachelor tenants at all, but this must be an exception: in fact, these young men, though their sexual morals might give offence to the puritan, are rather above the average in good citizenship: they are mostly from the far south, people who have come up here, not to spend what they earn—to get on to a cash standard of living like the coastal tribes—but to earn enough to set them up on their return home. They are not exactly target workers. But they are immigrants with no intention of settling down permanently; they do a tour of duty and go home for leave in between; many intend to bring their wives when established (in which case they would move into rooms of their own); they share to reduce their expenses, and thereby enable themselves to take on jobs at pay which otherwise would be below the subsistence level (e.g. the 45 Shs. per month one is getting as office messenger with a well-known Indian advocate) while they look around for something better. They have more or less got a corner in one street, where two got jobs in a stores, one across the road as messenger to an advocate, and another as his houseboy while another is houseboy to his neighbour. Leaving out the Arabs five out of the eight men are Christians, with primary education, and literate; so although it looks like a hive of teddy-boys it is in fact the opposite, more like a youth hostel, with poor but serious people living cheaply as they start at the bottom of the ladder—but intending to climb.

There is the usual mixture of tribes: of the Arabs one, the owner, is a Seiyid from Shibam in the hinterland of the Eastern Aden Protectorate. The other Arabs are coastal men from tribes to whom it is as traditional to come to Dar es Salaam as it is for the Nyamwezi; then there are the three Northern Rhodesians, come up here to get clerical work (which they say an African cannot easily get on the mines); a Makonde and a Yao sharing; a Sagara and a Luguru sharing;

an Ngindo couple; and a Mwera pair of boys; the accent is thus predominantly southern.

The Arabs all went only to Koranic school, but are all literate in Arabic.

The three Rhodesians all completed the primary course and are literate in Swahili (Roman script); the same is true for the other southerners, the Mwera and the Makua, the Yao from Lindi, and the Sagara from Kilosa. But the Ngindo and the Makonde both from Lindi are uneducated and illiterate.

Another example may be quoted, to show a better-than-average house, in Ilala, and its shifting population.

This house had a lot of changes between August 1956 when the first questions were asked and December when the second set were put.

In August there were in the eight rooms ten souls. In fact apart from one man, there were 'single' persons living in every room. Actually only one apart from the old lady who owns the house was in fact single; two wives have since returned from a sojourn in the country, one man, then single, has been found a wife by his father to look after the three foster-children whom he won in a court case, and he has gone off to Temeke Walesi to live in his father's house. Two have left and their rooms been taken by other rent-paying tenants and one has left and his room been taken rent-free by a relative of the owner.

There were in August five tribes represented, Bisa, Zaramo, Sagara, Luguru and Rufiji. There is no great difference between any of these, at any rate between their representatives in this house; all speak Swahili all the time, and the old taboos here fallen into disuse. They are in fact Dar es Salaam-ites rather than members of this and that tribe.

The house is of very good standard; the owners originally had a house in Mnazi Mmoja, but in 1921 after the big fire this space was cleared of all houses, and they were compensated and moved to Ilala. There they built a plain house of mud and wattle walls, mud floor and thatch roof, but over the years they have improved it with cement floors in all the inside rooms (but not in the courtyard rooms), and have plastered the walls with clay and painted them over with green, yellow and red paint. The roof is of good new corrugated iron (having in between been of flattened petrol tins). The whole thing cost

2. Types of semi-detached 'Quarters'.

something like £200, over a period of years. To balance this expenditure the owner now gets 25 Shs. for each inside room and 20 Shs. for the courtyard rooms, a total of 140 Shs. per month or £84 per annum. There is at present little more that can be done to the house to bring in more rent, as electricity or piped water are luxuries that very few Africans are yet prepared to pay extra rent for, whereas there are many who will pay the extra for a cement floor, iron roof or coloured walls.

It is interesting to see the type of person who lives in this better type of house: there are a railway wharf cleaner on 120 Shs. per month; a compositor for the *Tanganyika Standard* newspaper on over 210 Shs. per month; a dockyard painter on 90 Shs. per month; a headman for the Landing and Shipping Co., on 210 Shs. per month; a mason for Tanganyika Engineering on 7 Shs. per day; and one at present unemployed but who was recently getting 90 Shs.

All except the compositor were uneducated and illiterate. The compositor's stepchildren were all going to school. He himself had completed a middle school education.

People such as these, well settled in Dar es Salaam, have friends in many places, and little need to rely on others in the house. The house to them is just a block of flats, and they found great difficulty in recalling even the names of those who had moved out three months earlier—they had never seen or heard of them again. To these successful, established people, the house was far less of a home than the other crowded house in Ilala with its patriarchal owner.

INTERLUDE

Mr. K: Brother, to get paid early in the month cuts both ways: as you know this month we in the Posts got paid on the 19th of December. Well, you know we were in Christmas from 22nd December onwards, whole holidays. Well then, I went off to Morogoro and broke into my notes one after the other, leaving about 60 Shs. I got back here on the 1st, and today I am spending the bottom dollar: what I'm going to use for money for the rest of January I don't know. And the worst of it is that I didn't set anything aside for the rent—that's what's got me worried.

Mr. A: How many years have you been in that house?

Mr. K: It's about a year and a half now.

Mr. A: Oh well, if you've been there so long nothing will happen.

Still, it doesn't pay not to see to the rent of the roof over one's head and the shop where one gets one's food.

Mr. A: In our house there's continual quarrels, especially the women. There's one woman whose husband works for Indians, and every day she cooks porridge and sells it, or bean stew. She sees the other women in the house cooking rice, meat and fish and *chapatis*, things with fat in them, while she has tea and a couple of buns, and no milk either. The other women get fat on their food and they make narky remarks about her and joke and talk about her. Even more with clothes: many of them get a new lot of clothes every second month, while she may go up to six months without a new thing. This is the big bone of contention in a six-roomed house. What do you think? Next day the woman tells her husband she wants a divorce. What do you think the end of the story is?

Mr. K: I think it is all the fault of the husband. As I see it he'd best move out, wife and all, as they are out of their depth in that house, and his income does not match that of the others; so he'd best look out for a house of people of his own standard, then he wouldn't get all this trouble.

For instance if a clerk on 75 Shs. lives in a house with a man getting 400 Shs. it's just asking for trouble. If he isn't quick to move he'll be punished twice over, losing his wife and quarrelling for nothing.

Mr. A: You're dead right, he ought to get out. A couple of months back there was trouble like this in our house, but it was caused by differences in religion; one tenant was Christian, the rest Muslim. One morning he cooked some bacon and all the Muslims complained and refused to let any of their pans be used or any of the ladles. But they moved out and there was no further trouble. Always these troubles in the house come from the women more than the men.

Even in the type of house where almost all are of the same tribe, and many are interrelated, the community of feeling was less than one would have expected. Take for instance a house at the far end of Ilala, thatch roof, mud floors, mud and wattle walls, a poor type of house typical of the unimproved houses which a few years ago formed the bulk of the mainly African areas.

In this one which has six main rooms and one in the court-yard there lived 26 souls, 19 Zaramo all from the same village, 6 Rufiji and 1 Makonde. One of the Rufiji was the owner's relative and agent, living rent-free with his wife and female cousin; another Rufiji was a rent-paying tenant, with his wife and five children all living in the same room. Two of the young Zaramos shared a room; a third had his wife and two daughters in another room; one of the young sharers had, in a separate room, a sister, a cousin, an aunt and a brother's wife; and in the courtyard room a bachelor put up his brother and cousin free, while the last room was used by a single man, whose wife and child were away. Thus there was a criss-cross of relationship; they were in two types of job, some labourers and some house-boys to Indians, while one was a petty trader and one was temporarily in prison; incomes varied within a narrow range between 75 Shs. without food to 60 Shs. with. All were un-educated and illiterate. One would suppose that so homogeneous a houseful would by living together quickly merge into a compact community. But the owner's agent said he would prefer people of other tribes, partly because in a houseful of such people, employed in the two main categories of unskilled labourer and domestic, where turnover is quick and perman-ency rare, he is constantly being called upon to come financially to the rescue, to postpone payment of the rent, or provide food. He summed it up by saying: 'My relatives' needs are many.' The other Rufiji went further and said that he would be worse off with a job at home, because all his relations would beg from him *all* the time. The others, the Zaramo, coming all from the same village as they do, have more in common, and say they prefer to live in a house of people of the same tribe, as they can then talk to each other in their own language, observe their own taboos without embarrassment, and carry letters and gifts home for each other when they make visits; on the other hand everything they do in town will get back to any wives or imperious parents whom they have left at home, and this is a point which often outweighs the others, so that some prefer to live in obscurity and licence among strangers. When it came to friends most said their closest friends were people they knew from their work, while others had first met their friends at previous rented rooms, though they were now, owing to the general drifting and eddying, living elsewhere; if friendship be judged by willingness to lend money, all relied for this on relatives and none on friends outside the extended family circle.

The most noticeable characteristic of the Swahili house is that it contains within itself both 'first-class' and 'third-class' accommodation, rents and all that go with them; the people in the front rooms are often paying twice the rent of those in the back; they may also be twice as well off, though as will be shown later that is by no means certain. Some of those who live in the better-type houses, with an attempt at a higher standard of room, will have as part of the same house others who make no such attempt: they may not see much of each other, particularly if they are not otherwise connected by tribe, temperament or job; but their wives or girl-friends will sweep the corridor in turn, will wash dishes together and use the same fire, will sit and talk the morning through together. The men may not make friends with the others and may have their own friends outside, but they cannot fail to be affected by the close living of the other families; perhaps his wife complains of the better food of the other families, or the more frequent provision of a new garment; food particularly can be a frequent source of friction, for although the men and their wives eat the evening meal each in their separate room with no attempt at sharing, the women who eat the left-overs the next morning are more likely to share, and certainly they will eat openly so that each can see what the other had.

The population is fluid in another sense besides that of moving into and out of town: it is also moving around inside the town to a noticeable extent. In a random sample of 132 families who had been surveyed in August 1956, 31 were found to have moved room to another house by December/ January: that is just under a quarter in four months.

There are many reasons for which people move house, of which the most common is that the constant quarrels and upbraiding without which rents cannot be collected have eventually made friction between landlord and tenant intolerable, so that either the landlord has turned the tenant out, or he has voluntarily left for the sake of peace and quiet. (This friction over the payment of debts is found in other spheres also, and is believed to be the most common single reason for domestic servants leaving their jobs, when advances are either refused or their repayment insisted on; many give the stickling by Europeans for the payment of debts—to a much greater degree than by Indians—as a reason for preferring a job with an Indian.)

Another common reason is friction deriving from the presence in a house of a young bachelor, particularly if he is on a night-shift so that he is in the house while the other men are away at work, leaving their wives in the house. The jealousies thus set up, by no means always unfounded, often induce one or other party to move.

A reason often given, but which I suspect to be a contributory reason only, is the poor repair of the house, particularly the roof, and the landlord's refusal to repair it. When rain comes the tenants are made uncomfortable and move.

A reason which crops up surprisingly often is that the house has been sold; it is often the case that the new owner will prefer to clear out completely the old set of tenants; this happens particularly in the case of a house which is bought to be improved, whereupon rents are raised; often the price of the house, or part of it, has been raised by a loan from an Arab or Indian trader, who makes this loan on the understanding that he will rent half or the whole of the house and recoup his loan out of a reduced monthly rent (which is still very much higher than what the African tenants were previously paying). Even where no improvements are to be put in the new owner would find it difficult to take over the financial situation which often includes several months' arrears of rent.

Considering the close juxtaposition of a tenant to the other occupants it is surprising that a prospective tenant makes no inquiries at all about the other tenants, and most express indifference even as to the tribe of the others (Zaramo and other coastal tribes even go so far as often to prefer a mixed-tribe house as they say quarrels over borrowing and repayments, differences over food and so on, are fewer; on the other hand the more far-flung tribes prefer to live near each other for mutual support).

In a recent essay competition the most common cause of constantly moving house was given variously as:

Petty restrictions by the landlord.
Failure to pay the rent.
Jealous (or justified) suspicions of bachelors.

Quarrels between women in the kitchen.
The insecurity of a house against thieves.
The raising of rents.

Each competitor had his own list of the causes of moving, and none of them agreed on their relative importance. One list ran as follows:

Petty restrictions: for instance, insistence on a tenant returning by 10 p.m., the landlord thereafter shutting the front door and getting angry if he has to come to answer it for a late-comer; or refusing to have people in the house who like a party, or who bring friends in till late and sing and shout.
An overbearing attitude of the landlord to the tenants.
The inquisitiveness of landlord and other tenants into one's food, furniture, clothes and entertainment, followed by remarks if yours are better or worse than theirs.
Quarrels over the chores of sweeping-up the common courtyard and latrine: this is an oft-repeated source of friction.
Personal defects: a quarrelsome nature, dirty habits, rudeness, or being a bad rent-payer.
Becoming crowded (cf. the man with a growing family, or who lives free with relatives).
Finding the rent more than he can manage.
Leaking roofs, etc., and the landlord's refusal to repair.

Others added other causes:

Flirtations between male tenants and other men's wives, or alternatively the suspicion of a husband that his wife is flirting, or worse. The sale of the house and the desire of the new owner to have nothing to do with people he has not chosen himself. A man with a rise in salary wishing to move to better lodgings. People welshing on their debts (when too many creditors know their address). Quarrels with the other tenants. A tendency on the part of the landlord to scrounge on the tenants for food. Quarrels between the women alleging theft of salt or firewood left in the kitchen. Differing standards of food leading to narky remarks. A landlord who dislikes children. Incompatibility of character of landlord and tenant. Quarrels over a bachelor's lady friends who do not sweep out the bathroom. Fear of a father to leave his growing daughter in a house with unmarried men. The insistence of a landlord on being paid on the nail, or even before the end of the month, when he himself tends to get short.

All in all then, the big six- to nine-roomed Swahili house, with its first class (in the main rooms) and tourist class (in the courtyard rooms), can generate a lot of friction, much as do flats in a European town: most of these causes of friction boil down to lack of privacy, and this lack of privacy is felt the less when a man is on his own, or poor, or uninterested in a high standard of comfort, and felt the more when he is better paid, better educated, more ambitious of improving his lot; it is felt particularly by the up-country Christian educated man with a stable marriage which he is loath to lose, and a tendency to put money into comfort and food: for he will find his standards consistently above those of the others in the house, who have spent their money on other things and envy him his food and ability to pay his rent at the end of the month. It is this type which prefers Government Quarters. But they are a minority. The majority are coastal Muslims, uneducated and illiterate, many of whom have no ambition for a permanently improved standard of life, only for ready spending money, which they are reluctant to 'waste' on food or rent. They have traditional habits of loosely knit marriages or less, and have, therefore, less to lose. To them the Swahili house gives what the Quarters cannot give: companionship at all times—a sort of ready-made club—help in sickness, and what ought to be a cheaper form of accommodation (in fact, however, it is Quarters which are still the cheaper).

INTERLUDE

Two anecdotes

A man went to the Sewa Haji Hospital and found his child had died. He took a basket and put his child's corpse in it, and covered it with a shawl and rode off with it on his bicycle to get the shroud and soap. He got the soap and put it in the basket, and leaned his cycle up against the wall while he went to get the shroud; while he was in there a thief saw it and thought it belonged to a laundry-man who had a basket full of clothes for washing; so he took bicycle, soap, basket and all. When he got to the Oyster Bay police station he was stopped and the askari told him to uncover the contents of the basket. Collapse of all parties when the corpse was discovered.

.   .   .   .   .

Thieves made off with a goat. They dressed it in a *kanzu* and put a cap on its head, and each took a leg and carried it upside down. They kept putting salt in its mouth to keep it quiet, and so they carried it through the streets of Magomeni, saying, 'Juma, we told you you couldn't hold your liquor, now we are having to carry you home, what will your wife say?' At the main road they got a taxi and drove off towards Kawe. As they got to Pepino's the salt ran out and the goat let out a squawk: 'Who made a noise like a goat?' asked the taxi-driver; 'We didn't hear anything', they replied. But the driver stopped the car, and saw the goat's head with the cap now fallen off, and took them all to the police.

Quarters

A much smaller part of the population, some 6 per cent., lives in what I have termed Quarters (this being the term used in Swahili and most generally understood); until after the last war there were no houses of this sort, but only either the big 'Swahili' houses which have been described, or servants' accommodation in larger houses, mostly belonging to or occupied by Indians or Europeans. When in 1946 the end of the war brought a very heavy inflow of African, as well as other, immigrants to Dar es Salaam, there was suddenly a very severe shortage of housing, resulting in the springing up of 'shanty' towns in vacant or apparently vacant plots. To combat this British funds from the Colonial Development and Welfare Fund were applied to building numbers of Quarters to be rented at as low rates as might be without actual subsidization. These were in the form of one-room, two-room and three-room bungalows (in Ilala) or semi-detached villas (in Temeke) or terraces (in Magomeni). Whether detached, semi-detached or terraced, each flat was self-contained with its own kitchen and latrine, and separate front and back doors each. The degree of privacy varied as would be expected, being comparatively low in the Magomeni terraces where the internal walls did not go much above head height and allowed sound to carry between flats, but to balance that was the additional privacy (as compared with the Swahili house) of one's own kitchen and latrine.

In these flats it is most unusual to find any mixing of tribes: their occupants are strictly single families, together with any relatives who are seeking their shelter. This is not the result of any official prohibition by the landlord (the Municipality) of sub-letting, but rather of preference: people who leave the Swahili houses for the Quarters do so particularly because they want privacy; such people are of course a minority, because the ordinary coastal men are not so addicted to privacy; the inhabitants of the Quarters are quite untypical in this as in many other ways; they are far more Christian (60 per cent. compared to the 15 per cent. average of the town as a whole), educated, and of settled family habits, with stable marriages. Often they come from up-country tribes, some of them with only small communities in Dar es Salaam; such are to some extent a people apart, and many do find their friends among neighbours like themselves. Their flat is the basis of their existence, though their area of Quarters, and their particular terrace or group of villas, seem to call forth no particular sense of belonging. Such associations as Tenants' Associations have a fluctuating existence, depending on the energy of one or two committee-minded persons, and these areas are notorious as being those which take the least interest in the affairs of their respective Ward Councils.

This is hardly surprising when one considers the type of person who rents a Quarter: he is a person who has come to Dar es Salaam with something to sell—his education, or skill as artisan; he has no intention for the most part to settle here, but to pursue a career until he comes to the end of his working life and then retire—back to his home up-country, which he visits regularly at intervals of two or three years, usually on paid leave, for many are Government or High Commission servants (though this again is not mandatory, and the Quarters are open to all). He has no call to immerse himself too deeply in town affairs, which tend to be dominated by tribes other than his own, by people less educated and with manners foreign to his own. Apart from his own family in their flat, the centre of his life tends to be his firm or office, and perhaps his tribal association if he is, like the Pare or Chagga, one of a small compact community. Even when the tenant is, as in one example, a Zaramo, he is to some extent marked off from others of his tribe by being a Christian, with a Christian and educated wife, and comparatively fixed ideas about divorce. Even so settled a citizen as 'John Petro', who came here to join his parents at the age of 20 and has been here continuously except for leaves for 21 years, first as houseboy and now as craneman, a Mwemba from Northern Rhodesia, Catholic, married (to a Digo from Bagamoyo) with one child, says that his best friends in town are those he met at his work, none of them from his own country, and none of them living in the Magomeni Quarters.

The atmosphere of being a career-worker here 'for the duration' seems to affect even such apparently typical coastal people as 'Juma Omari', a Zaramo from the Mbagala country-side just outside Dar es Salaam, his wife from Mjimwema, who, though more educated than most Zaramo, having completed the primary course, is otherwise hard to distinguish from the 'average man' depicted by the statistics; he says that he is here 'so long as he has paid work, and when he has enough put by to retire with he will go back to his village outside'. He too says that his best friends were all met at work (he is a mason for the Water Supply). Most of these Zaramo, Rufiji and so on who live in the Quarters are better educated, higher paid, Christian, or in some other way marked off from their fellows: others such as 'Charles Otieno', a Luo from Kenya, are also differentiated by being 'foreigners', and find their friends to an even greater extent from among the others of their kind, who tend like themselves to live in Quarters: but they do not live in groups, or in the same lot of Quarters; Charles's friends all live in Quarters, but in Temeke and Ilala while he lives in the Magomeni Quarters; all he met at work, and without having known them before.

INTERLUDE

A married woman of the professional class

I am a teacher and so is my husband. We are just married, and have one of the Ilala Quarters, that is, a bungalow on our own.

As we both go out to work we have breakfast and supper together, but not the midday meal, since our times of work are different.

Breakfast is at a quarter past seven, my lunch is at one and my husband's at half past two; supper is at half past six, but we have tea in between at four.

Our breakfast varies: it may be tea and a slice of bread and butter and jam; or cocoa and buns; or eggs, or toast.

Lunch is the big meal: rice and spinach, or meat, or fruit, and a glass of milk.

Supper is light, soup and sweet potatoes, or cassava with coconut, followed by coffee.

My day begins at 5 a.m. I get up and open the doors and windows, heat some water for washing, and sweep the courtyard, and wash up last night's dishes. Then I make tea, and sweep out the sitting-room. At twenty to seven I wake my husband and he goes to wash, while I do out the bedroom, opening the windows, dusting, making the bed, and dusting off again and tidying up. Dirty clothes are put in the basket ready for washing. When I am finished I wash (my husband changes the water), then I dress and we eat breakfast, and go to work. We leave behind a 'help' who completes any housework left over.

In the afternoon I wash clothes and iron; sometimes I tend the garden; then I make ready the evening meal, and go to get water from the standpipe.

The morning chores take about an hour and a half.

When my husband is out I have no permission to go out anywhere, except to the Guides, or the Police, or if I am called away urgently, I must leave my husband a note to show where I have gone, and why.

I do most of the shopping, but sometimes when we are both off duty in the evenings we do it together. We shop in the evenings, except on Sunday mornings, when we shop at ten in the morning.

My husband gives me his salary to manage, and tells me of any bills incurred, and the amounts he used to spend before we were married.

We prefer to live in Quarters rather than a Swahili house, because there is room to spread yourself, and you don't get into bad habits from the other women; there is no noise or jostling, and you can keep the place clean.

A proper marriage shows itself in both sets of parents knowing and approving it, with many witnesses present, all friends, a marriage for life. When people live together illicitly there is less tolerance, and a greater readiness to divorce. And when they quarrel they don't mind what they say and there is little mutual respect. Often it is those who have been married once that live together so. Others are afraid to marry, having been told that divorce is not allowed.

Again, some children when they begin to grow up are told that they should not continue to live with their parents.

I prefer traditional to ballroom dances, just because they are traditional and are danced by people of the same tribe, not just anyone. And as they are traditional anybody who is an outsider will be unable to create a disturbance; the elders are there too, to see that everything is done properly. I prefer this because people then dance in an orderly and organized manner.

There remain two further categories of house: the Rural and the Village. Rural are by my definition those which have an adjacent subsistence plot. They lie, as is to be expected, on the outskirts of the town, and are in fact part of the town only because the Municipal boundary has been extended beyond them to provide for possible future development. They are thus part of the countryside beyond, from which they were administratively excised when the boundaries were thrust further out. Although their headmen now report to superiors in town instead of in the Kiserawe District, life has not otherwise changed; they shop occasionally in town, as they did before, though the town is constantly coming further out to meet them; they market their surplus products in town as they always did; they brew their own beer or tap their own palm-wine, or buy from the local purveyor, as before; for companionship they go to the same relations, or coffee stall or dance ring, as they and their friends have always done; their administrative structure has been built to another apex but it is intact; the headman consults the same elders and wise men as he would have done had the Municipal boundary still run to townwards of them; they have still the village mosque and Koran school, though for modern schooling they would now be expected to send their children to a town primary rather than one in Kiserawe District (the rule of course is not strict and there is much interchange over the border according to convenience). With administrative, social, religious and economic setup unchanged, it is not surprising that the Rural areas of Dar es Salaam show far more signs of being true communities than the truly urban areas nearer the centre, for they are 'natural' groups which have grown up without planning interference whether for good or ill, have evolved their own social-administrative systems and taken their trade to its natural market.

This is so although the Rural communities are not in fact composed of the same people: Zaramo are being drawn in to town not only directly but by a gradual approach, nearer and nearer to town, where the diminution in the fertility of the soil and in the availability of land is offset by the better prices of the products and convenience of nearness to the amenities of town; in addition many of the other tribes who are drawn to the town life but are unable or unwilling to go completely urban by taking a job and relying on it exclusively for income settle instead on the outskirts and become part of the original nucleus. Their numbers are swelled when there is a wave of unemployment, or after a strike, or a recession, or a sudden influx such as was caused by the announcement of the minimum wage, when many hang on by 'going to ground' in the surrounding countryside, helping relatives with the field work, or—if the season permits—starting their own fields. Most of these houses are in rural style, the bare necessities, two or three rooms, low-built, and made of materials cheap to buy or easily won from neighbouring and ill-guarded coconut plantations. They cannot in any case be called shanties, for they are normal rural dwellings such as they would build for themselves at home, far out in the country, nor are there any large clusters of them squeezing out the fields and becoming a village, except perhaps in Mtoni astride the border, and Kipawa (in this survey these two clusters have been classed as Village). As in other, purely rural areas up-country, when alien tribes infiltrate into the territory of the resident tribe they become absorbed, submitting themselves to the jurisdiction of the existing leaders, attending the same schools and dances, and by their acquiescence in things as they are actually serving to reinforce the existing state of affairs. So when a Zaramo or a stranger from further afield builds his house in a Rural part of Dar es Salaam he is absorbed, once having submitted to things as they are: attaching himself to the inevitable relative, who himself has his well-known place in the setup, he knows at once where he is. Unlike the stranger who attaches himself to a relative in, say, Kariakoo, and who is adrift clutching only this one spar until he can find footing for himself, a stranger coming to a Rural part fits himself into an already integrated structure of which each part knows its own place and function; by attaching himself to the one part which he previously knows he has attached himself to the whole. So the Rural parts have grown from the earliest, purely Zaramo settlements almost untouched by the then distant town, by accretion of aliens and more Zaramo without losing their nature as communities.

INTERLUDE

Msasani: Kijito Nyama: a rural area

The natural vegetation of the area is thicket interspersed with sedge, sandy watercourses, and the occasional baobab: now that it has been almost fully settled the baobabs have been reinforced with mangoes and cashews, the thicket (which gave the stream its name, from the hunting of gazelle) has gone from all but the watercourse itself, and the swamps are growing rice, the drier areas being under cassava and sweet potatoes. A day or two ago when we were across the road in Mwananyamara—where at the far end the thickets survive—a Nyamwezi with me pointed to them and to a few rows of cassava and said: 'this year the Nyamwezi are trying it out, next year you will see all this cleared away and the country full of us.'

Across the Kijito Nyama stream-bed, in Kiserawe District, the scene is the same, the population becoming rather thicker as one approaches the Tanganyika Packers. The whole of this area is now well populated in rural fashion.

Even in this rural atmosphere, with aged grandmothers harvesting the rice, there are reminders that the European houses are not far off: a child's pot and a well-upholstered figure betray the ayah who has her own field. She works as far away as Mustabe (Oyster Bay) so is presumably 'resting'—gone sick perhaps for the duration of the harvest. The two oldest inhabitants of the area, both Ngoni, have made no concession to modernity, but an equally aged grandmother, ears pierced and ready for anything, has a few words of English, her husband being a houseboy in Nairobi. 'Baswezi' are singing a song as they reap the rice, and put in a verse about the 'Mzungu' as we pass.

By one house there are two bushes of henna, for painting red the fingers and soles of the feet. For rouge and lipstick the European articles are used. Other houses have sugar cane, sunflower and a patch or two of millet for beer. One or two of them are grinding millet today for this purpose. The only millet beer premises in town are those of Kariakoo and Ilala, so the up-country people who inhabit the fringes of Dar, and prefer this beer to palm-wine, have their beer clubs just outside the boundary, in Kiserawe District. Palm-wine on the other hand is obtainable readily everywhere; my guide, the ward councillor, went off to tap a few trees yesterday after our morning's work, as his living. Almost every other house in some parts has a few gallon tins of it lying about ready to drink or to send to the clubs.

There is a lot of mutual help in the harvesting, the helpers coming back on the next day, when the grain is dry and ready for eating, and having a good feast on the proceeds. The rice is laid out on mats (in some cases on the bare ground) to dry in the sun for a day, and is then ready for husking and cooking. The quantities grown are not great, and it is said not to last long although little is sold. Partly this is due to the 'locusts' who soon know when the harvest is imminent.

The pioneers of these parts off the roads are the bakery vans. They go everywhere on their daily rounds, delivering loaves to the Arab shops. With many of the population unmarried the easy-to-eat loaves are in steady demand, many combining dry bread and tea for days on end as their only food.

Mikorosheni, the largest division of Msasani, is partly a true village, many of the central houses dating back to the early thirties and beyond, and partly the relic of the hutments round the quarries that once housed the quarry labour. One part is still called the Kambi:[1] it has 28 houses, many of them only a single small room, but the impression they give is certainly not one of poverty— on the contrary, they are often brightly painted, and the inmates are for the most part houseboys, and 'ayahs' both real and professional. There are also some really poor ones, ladies with no husbands and to all appearances not drawing a very good type of clientèle. In this 'houseboy village' there is a great variety of tribes, many Nyakyusa, Yao, Luguru and Zaramo. The head of it is a cycle repairer. The whole place, compact, well kept, and well off the road (though there is a track running through it), hums with life, the keynote being struck by the notice outside one house, in the shape of a cross: 'The house of cowboys'.

Some roofs were being thatched with '*miyaa*' the dwarf palm of which mats are made: it is said to last much longer than coconut thatch, up to ten years.

There is a two-classroom school started by the local people with Social Development Department help; it still holds the first two Standards of schooling, the others now going to the Education Department school which has been opened. There are also adult literacy classes.

[1] *Kambi*: camp.

As they put it, 'Arabs are not allowed to build here.' Almost all the shops are Arab, and they rent part or all of a house for this purpose. There is in fact nothing to prevent an Arab buying a house openly; but new building is supposed to have been stopped for all races.

Despite the wealth of coconut husks no rope is made in Dar es Salaam, so they say, and as a result it is more expensive, though better, than sisal; some comes from Mafia, some from Zanzibar. The husks here are all used for firewood.

In the tidal flats near the salt pans shrimps are caught, and also a type of sardine-sized fry.

Sisal poles from the nearby estate are much used here, for latrines, kitchens, and even for main poles and roofs. They say that a house made of them stands up long after the pith has rotted right away.

An Ngoni woman walks slowly along the main street shouting ruderies over her shoulder at her husband, a Zaramo, who follows twenty yards behind, shouting back as occasion offers. '*Ulinipiga kidachi*' (you beat me like a German), she says, 'why should I return?' Nobody pays much attention except to mutter, 'difficult, these Ngoni women.'

Msasani, besides its connexion with Oyster Bay and the domestic business, has Leopard's Cove (Kichanga Chui) where crowds of Europeans go at week-ends, and outrigger canoes can be hired out to go to the islands; there is also a steady traffic down to the Msasani bay, not only to the beach huts beyond the Municipal boundary but to the beach in Gongoni, and there is a fair trade with visitors and with the Arabs and Indians in coconuts, fish and other produce. Whether as a result of these contacts, which bring out the predatory commercial instincts latent in all of us, or because of their pretensions to Shirazi[1] blood, the fisherfolk by the shore are noticeably less forthcoming than others. Or it may just be the sturdy independence of the self-employed.

A notice points the way to the 'Shirazi ruins'. Otherwise one would hardly notice them, as they are mere mounds of cactus and bush, with an occasional stone appearing in a gap in the vegetation. A more interesting ruin is the huge mosque which a past Jumbe started to build, in stone, but died too soon: it has never been finished. There is a row of genuine 'Shirazis' on the foreshore, with the true yellow skin and semitic features, unlike so many of those who claim the name and make guttural sounds to prove it.

Outside a house a brassière hangs drying on a cassava bush, a symbol of the 'town-in-the-country'.

---

[1] Families of mixed blood who claim Persian descent.

The remaining type of house is that categorized as Village. This term is intended to cover both original villages which have become engulfed by the advancing town, such as Msasani, originally a fishing village pre-dating Dar es Salaam itself; and clusters of houses which have sprung up within the town as a result of urban conditions. The latter class includes parts of Kipawa and Mtoni where a rural scatter of huts has as population pressure increased become a village, squeezing out the subsistence plots; and places such as Toroli in Keko which sprang up purely as shanties at a time of great and sudden shortage of housing, but have since begun to evolve with improved houses into villages within the town.

Where a Village is an engulfed original village, its case is very similar to that of the Rural areas, where the originally fairly homogeneous population (in Msasani the Shirazis) has been supplemented by accretions both before and after being engulfed. This original population remains the 'owners' (*wenyeji*) of the Village, and the others as they come and settle are expected to fit themselves into things as they find them; to accept the original spokesmen as their own, and to fit themselves into the order of esteem which has grown up through generations.

On the other hand, when a Village has arisen as a shanty town one would suppose that these considerations would not apply; for the shanties sprang up so quickly, in the immediate post-war period, that it seemed like a rush of new immigrants similar to those who flow in, in a single month, when a new town-planned suburb is demarcated and opened up. In fact, however, there is a vital difference: in a town-planned suburb, such as Temeke, the land acquired by Government is empty one day, and the next day—so to speak—parcelled out to a large number of newcomers none of whom receives his rights to the land much before the others; they all move in together as Government's tenants, in a single undifferentiated block, with no leaders or led, no traditional elders, in fact no framework of society into which a newcomer can fit himself in his appropriate place. In no case did the building of the shanty towns happen in this way: even in Keko kwa Magurumbasi, and Toroli, there was one man who first settled (in the case of Ali Magurumbasi he settled, long ago, by no right in the eyes

H

of the law, as the land belonged to the Sultan of Zanzibar whose permission was never sought) and others who followed him, receiving his permission to do so and thus becoming in a sense his followers; others followed them and acquired a similar status in relation to those whose permission they sought; in time the nucleus of a Village with a recognizable structure of society was formed, and it was round this nucleus that the shanties were built; so that although the original villagers were to a large extent flooded out by the large number of newcomers, many of whom squatted without any permission from an earlier squatter (let alone permission from the owner of the land!), there remain still some recognized leaders and led. These shanties are an extreme case: intermediate are the old villages which although they did not pre-date Dar es Salaam, date back for a long way and were originally settlements, not part of a continuous block of urban housing but satellites of what is now the central town; such villages are Keko kwa Mzee bin Akida, originating from the Arab garrison; Keko kwa Birali which was an old halting-place for the travellers from the south; and Chang'ombe kwa Wanubi which was a settlement of demobilized askaris of German times; Kigogo was rather more recent, formed as a settlement dependent on the Msimbazi Mission, at first settled mainly by the Mission's converts and followers. Buguruni, the biggest of them all, was founded around a nucleus of landowners who lived on their freehold plots and permitted others to settle around them; again a sudden tide of settlement in the post-war period to some extent swamped these original leaders, but the original structure of society is still there, though there may be a disproportionate number of persons who ignore it and do not take their place in it.

So in the Village areas a newcomer can relate himself to his new surroundings not only by his tribe and his relations, but by a kind of tacit compact with those who got there first, an echo of the tacit compact into which each newcomer to an up-country village enters, accepting the leaders whom he finds there, both as persons with a right to speak for him to Government, and as having a right to such respect as he accords to established authority; accepting the subordinates of these leaders as persons deriving their authority by rightful process;

all these rights in their turn deriving from the prior right (whether 'legal' or not) to the land.

INTERLUDE

Keko kwa Mzee bin Akida: an old village engulfed by the town

This village dates back a fair way, but not so far as its neighbour at right angles, Keko kwa Birali. It has 71 houses and a population of some 650 souls.

Its origin lies in events to the north-east, when Seiyid Majid agreed to undertaking a protectorate over this part of the coast, and brought a garrison of Shihiri (not Baluchi) askaris, known as *viroboto*. They were barracked on the far bank of the creek, where the old King's African Rifles lines later were, but the commander, Akida Askara, also a Shihiri, took as his own the creek sides and planted them up with coconuts, giving the original Zaramo a sweetener which he considered to be a sale of land. The barracks were centred by a soapberry tree.

When he settled in as 'governor' he planted up the creek with sugar cane and the side and top with coconuts, and the latter has ever since been recognized, first by the Germans and then by the British, as freehold, while the creek, being under annual crops, was not.

Akida Askara had two sons and a daughter. One son, Abdallah, died young and had no children; the daughter Bibiye lives there to this day, and has borne two children, one of whom died, the other a young man called Shebe. The third child (of Akida Askara) was Mzee, after whom the village is named. He in his turn had three children, Mohamed, now in Morogoro working for Daresco, who has a small child called Matata. His sister Mkuu binti Mzee had two children, who live in town; and the other sister went when young to Zanzibar but now lives in town with one child. None of them has any official position now, but the land belongs to them freehold, and each house owner has to get their permission to build and pays an annual ground rent of 10 Shs.

The head of the community is Mwalimu Pazi, who came originally from Chamazi, where he still has a plot of land and relatives. He joined the railways as a blacksmith and went to Kigoma to ply this trade on the steamer before the first great war. After the war he settled in what is now Keko kwa Mzee bin Akida (that is the south-western side of the small creek which crosses the Kilwa road) but was then cassava fields. That was in 1919, and he was the first to build a house there, by permission of the Mzee bin Akida family. He went there because he was a caretaker for the railway houses in Gerezani, across the creek. He did not have to pay anything for the plot of land, and he still lives rent-free, though his sons, who have built further along on the same freehold land, are charged rent.

After he had settled there others followed, including Bibiye herself. The Chinamen came comparatively recently, and the Luguru who together with them grow vegetables in the creek.

None of the Shihiri barracks is still standing, having been demolished to make way for the King's African Rifles.

Mwalimu's son is joint head of the community, having spent 18 years here. He has another son at Tanga, working as a clerk.

Originally the graveyard of this community was where the petrol dump now stands, but the remains were exhumed and transferred to Temeke. Now people are buried just below the road facing on to the creek.

Other groups

It will already have been noticed that time and again a person says that his best friends are those whom he met at his work. The term 'best friend' will of course have different connotations for different people but is well enough understood, whether as meaning the man one talks to in the evening, the man one sees most of—even if not out of working hours—or the man with whose temperament one has most in common; it does not usually mean the man who will come to one's aid when in difficulties—this is the relative, the sheet anchor of a man's existence. In one sample men were asked how they met those who are now their best friends in town, and their replies were in this proportion:

At my work	43
From home	33
In this house	29
Same tribe only	16
Only relatives	10
In previous houses	8
Fellow pupils	5
Same street	4

One each: religious group, tribal association, same age (and old men), football club.

Most jobs are ideal for getting to know people: the majority of workers are unskilled or dockers, or masons or carpenters working on construction sites; in addition to working side by side these take the lunch hour, during which most simply rest on the site, talking in the same gangs in which they have worked. It is natural that from these repeated contacts some lasting friendships should sprout.

Many of these groups re-form in the evening into small clubs, or 'schools', where small-scale gambling takes place, for penny points, on *bao*,[1] snakes and ladders, dominoes, or cards. Particularly these clubs are used by those who are paid daily or by the job, for they have ready money. The sums lost or gained are not large, and often the rule is that a man who loses must drop out to give another his turn, thus curtailing still more his losses. A newcomer to town is certain to be taken by the relative who is putting him up, or at the latest when he makes an acquaintance at his work, to one of these clubs, where at once he is accepted by a group of up to twenty, whom by constant meeting he will quickly get to know well.

Others, according to taste, take to the football clubs, whose players are a small minority, with a large, inactive but enthusiastic following; many of both players and followers get into the habit of meeting in the evenings for discussions about football or anything else that may be of interest. Many of these clubs, whose signboards are to be seen all over town, in fact meet only as social clubs, the football side of them having dropped out through lack of organization or the transfer of the first enthusiasts. Most often they are based on tribes or localities, but a number are 'works' teams, or departmental teams, though these have not so strong a social side as the tribal or village teams. The clubs have many of the opportunities for the practice of internal organization, and the failings, of more august associations, and in some the frequent changes of officials, walkings-out from meetings and intrigues form a microcosm of larger politics.

Jazz clubs tend more to the dominance of those who actually play an instrument, but they too have a social side and the members often stay together for years. Again there is a struggle for leadership among the organizers, and constant permutations not unconnected with money: for the bands are beginning, the

[1] A game peculiar to Africa.

best of them, to enter into comparatively big money now that takings may be £80 a night gross.

We have traced our way from the larger groups down to the smallest: it is now necessary to return to the largest of all: the Africans. For the fellow-feeling for 'us Africans' is beginning now to become one of the strongest: not translated yet into practical help for each other, but at least into a sense of packing together against the rest. The branches of the only political party which operates in the African areas of town are beginning to be clubs where people gather to meet others like themselves. As these branches are opened in each village and section of a suburb they may well bring to those suburbs the cohesion which at present they lack, just as the new Village Councils, a fragmentation of the suburb-wide Ward Councils, will tend by bringing civic matters nearer to ground level to awaken in these villages more of a corporate sense.

INTERLUDE

Wealth and poverty

This account is apocryphal.

'I had arrived that day from Morogoro and saw Dar es Salaam for the first time. Till then I had lived with my parents not far from the town of Morogoro itself, and had heard from my brothers of the big town at the coast; many of my brothers and cousins had already been there and some were working there this year. I had seen the clothes they had brought back, some of them, and heard them speak of the wages to be had; they had described the street lights, the cinemas, the dance halls, the women and the clever town men; my father did not wish me to go, but I knew that if I stayed I would soon be expected to begin again the yearly clearing of the fields; the fare to Dar was small and I borrowed it from a young friend; one day, without saying goodbye to my parents—for they would not have agreed—I boarded the bus and went to Dar. I had sent no news ahead but knew where to go: my elder brother lived in Ilala and worked in the Commercial area, as servant to an Indian; he lived in a room at the back and got his meals from his employers; nothing was said when I found the house and he took me in; I helped him with his chores and he fed me and with his help in a few days, found a job like his, at 50 Shs. plus food, with another Indian not far away.

'That first evening my brother took me out for an hour when his employers had gone to the cinema; we strolled in the streets, Acacia

Avenue, Ring Street, Kichwele, Msimbazi; I was amazed at what
I saw and wished I had come down earlier: there was nothing like
this at home. Every house was bright with lights, electric in the
stone town, pressure in the wattle and daub; the streets were
thronged with crowds bigger than I would have believed could fit
into any town; there was an unbelievable and exciting bustle,
thrill and glitter; in the roadway passed car after car, nose to tail,
the drivers hooting and revving, gesticulating, cursing, the taxis
with veiled and hooded women, a glimpse of bright garments under
the veil, a flash of rings, the private cars with Indians and Europeans
leaning back at ease, big lorries still at that hour unloading their
bales at the shops and godowns; pawnshops thronged and packed
with more *khangas* than the eye could count; the young men
lounging at the corner, bright, cynical eye cocked to every passer-by,
resplendent in their evening best; confident in their affluence;
burly men in jeans, bold men in wide hats, arrogant men in strange
hair styles, parted in the middle, or brushed up high in front;
everyone radiated wealth, confidence, success; life in town must be
easy, the rewards great and quickly plucked: I was glad that I had
left the dark, quiet hut of my father, where I was only a boy, a
messenger, a fetcher, a labourer; this was Life.'

. . . . .

'I had been six months now in Dar; I had moved from the first
job, where the hours were long and the work unending, though
intermittent; I found another, and a third; the conditions were
little different, and the pay was actually a little less, though the
food was better. I had moved too from living with my brother and
had found a small back room in Keko which I shared with another
boy of my age, each paying half the 10 Shs. per month rent; water
from the stream was free, and we had an arrangement with a
cousin, who worked at one of the furniture factories across the way,
about firewood; I had settled into the rhythm of town life, a rhythm
of spring tides, dead low before payday, then a surge at the end of
each month, eating till I burst at a hotel, a blind with my friend, a
visit to the pawnshop to recover my pledges, and then back to the
grind of the month, relying on the food I got free from my employer;
at the half-month came the neaps, a small dip of extra poverty, then
a small advance of pay, enough for a few good meals outside and a
drink and a dance, till the dead low approached again and all I had
went into pawn and I lived a life as quiet as I once did at home.
Each evening when work was over I went out in the street and stood
and watched; there were always the same sights, the same procession
of cars, the same well-dressed women in taxis, the same wide boys

and flush boys; where did they get it from? There was a trick some-where. I was worked as I had never worked before, but the money, for all that it came in, in handfuls that I would not have dreamed of, went out again as fast and there was nothing left to me but the bunch of pawn tickets, a grubby vest and shorts, and a few brief memories of the last high tide.

'Sometimes I thought of going home, particularly in those last "tight-stretched days"—as the local slang has it—before payday. But then I thought of what my father would say, and the other lads of the village; "thought you'd make your fortune, did you? Well, what have you brought? Was the big town too much for you?" No, I could not go home like that; I must do just one or two more months, buy some really good clothes, and show them I can beat the odds. But somehow things always got ahead of me, and the clothes never stayed with me more than a few days, never enough to get clear. I began to see that people like me never had a chance.'

The primary object of the average immigrant African is to get cash. A strong secondary object is to break out of the bonds of gravity that tie him so firmly down to ground level at home, and soar away in a new and freer orbit, vying with the other bright stars in the firmament, of whom he sees pictures and hears accounts even in his country quiet. The big town does certainly give opportunities for the free expression of one's personality which are not to be had at home, under the sardonic eye of one's parents, one's older relatives, and the elders of the community. In a world where every man is for himself there is nobody to tell the young immigrant to pipe down and listen to his elders and betters. The fear of envy which in the country makes even those who can, think twice before wearing fine clothes or making too much of a splash, is non-existent in town. A man from Nzega in the Western Province gave as one of the attractions of town that one was free of witchcraft used as the weapon of envy over clothes: but he added that witchcraft still existed in the town, was still based on envy, but here envy of those who *ate* better, and ate more regularly.

Freedom to display oneself is here; the means of display are also available in great abundance, cigarettes, sunglasses, clothes, shoes, drink and women, and of course taxis. These things are here in an abundance that maddens—for not one of them is available except to the man with money in his

pocket. To the man who is unused to dealing in money—
and many from the south and west use money hardly ever
except to pay their tax—it is like watching the guests go in to
a great feast for which one needs a special card of entry, a
card which they have not got. They can get one, the lucky
ones who get odd jobs, or even a steady job at a regular wage,
but the card suffices only for one entry to the feast, one wild
splash with a dozen bottles of beer, or one evening with a girl
at the cinema, complete with taxi, cigarettes and drink, or one
visit to a shop to buy a fine pair of shoes, or a hat—but not
enough to get the whole outfit, or to keep the girl more than
the single evening, or go to the bar day after day, as some
others seem able to do; so there is a growing sense of frustration,
there is always somebody else enjoying something one cannot
have oneself, the monthly splash is soon over, and the remainder of one's pay is overpledged with resulting short meals, the
pawning or sale of the shoes one bought so recently, a retreat
eating up all the gains of the small advance: to cut a bit of a
figure for a day one must cut a very poor figure for many.

So frustrated in one of the important aims of the migration
to town one seeks whose fault it is: where there are poor, it is
clearly the fault of the rich, for do not they make their money
from the poor? Clearly it is only the low pay given by Government, the firms and the contractors which deprives each
immigrant of his due enjoyment of all the pleasures of town.
One can see this in the life of the lucky dockers, those carefree
men who receive more than seven shillings a shift, three times
the wage of the ordinary unskilled labourer: the unskilled man
cannot help be envious of the docker who eats daily at the
hoteli (being paid daily[1] he never lacks while working), and
it is well known to all that a docker never lacks for a girl or a
drink. If only all labourers were paid like that: but the employers want to keep them down. The shopkeepers too, with
capital and stocks of enormous size, standing surrounded by
innumerable *khangas*, shirts, flour, rice, stoves, shoes, all the
things one cannot afford, it is partly their fault for charging so
much. With so much stock they could surely afford to let it
go a little cheaper. They overcharge for what one buys, and then
when one goes to pledge a shirt or a vest or a pair of trousers,

[1] Dockers are now normally on monthly terms (1962).

they give the smallest amount, far less than they cost to buy. One is in their hands, they make on every transaction and one loses. Then the servants in the houses, working for a pittance, have to handle meat and fish and butter and drink and do without themselves; their employers have so many sheets and towels and shirts that they have to be counted, yet if one is missing there is the devil to pay: why cannot there be more of a share-out? Why does one have to take one's cut out of the food by stealth instead of by right?

So goes the old egalitarian train of thought, less sophisticated here than elsewhere but not a whit less bitter for that. The wages, which on hearing about them at home seemed so high for one's needs, are here so low in relation to one's desires; and what worker in the world is going to admit that they are reasonable in relation to output?

To the basic tensions of the poor man with expensive tastes and of the poor man set among rich men, is added the tension deriving from the poor being African and the rich being Indian, European and to some extent Arab; there are of course some rich Africans, and some poor Arabs and Indians; but they are so few as hardly to blur the outline: it is a clear-cut division between the poor African and the rich 'White Man' (the term in Swahili is made to stretch over all three non-African races). This leads naturally to a further train of thought: why should these people from overseas have all the wealth and I, from the country, have none? Am not I entitled to it all, and are they not mere interlopers blocking me off from my rightful heritage? So the natural antipathy of one race for another is fed to the stream of resentment of poor against rich. And to that is fed yet another irritant: that at least one of the alien races, the European, is in authority, fixing the low wages, opposing the strikes, arresting those who steal, harassing those who do not pay their tax, repatriating those who cannot give good account of themselves. All the restrictions which seem to be aimed at preventing a man from making a few pence—no hawking without a licence, no begging, no three-card-trick stands—are made by these people who combine the three attributes of being rich, alien and in authority, all three sitting ducks for the frustrated, the discontented, the simple and bewildered.

In a town where so many have spent too much on the pay-day blind, and as a consequence go short at the end of the month, the murmur of grumbling is to be heard in every house, coffee shop or street corner; much repetition enlarges the grievance and fixes it firmly in the mind as a fundamental truth on which other theories may be built.

Corruption

The presence of corruption like some Egyptian dragoman hanging unwanted at the elbow of every transaction can be horrifying. But to the African it is nothing new. The very word used in Dar es Salaam, or one of them, *kanyagarubuga*, deriving from the payment made to the headman who measured one out one's plot of land, points to the continuity of centuries. The means and the circumstances have changed in town: one pays here to get a job, unless one is lucky enough to meet the Indian or European employer face to face; one pays to get favourable attention, or attention at all, for an official application; one pays to get to the top of a queue for rented housing, or a plot to build one's own; one pays to avoid arrest or to gain a further respite from the payment of tax; wherever there is a slice of power in a man's hands, to give or withhold, it has a price, and the price is exacted. This is not resented; or let us say it is resented in the same way and to much the same degree as one resents the income tax or a licence fee. It is unpopular (with the payer) but is recognized by Africans as the normal course of life. The European dream of eradicating it is only a dream, and the European method of limiting it by strictness of routine checks depends too much on detailed efficiency to have a very long life ahead of it.

In Dar es Salaam it acts as an exaggerator: when a man is down and in search of a job his task is made the more difficult by the necessity of finding the grease for the itching palm; when he is up and in a position of authority it is an addition to his income; in the middle the middling fleas probably get as much blood as they lose. In general its effect is to strengthen the ties of kin which already hold a man's life together in town as in the country, by increasing the importance to a man of the help of his relatives, who alone may give what he wants free.

Bribery is only one branch of the universal trade of corruption; another is racketeering, whose most profitable field is societies of all sorts, from the main political parties, which from the beginning have foundered on repeated embezzlements and are not immune from them today, through the trade unions, none of which can present a balance sheet without considerable previous comings and goings, through the tribal societies, some of which have died completely owing to the general distrust of their members who have been robbed of the common funds too often, to dance bands and football clubs. To take an uncontroversial example one may instance a certain club, which is formed from a few educated and sophisticated leaders and a less sophisticated rank and file.

At a meeting if a member queried the accounts (which were never written) he was easily quelled by the leader, who, speaking in English, accused him of preventing the advancement of Africans. Recently the club subscribed £20, which was taken by the small inner group, and never accounted for in writing. A little later they received an offer from Germany to send two men for training, and the leaders—after appointing themselves as the most suitable to be sent—asked for a subscription to cover suits and other clothes in order to make a good impression; one member had the temerity to ask what had happened to the £20 so recently subscribed, and was told that a European (who had in fact given his services free) had taken this as fees for teaching the club members. When this came out an attempt was made to get members to take the matter up with the leaders, but such was their exclusive solidarity that no member would make a move, knowing that not only would all members back the leaders up in denying the racket they had suffered, but that they would in turn be counter-attacked and driven out of their club for being informers. An example like this, which could be multiplied a hundredfold from every level of life, illustrates that all the criteria of a fertile field for large-scale racketeering are to be found in Dar es Salaam as it is today: a marked divergence in the degree of sophistication as between a few educated and the many uneducated; general understanding and condonation of dishonesty; and the semi-political feeling that however much they have been gulled and robbed by their fellows it would be letting the side down (quite apart from requiring great public spirit and courage) to bring them to justice.

The tensions described in this chapter are the stuff that many dreams are made of: to the trade unionist they give an already convinced audience to any talk of the iniquities of employers and the wage levels; to the nationalist they prepare the way— to an extent that few rural areas can—for the theme that if only the alien authority is removed wealth will accrue to the African poor; on a less legitimate level of thought it prepares a receptive mind for those to whose profit it is that a mob should attack a shop or a gang loot a cargo. The pilferer, the thief, the embezzler, to be found in any city, are in the eyes of many— including themselves—hardly criminals but are 'winning' something which nobody will miss, and to which they are in any case in some way entitled.

The irritants described are made the less bearable by the belief, which is so common, that as the Government—or the non-Africans—made the town, it is the Government's duty to provide jobs for all who go there (since employment is the *raison d'être* of the town); when it is found that there is not enough work to go around, and when, say, a boy of Standard 8 fails to get a job, after having paid school fees for all those years, he feels that he has been let down. The argument often then proceeds to the conclusion that they are deprived of jobs by a deliberate intention to keep Africans down. It is then said that the best jobs are kept for non-Africans solely through a colour bar, and the charge of corruption and inefficiency is used simply to get rid of unwelcome competition.

INTERLUDE
Clothes

Why does a man come to Dar es Salaam? To get money. Money for what? That depends; certainly there are many who come to get capital, to invest in a wife, land, the tools of a trade, a bicycle or other productive goods; there are also those, a large class, who come for a career, at rates of pay which enable them to reach and maintain permanently a higher standard of living. But the biggest class, drawn from the uneducated, unambitious coastal tribes, come simply to get spending money.

When such a man has a wad of notes in his hand, he spends it: that is what he came for; had he wanted food, there was more food at home than he could eat, and he would have stayed at home; had he wanted the quiet companionship of family and old friends, there was only too much of that at home; to move to a better room at a higher rent appeals to few—how many among the crowds that throng the streets would ever come inside and see how well he lived? But to make a splash, to show that he has beaten the odds, has pitted his wits against the world and won, how better than to buy clothes, fine clothes, bright, unusual clothes, and wear them through the streets?

So here in town clothes make the man; they also reflect his attitudes to other things, and give a clue to the sort of man he wishes to be, or at any rate to seem. To begin with there are two divergent modes of dress, the Western and the Arab; the latter derives from the imprint of the Arabs who brought the first civilization to these shores: an Arab was then powerful, rich, educated, and backed by the magic of a successful religion; his views and his ways were worth imitating as a means to success; Islam took firm hold, and still does, and the outward and visible sign of Islam here is the *kanzu* and the *buibui*, both worn as outer garments over almost anything; the *kanzu* is often topped by a coat, seldom now the *kizibau* or waistcoat, more usually a second-hand European jacket. It is almost a uniform at times of religious festivals, Ramadhan, or Friday mosque; the sandals of the older generation now give way to European shoes, often with socks; under the *kanzu* may be a loin-cloth, or a skirt and shirt or vest, or shorts and shirt, or even long trousers and shirt. At its best, clean, ironed and fresh, the *kanzu* is a garment of dignity, suited now as of old to a gentleman of leisure on his way to the mosque, or to sit with his friends for an unhurried discussion of the world's affairs. It is less suited to the hurly-burly of city life, to manual labour or the work of an artisan; to the poor man who cannot afford much for laundering, or the bachelor who tends to let things slide. At the street corners where the young men wait for odd jobs may be seen *kanzus* dirty, crumpled, torn, worn two or three one on top of another, striped with old sweat, an echo of old values now disregarded, of new half-learned.

The little cap which the Arabs wore as a first covering under the turban, and the only covering in the house, is now the favourite headgear of those who wear the *kanzu*. Many are delicately worked with fine stitching, and cost up to sixty shillings each, incorporating as they do the work of several weeks; this slow art too is being squeezed out, and few but the older men any longer have the time or the slow pulse to spend these hours on a cap whose mass-produced substitute can be bought for one or two shillings. The gleaming, laundered and starched caps now more nearly earn the slang name of *muhogo*[1] or *mtama*[2] which is given them for their yellowish colour.

But the *buibui*, the garment devised by men to disguise any shape the good God had given their women, which requires to be held on by hand and induces the waddling walk of the Swahili woman, continues, though its form is often changed, and the clothes it hides have often changed to full Western dress. Many are now short, even sometimes above the knee (lest passers-by should miss the fact that the wearer has graduated to nylons); there are fashions in the way of fastening, one now current, folded round the face to leave a small opening, is called 'the lemur fold'. Although many, even among Muslims, go about in the streets without the *buibui*, wearing *khanga* or gown, it is still the 'safe' dress for a woman to wear. But the original purpose of the men, to prevent their wives' beauty appearing before other men, has tended to recoil upon itself: as they wryly joke, a man's wife may perhaps pass him in the street without him knowing, on her way to an assignation with another, wrapped in her all-over mask.

Cheaper to buy are *khanga* and vest or round-necked shirt, worn by some even in the street, and by most when relaxed at home; for a woman a *khanga* is the obvious dress for housework and any field work. Only when she goes out must she wear the *buibui*. In the house also are worn the flapping slippers called *mitalawanda* or, more evocatively, *la haula* (a shortened form of the Arabic expression 'there is no force or strength but in God', an expression of surprise and dismay, but here onomatopoeically echoing the flapping noise of sandal against foot); these, once clogs, then leather, now come in bright-coloured plastics and a variety of designs.

Plain *shuka* (skirt) and vest are seldom seen in town except among the poorest (or the Arabs themselves), or an occasional politician trying to divest himself of Western influence and get back —if not to a state of noble savagery—at least back to the stage after the Arabs had brought clothes to naked Africa; the effect of this is sometimes spoiled by the carrying of that white man's burden the brief-case, symbol of the organizer.

So much for the Arab style of clothes, a style which must rest its appeal on a desire for restraint and modesty in dress and bearing, and hark back to a life of quiet and ease and unhurried dignity.

The Western style, with its variety, its unlimited scope for display, the expense of its chic and the convenience of its standard clothes, has made way out of proportion to the small numbers of the Christian or the educated who might be expected to use it.

Among clerks, teachers, laboratory assistants, and those in

[1] *Muhogo*: cassava.   [2] *Mtama*: millet.

responsible positions office dress is identical with that of their European (or Indian or Arab) counterparts, that is, white shirt and shorts, stockings and shoes; though white is perhaps not a sensible colour in dusty heat, the materials are cheap, and the man on £10 a month can wear exactly the same as the man on £100 a month without being extravagant. Long trousers and a shirt are rather more expensive, and consequently less common, but add a cachet particularly when worn with the long sleeves and tie that are cheaply bought at the price. The 'full-suit' (the word has passed into Swahili, and is used even to describe the thatch-sided shanty hut) is relatively very expensive, and its owner has demonstrated to the world that he is a man of wealth and position. This being the motive behind so many of those who are drawn to town from the coastal districts, Western types of clothes offer the chance that they have sought. There is no man who can be sure that he will be the best-dressed—there is always scope for more display, more expensive clothes, a firmer stamp of success.

In a town like this where most are young or middle-aged, and male, there has grown up, as elsewhere in East Africa, the cult of the cowboy, the African equivalent of the English teddy-boy. The young man from the country, or the young man from the town, soon acquires the idioms of tough speech, the slouch, the walk of the 'dangerous man' of the films; the ever-popular Western films teach him in detail the items of clothes that go with the part, the wide hat, neckerchief, particoloured shirt, often with tassels, jeans, and high heels, or at least the *kilipa*[1] or heavy shoe in suede or plain leather with double crêpe soles to give added height. After the first years of direct imitation local fashions have added their own peculiarities, such as the *uchinjo* jeans drawn down tight to well above the ankle, like shrimping pants, and drain-pipe thin. With such an outfit, sometimes costing as much as a hundred shillings when bought all together, goes—as with the outfit of the teddy-boy—an attitude of mind; it is the revolt of the adolescent, in age and in culture, against the authority of elders, of the established, of the superior and supercilious. Outré dress is its most innocent form. It often takes others, the almost anti-religious movement of which one still hears echoes, which called itself the Mabantu, which challenged the authority of the Sheikhs; the groups and gangs who occasionally defy administrative authority, and in their lifelong struggle to avoid paying tax are waging an unceasing though usually personal and defensive battle of wits with the Jumbes and police; and rowdyism at dance halls. The cult of cowboy clothes is the safety-valve of the

---

[1] Phonetic spelling of crêpe (soled).

dangerous mob element which is likely always to be part of Dar es Salaam. They are unformed *Hitlerjugend*, as yet, their uniform jeans and wide hat, their march the gun-on-hip cowboy slouch, waiting for a *Fuehrer* to give respectability to their longing to be admired, to be feared, to have a place in the sun.

The women who have the money and the independence to dazzle with their style (and in this town of loose and shifting liaisons there are many such) can do so only through the medium of Western dress; in the old style one can buy a new *khanga* more often, but there is not much to choose between one *khanga* and another, and the difference in price is a matter only of a few shillings; in Western dresses, called *gauni*, there is a world of difference between one dress and another, and in the prices of them. At dance halls Western dress gives the man an opportunity to display with black dinner jacket and white trousers, and bow tie, fame enough, but the lady in the long evening gown, with sequins, is rewarded by the look of still greener envy in the eye of her neighbour clothed like a country cousin in a *khanga*; moreover while the *khanga* is being held in place ever more awkwardly as the tempo of jive hots up, she of the sequins can devote her whole attention to her chosen part as queen of the halls.

In daytime these Western dresses are hidden, all but a glimpse to prove they are there, by the ever-present *buibui* as the wearer goes down the street. Of course it is only the better-off, the prettier who have the more generous boy-friends, who can afford the best (and use the Acacia Avenue Bata for their shoes at an enhanced price instead of the Kariakoo branch with its equally good stock but less chic address). The majority of the wives, relatives or independent women in town use the *khanga* for most of the day, or a second-hand dress of some cheap cut and material. And some of the richest women in town, the widows and beer-brewers, the landladies and fish-sellers, are so well established that they can afford, like county ladies in the *Tatler* in their tweeds, to wear the old-fashioned *khanga*, cheap and serviceable, and wear it with finality.

Hunger

Most Africans in Dar es Salaam believe that they go hungry often. For instance when the sample of 4,891 persons of all ages, of both sexes and ranging from 45 Shs. to £45 a month in wages, were asked to state the number of meals they had, in the preceding month, firstly around payday and secondly in the days immediately prior to payday, which are called *sika zu mwambo*—the tightly stretched days—some 700 persons claimed

I

to have had nothing at all to eat in the worst day; a further 500 claimed to have had no more than a cup of tea. Of course the form of the question invites exaggeration, as *siku ya mwambo* really means a day when there is nothing to eat, and, therefore, one is obviously expected to reply that one had nothing; nor is there any reason why the persons asked, the great majority of whom were in employment or dependants of employees, should lose an opportunity of influencing Government by claiming a state low enough to induce another rise in wages. Exaggerations were in some cases taken so far that some claimed never to eat, even at payday; even dockers, who are mostly paid daily, claimed to have to go without food some days—presumably those on which they did not work, for the average docker works only every other day. The truth is very hard to find; the domestic budget survey has encountered a few examples of people actually going hungry at the end of the month, but not to the extent of it being a regular thing. But of course if one once goes hungry that day will be remembered for many months, and any rash interviewer will be told that the subject 'always goes hungry at the end of the month'.

The medical authorities at the Sewa Haji Hospital have found no clinical signs of widespread malnutrition; nor has the Municipal Health Visitor whose care is particularly the small children: the only examples she found were in fact *outside* the town in a rural village. For the most part the very small children in town are adequately fed—though the choice of food is not always wise—and those who get least are probably the children large enough to feed themselves without protection but not large enough to get their fair share in competition with their elders. In general it may be said that when a man is supporting a wife and children the responsibility steadies him up considerably; he will seldom go so far as to disclose to his wife what his salary is, or to take home his earnings whole.

'We were going round asking people their salaries, trying to see what difference had been made to them by the recent minimum wage award. We came to the house of a man of some education; we explained what we had come for. He hesitated, looking sideways at his wife who was also there. He thought for a moment and then asked for a pencil and paper. He sat with it, and was about to write, but his wife, who was also able to read, moved to his shoulder and waited to see what he would write. He pondered for a long time, and eventually wrote down his salary in £ s. d., hoping thereby to make it unintelligible to his wife. Though both were relatively educated he had not reached the stage of letting his wife into the secret of what his earnings were.'

He will very often take his evening (the main) meal in a *hoteli* in order that he personally may eat better than the whole family can afford; but at the same time he does tend to make the money last better through the month. This is reflected in the preference of married men for a fortnightly wage, rather than a monthly, for the mid-month payment is mainly used for real necessities, of which food is the most important, while the end-month payment goes to repayment of debts, clothes, and pleasure in addition. Conversely the single man with no family responsibilities tends to have his evening meal always at a *hoteli*, and probably does not bother to have anything else but a cup of tea and slice of dry bread for breakfast on his way to work; if he is feeling hungry he may eat a cob of corn or a cake or bun at midday: this is the meal which is most expendable, as it is in the country—or indeed in the City of London where it is closely paralleled by the bun and glass of milk.

In between the family man and the single is that class, statistically most elusive, of men with unmarried wives. These may be companions of a very short stay, or they may have lived together for years; in either case they require to be fed, and fed regularly. Such are the companions of dockers, artisans (mostly weekly paid) and some of the more regular building labourers. There being no great compulsion to stay with their 'husbands' their bargaining power is great, and these households are reputed to feed regularly and to spread the earnings fairly evenly over the month.

Be the truth as it may, the conviction remains in the minds of most Africans that they are often hungry. When asked what the worst feature of town life was a huge majority said 'hunger', often coupled with 'unemployment'. Hunger in this context does not necessarily mean literally lack of food, but embraces the whole idea of shortage of cash, unemployment and uncertainty what the morrow will bring. Its opposite is often 'money' or 'work'. This feeling that they are often hungry is a constant irritant. One of the most common causes of quarrels in a house is over differences in the amount of food available to the different households in it; it is also one of the commonest causes of a rift in the marital lute; in the employment world, according to the Labour Inspectors who hear some 3,000 'small disputes' a year, it is one of the commonest causes of a change of employment—indirectly, in that having spent his pay an employee then asks for an advance, and if that is at some stage refused he leaves.

It has been said above that the man with his wife and child in town tends to eat more regularly, if only for the children's sake; there is another family, and other obligations, which are if anything more common than those to the strict family: a man's obligation to shelter and feed the members of his extended family, his cousins and nephews, uncles and some less closely related. The advent of a swarm of 'locusts' as these are jocularly called, is often a time of shortage, for they seldom give a man notice of their coming, and though they usually in their own interests try to time their arrival for payday, and normally bring some presents, it often happens that just when a man is at his lowest (perhaps having used his payday income to pay off debts) he is faced with the obligation to support two or three relations; if he possibly can he will provide them with some food, if necessary by still further pledging his credit, but whether the hungry day strikes him then or later, it is one more burden.

The reason for this heavy swing of the pendulum from comparative affluence and extravagance at payday, to penury and hunger just before the next, is (given the present range of wages) that so many Africans arriving in town have hardly seen money before; those young men who have begun to pay tax have probably done a month's work in the year for pay in order to earn it, but have in most cases done only the minimum required to complete the tax, leaving little over with which to learn the management of money: certainly very few indeed have used money to such an extent that they are able to calculate how long it will last and to allocate it throughout a month or a fortnight; the inability to distinguish between capital and recurrent which has ruined so many hopeful shop-keepers, is matched by an inability to distinguish between an income sufficient to cover the necessary expenditure, and a surplus. So when the country bumpkin comes to town, who used to eat and be housed free, and needed money hardly at all, he is delighted and carried away with what appear to be large sums put into his hand, and does not stop to reckon the cost of merely keeping alive until the next lot comes in. He is abetted in this by the way all those about him do the same: everyone, it seems to him, has a big splash at payday, so it must be the correct way to go about it. Only the women are exempt from this rule, perhaps because in the country it is so often they who take the little baskets of produce to market and exchange them, with or without money passing, for other goods. Most women seem much more cautious over money in town than the men, and many have managed to save quite large amounts, enough in some cases to build a house with, from the sale of small quantities of firewood, fish or beans, a few cents at a time. Few men could resist the temptation to spend these earnings at least as fast as they came in.

In this survey no attempt was made to examine the diet of typical households, whether of single or of married men; nor to study the distribution of their expenditure over items of food and over the other items of a typical budget: for at the time of the survey a domestic budget survey was being conducted by the East African Statistical Department.

From observation during the survey, however, it appears that there is a fairly well-followed pattern of meals: working men usually have a cup of tea and a slice of dry bread at one of the roadside tea-vendors who are to be seen in almost any street, or at the Municipal tea-house where stallholders sell tea and bread or rice-cakes in the same way. As in the rural areas few eat more than a slice of bread with this meal at any time of the month, however flush, and the breakfast cup is usually one of the last to be dispensed with when the money runs short. Thereafter the worker has nothing (unless like the dockers afloat he gets a meal on the job) until he knocks off at half past three or four, except for drinks of water. A lunch-time meal is the exception rather than the rule, except as a treat around payday. Instead he may buy some peanuts, or another cup of tea and a bun or cake or corncob, or he may have nothing at all. On coming off work he will often have a reviver, an orange (which is sold in the market and by many vendors, ready peeled) or a cup of tea, or a milk-coconut, and will then settle down to chat until the time of the evening meal, which is taken at between a quarter past six and a quarter to seven. If he has a wife or a mistress she will cook the food which he has brought back with him, shopping on his way back from work (prices are lower in the evening), but if he has not he will eat at a *hoteli*, which is not a place to stay but a restaurant: it may be in a building of good quality, at tables with napery, well served, in which case it will be expensive; or it may at the other end of the scale be a trestle-table in the street, with bare board and tin mugs and plates. A good heaped plate of rice with some meat and beans will cost a shilling, but there is considerable variety to be had both of menu and of price (and the quality of the cooking). It is of course cheaper, though more trouble, to cook for oneself, and many bachelors do, using usually a primus.

While the men go off to work, the women keep rather different hours of meals: they do not usually drink tea first thing, contenting themselves with serving it to their menfolk and getting them out of the house. They then repair to the courtyard where they wash up the dishes from the night before; after that, and sweeping, they are ready for their first meal at mid-morning, about ten o'clock, and very often all the women of the Swahili house will gather and eat it in company, though they will not necessarily share what each has. The left-overs from the evening meal form the main part of this, with tea. They may or may not have another similar meal at midday, but after that they do not usually eat again until the evening meal, when each prepares her husband's food and takes it into their room to eat privately.

It is sometimes thought that the heavy swing in expenditure could be partly avoided by paying people at shorter intervals, either fortnightly or weekly, and the survey was asked to discover what preferences were held in this respect. This question was, therefore, included in the original questionnaire of August 1956.

It is not quite so easy to answer as it looks: few are able, without much discussion, to distinguish between a monthly wage (often with an advance or loan half-way) and a fortnightly; or between a monthly wage with an advance or loan every Saturday, and a weekly wage; there was, therefore, considerable overlapping. Subsequent inquiries myself convinced me that what most people wanted was something to keep them going (for food and the essentials) during the month, with as large as possible a lump sum over at the end to cope with rent, funerals, clothes and other lump-sum commitments.

The preference varies according to the way the worker is at present being paid—daily, weekly, fortnightly or monthly.

The bulk of the daily paid are dockers, though a number belong to the 'ex-dockers' class of people who, liking the freedom of the daily casual labourer, prefer to stand at the recognized street corners and pick up single jobs, often working regularly for much of the month, but always able to stop when they feel like it.

The weekly paid, most of whom are in fact paid on a card basis but with a weekly disbursement, up to the amount earned to date, are mostly artisans, particularly those on construction work. Like the dockers they are well spread over all areas of the town.

The fortnightly and monthly paid, as explained above, are hard to disentangle, but those who feel that they can always get, and usually do get, a substantial advance of pay at mid-month are here deemed to be paid fortnightly; while those who either must or usually do get their full pay (less occasional *ex gratia* advances) at the end of the month are deemed monthly. Rather fewer like this latter method than get it, and there is a small but definite swing over to fortnightly pay, reinforced by the swing to fortnightly at the expense of the daily paid.

An attempt was then made to get behind these figures to see what sort of person preferred each method of payment, in the hope that this would give a clue to their reasons: for all those interviewed gave only the two reasons—that they liked frequent payments because it prevented them going without food through failure to manage their finances; or conversely they liked a single lump payment to cover their big commitments and have a bit of a splash.

The first rule appears to be this: that by and large people are being paid the way they like it; in the statistical tables (which are not included in this edition) this shows up in converse form, that people like the way they are at present being paid. Thus of clerks who are being paid fortnightly 69 per cent. prefer it so, much the biggest group; while of clerks who are being paid monthly 58 per cent. prefer it so, followed by 25 per cent. who would prefer a fortnightly payday; the same preference for the present methods of payments can be seen in every group.

The second rule is that, after allowing for this, there is a general swing towards fortnightly pay; the case of the clerks has been mentioned; of the unskilled, 28 per cent of those paid daily, 30 per cent. of those paid weekly and 43 per cent. of those paid monthly, would have preferred fortnightly. Similarly with the other groups, messengers, factory-hands, artisans, domestics and others.

When attention turns to the differences in preference between the various wage grades, it is found that up to about 120 Shs. per month a fairly high proportion like the mid-month 'subsistence' payment, to cover necessities, but that over this wage there is more confidence in their ability to last out and the preference, therefore, swings slightly towards the single monthly payment which enables spending of a capital nature, on clothes, etc.

The sample was differentiated also by tribe, and certain tribal preferences appeared; but they were of significance only in a few cases, and even there the difference was due not to the tribe as such but to the fact that the Dar es Salaam communities of some tribes are above the general average in education or tend more to clerical jobs, or to stable marriages. It was, therefore, necessary to dig deeper, separating out these causes of difference.

It then became clear that the higher the education the greater the preference for a monthly wage; in particular the bulk of clerks, and middle-grade employees, and almost all those in the upper grades, prefer the monthly wage.

A greater preference for a monthly wage among the married was observable but not nearly so marked.

No job

The great post-war expansion of Dar es Salaam's population has been based on an expansion of employment. As the main aim of the immigrant African is to get cash the wave of immigration would have expended itself long ago if the majority were in fact unable to get that cash: but at all times there has been a minority which has not been able to find a job, at any rate for a period which may last for weeks or for months.

Unemployment, however, is not at all a clear-cut term: employment—*kazi* in Swahili—tends to be used meaning 'a regular job'; but there are also a very large number of irregular jobs, loading lorries, shifting goods, stacking, which are well paid but last anything from a few minutes to a day; then there are the temporary jobs, construction, roadmending and similar jobs, which last perhaps for a month or so, and then lapse; all these are worth doing, and indeed the shorter the job often the better the pay (labourers are usually paid 1 Sh. to 3 Shs. to unload a lorry, which may be done in twenty minutes, and 10 Shs. in a day is not an unusual amount of takings. After these 'spot jobs' and temporary jobs, there are the innumerable opportunities for petty trading and many use paid work simply as a means of getting up momentum, as it were, after which they coast to a standstill on small trade; a docker, for instance, who does one shift and gets 7 Shs. 25 cents for it, can with this money invest in oranges a few miles out of town, and hawk them around the streets for some 12 Shs.; that gives him the money he needs for food for the next day, and cigarettes and so on, and the process is then repeated, usually with a slight net loss, so that after a week or ten days he has to return to the docks for another day's employment. In fact he has been 'gainfully' employed all the time, but his work sheet at the docks will show only three or four days worked in the month, unless he has hired out his registration card so that another can go and work (in which case the records will show him to be a very regular attendant, as in the instance seen where a man was recorded as having worked 45 shifts in the month!); there are plenty of young men who prefer the freedom of action of the street-corner station, picking up odd jobs at a shilling or two a time, to a steady job: you see more of the world that way, you can take or turn down a job as you please, and the takings are at least as good. Some of these also work only enough days in the month to get them by, from two to ten as a rule, and they may also invest the proceeds in small trade or merely make the money last. Those in the best position to get by with a minimum of paid employment are those who are enjoying the shelter of a relative, rent-free, and perhaps his food as well. Examples were often met of men who were out of work for months on end (particularly was this so after the December 1956 domestic strike), yet they were not thereby compelled to return up-country: there is hardly a soul in the town who cannot claim shelter and food for an almost indefinite period, thus avoiding the force of St. Paul's saying: 'if any would not work, neither should he eat'.

Thus the term unemployment is bound to be a very crude one, tending to include as unemployed those who have only the odd job once or twice a week; in the survey those who worked at a small trade were entered as employed, and a large number of unskilled labourers were found working 'in town', or 'for Indians', so that probably most of the more regular odd-job men were also included as employed. In an attempt to find some sort of a rule-of-thumb figure, if only for comparative purposes, a figure was obtained from the punched cards of 'males aged between 16 and 45 who when asked: did you have work last month said "no"'. This of course excludes those who have retired because of old age (though a surprising number of these older men were still in employment, even in such heavy work as docking) and also a number of youths who, presumably for tax-evasion reasons, put their ages down as 'less than 16' but were nevertheless in employment as unskilled labourers. The figure thus obtained was 18·6 per cent. When broken down by tribes it appeared that most of the members of the smaller tribes were, as one would expect, employed—for they are people who have come here for a career, arriving either trained or educated; among the major tribes the Pogoro (9 per cent. without a job), Makonde (14 per cent.), Ngoni (15 per cent.) had noticeably fewer out of work than the average; the Pogoro and Ngoni resemble many of the smaller tribes, in having a much larger proportion than the coastal tribes of Christian, educated people (only a third of their males were entirely uneducated, compared with the half that is the average of all tribes in Dar es Salaam); the Makonde are of two groups, the career men like those of the Pogoro and Ngoni, Christian and educated, and the contract labourers, who are also seldom unemployed, but for the different reason that when their services are no longer required it is the obligation of the employer to repatriate them. At the other end of the scale the Ndengereko (25 per cent. out of work) and Rufiji are typical coastal people, with more than the average who were entirely uneducated; a surprising entry in this list of out of work is the Yao (24 per cent.) who fall into the group of less uneducated tribes (a third uneducated), and with their long connexion with Dar es Salaam might have been expected to get what jobs were going. Another surprising one, though it is based on a very small sample and must be taken with caution, is the Manyema, 5 out of whose 14 working-age males were without work—a third: they too are a very long-established tribe, and have a high proportion of house-owners and wealthier persons; it may be indeed that this is the explanation of the comparatively large number without a job: that they are well enough off not to need to work.

It is to be expected that the unemployed will be found in those parts of the town where living is cheaper, particularly in those parts where rents are low; to some extent this is so: for instance whereas Buguruni houses 7·8 per cent. of the whole population it has 11·6 per cent. of the 'unemployed' (in Buguruni 44 per cent. of the rentpayers pay 10 Shs. or less, compared with some 17 per cent. in the town as a whole): similarly there is a bunching of 'unemployed' in Kinondoni and Msasani, areas where live many of the domestics, both in and out of work; although the survey was done before the domestic strike of December 1956, when large numbers lost their jobs, and before the introduction of the minimum wage had led to a pruning of staffs, there is probably always a surplus of domestics offering their services; the job of garden boy particularly requires no training and is much sought after as being the recognized apprenticeship for the better-paid job of house-boy and then cook. These Kinondoni-Msasani 'unemployed' are not of any one particular tribe except that no less than half the small sample of Zaramo and a third of the Mwera in the area were 'unemployed'. The Yao on the other hand were in this area all but one employed.

These 'unemployed' of Kinondoni-Msasani do not, as might have been expected, live in the 'shanty' parts of the area—

Kambini (the remains of the old quarry labour lines) and Mikorosheni: more than a third on the contrary live in the new town-planned area of 'Swahili' houses; a few were living with employed relatives in the Sisal Estate lines.

The distribution of the 'unemployed' differs little from that of their age-group as a whole, except that there is a small shift from Swahili to Village. The reason for this, as mentioned above, is primarily a search for low rents. This is not brought out by the comparison of the rents they pay and those for all heads of households. Fifty-seven per cent. of the 'unemployed' are on their own—heads of households rather than dependants; this is almost the same as the proportion of all males who are heads of households (58 per cent.) although it must be remembered that the base for this latter figure includes children and (to a lesser extent) old men.

As is to be expected, a slightly higher proportion of the 'unemployed' are single than of males as a whole, 45 per cent. as compared to 37 per cent.; the presence in the sample of a core who are not truly unemployed but well-to-do persons who have no need to work is echoed here again in the figure of men having more than one wife, which at 8 per cent. is slightly higher than the average for all males (6 per cent.).

With the search for low rents, and the building of rural houses, one would expect to find that a number of the 'unemployed' kept themselves going by a subsistence plot; but the figures do not confirm this, the proportion (of heads of households) with a plot in Dar es Salaam being exactly the same, at 7 per cent.

As for education or the lack of it, there is the expected small preponderance of uneducated among the 'unemployed':

	Nil	Koranic only	Standard 1–3	Standard 4	Standard 8	Standard 10	Over
All males	48	11	15	18	5	2	—
'Unemployed'	55	9	11	17	5	2	—

A noticeable point is the close correspondence of the sets of figures for those of completed-primary and completed-middle school education, in both the 'all males' groups and the 'unemployed'. Many in these groups feel, having had some schooling, that they should now get a clerical or other non-manual job, and finding no such opportunity at home, come into town; primary education has of course no sale in town for anything but manual or semi-skilled jobs, such as office boy, and Standard 8 boys are already a glut on the market, most clerical jobs requiring at least Standard 10.

The minimum wage

It probably takes some time for the effects of a statutory minimum wage—or even the existence of it—to filter down to all levels. It came into force on 1 April 1957 and in June an inquiry was made to see what effects were discernible already, that is, after one main monthly payday.

The minimum laid down for an adult male was 42 cents an hour if no food, fuel or quarters were provided: roughly the equivalent of a wage of 80–85 Shs. per month.

Those chosen for re-interview were those who in the August 1956 5 per cent. survey were found to be getting 90 Shs. or under. These had been further graded into those with stated wages:

> Under 60 Shs.
> 60 Shs.
> 61 Shs.–75 Shs.
> 76 Shs.–90 Shs.

Only those living in Kariakoo and Ilala were asked. In the event large numbers could not be found again, having since moved:

	Kariakoo	*Ilala*
Under 60 Shs. per month	50	27
60 Shs. per month	18	14
61 Shs.–75 Shs. per month	32	22
76 Shs.–90 Shs. per month	44	34
	144	100

total 244 not found again.

Of those not found in Ilala (which includes Buguruni) 18 were known to have moved to a different and unknown address in Dar es Salaam; one had become sick and gone home; one had died; four were known to have gone up-country, one was on remand, and two in prison. Seventeen had moved leaving an address which proved to be correct. The rest had sunk without trace, many almost or quite forgotten by those they shared the house with.

That left altogether 111 who were traced and re-interviewed; one further snag remained: no less than 24 had by now repented of a lie told in the first questioning, and confessed that the salary they then got was over 90 Shs. These are inserted in the table hereunder. The answers were then divided into:

The same salary as in August 1956
More, bringing it up to the minimum or over
More but still under the minimum
Less
Now jobless.

The results may be tabulated as follows:

	Same	Min.	More –min.	Less	Jobless	Total
Under 60 Shs.	4	1	2	—	2	9
60 Shs.	3	11	—	—	—	15
61 Shs.–75 Shs.	9	12	—	1	3	25
76 Shs.–90 Shs.	9	22	—	1	6	38
90 Shs. or over	10	8[1]	—	2	4	24
Total:	35	54	2	4	16	111
Per cent.	31	48	2	4	14	

This experiment would appear to indicate that the introduction of the minimum wage was fairly effective in raising to the minimum level the wages of those hitherto below it; but this is quite contrary to the impression gained by the District Commissioner who repatriates monthly several hundred boys and young men, mostly tax defaulters, and who believes from the answers they give to questions that the majority of them have had jobs—particularly with the small shop owners, Asians and Africans—whose pay has still been below the minimum. It is possible to reconcile the two samples, neither of which is

[1] In this case the meaning is that they received an increase in wages. With so many of the original sample not to be found too much reliance cannot be put on this table: it is particularly noticeable how many of the poorest paid (domestic servants to Indians, Arabs and Africans) had disappeared; perhaps this was the main effect of the minimum wage?

necessarily typical of the whole working population: for the sample just quoted, though originally a systematic random sample, has had eliminated from it most of the lowest paid, while those who are dealt with by the District Commissioner are just the type who disappeared from the survey's sample; the re-survey was in any case made too soon after the introduction of the minimum wage to be a reliable indication, and it would be an inquiry worth making at a later date.

In speaking of wages one must remember that there are two very different things, as in England: the wage-rate, and the total wage actually paid, including overtime; the domestic budget survey conducted by the Statistics Department shows how important this difference is.

The statistics of wage-rates paid are not given in detail in this edition. At the time of the survey—before the minimum wage order—the most commonly received wage was 90 Shs. Roughly combining daily paid and monthly paid as though 3 Shs. per day were the equivalent of 90 Shs. per month, 18 per cent. of all wage-earners received this wage (the great majority being paid on a monthly basis). Next came a block of 15 per cent. at 120 Shs. per month and third equal came 14 per cent. each getting 75 Shs. and less than 60 Shs. (the latter mostly domestic servants, many of whom received food). The block getting between 75 Shs. and 120 Shs., therefore, supplied half the force of wage-earners. There were considerable variations in the numbers of high- and low-paid as between the members of different tribes, which tied in with their varying education and skill. As might be expected, the highest paid tended to live in the Quarters, and the lowest paid in the Rural areas, the inhabitants of the Village areas being noticeably lower paid than those of the Swahili areas.

INTERLUDE

(Actual person, assumed name)
Mwinyigoha Mfaume

Mwinyigoha is the son of a wealthy man, who had five houses in various parts of Dar es Salaam; he has never lacked for food, but it cannot be said that he has ever had enough money. From childhood he has been looking forward to the day when he can get his hands on the capital sum and have all the things which he feels are his due and which yet he seems never quite to be able to reach.

As soon as he was old enough his father got him a good job, in the Police; he was first an askari, but passed several tests, marksmanship and then driving, and by the end of eleven years' service had two stripes up.

However, his career was not the model that this might suggest, for he was fond of a party and apt to become quarrelsome when the drink had taken hold. For all the pay coming in so regularly all these years he never had enough for his purposes and, in default of an early legacy, had to look around for means of supplementing it. It was on one of these occasions that 'regulations' first caught up with him; His Excellency was on safari in the Western Province, and was due that day at Sumbawanga: he was driver of the lorry taking the tents and luggage, and was sent on ahead; he went at a rip-roaring rate, and arrived in such good time that the tents were unloaded and luggage away with time to spare before the main convoy could arrive; so Mwinyigoha decided to take a few passengers into town on his own account; unfortunately he miscalculated the time required, or the speed of the convoy, and on his return was met by destiny, which saw to it that he was returned to the ranks and posted to Sumbawanga itself; somehow it was only a matter of time before he was up again for furious driving and the taking of passengers, and this time he was out altogether.

Since that time he has had no regular work, but used to serve behind the counter in one of his father's shops; recently he has given this up, as his father has brought in an Arab as tenant. For the past nine months he has had nothing to do.

All the same he is an important man in the village, where he is the chairman of the 'young men's council', a post which unfortunately carries no stipend. His father has now died, and the inheritance has gone to his uncle, at least one step nearer its proper destination.

He told how his father's inheritance was still in the hands of the administrator general, in trust for his young sisters. Each had been allocated one of the houses (he two, being a male), but could not sell. He said there was a herd of cattle at Kunduchi, and he and another took week and week about to cycle out from town and bring the milk in for sale. He had recently moved into town, to his Msimbazi Street house, from Kipawa.

One of his neighbours gave a slightly different version: he was gradually going through his father's fortune as fast as these restrictions on spending would let him. He had moved into town following his latest girl-friend, having installed her in his house. They were not married, and the union would last as long as he could amuse her in the manner to which she was accustomed. He had no herd of cattle, in fact not a single cow, and was presumably working as a milkman temporarily, but the neighbour did not believe he could work for a week on end. The house in Kipawa with a shop was gradually passing into the hands of the Arab who had been installed there in April this year, as Mwinyigoha was continually pestering him for loans, which were entered up against future rent: eventually the sum would be too much to repay and a settlement would be made turning the house over to the Arab.

•   •   •   •   •

So he moved into town to his house in Msimbazi Street where he had installed a mistress. For two or three months I saw nothing of him, but now he has got a job as driver of a lorry plying between Dar es Salaam and Iringa, and down to Abercorn. He says that he will do that until he has roofed his house with corrugated iron (he has paid 1,000 Shs. cash to an Indian, and taken 1,500 Shs. worth, enough to roof the whole house, on condition that he will pay back 100 Shs. per month and pay interest at 10 per cent. a month on any arrears) and installed electricity. After that he says they can sack him.

His pay in this job is 175 Shs. plus subsistence allowance, which is paid as a sort of bonus: he may get 5 Shs. a day, or he may not, and he gets it on safari only. Of course, he says, the salary is not much, it is the pickings, taking extra passengers at one, two, three or five shillings a time, which usually amounts to as much as his salary for the days of the trip, or more. They are toting beans these days. It is a high life, big meals and big drinks and lots of self-esteem as he propels his tons of machinery and beans powerfully around the world: it is a satisfying life, but sooner or later one oversteps the mark, gets into an accident, gets run for driving too fast, or overloading, fails to turn up after a particularly good party *en route*, and then one is back in the ditch again. However, there is nothing one can do about that, but enjoy it while it lasts, and the devil take the hindmost.

He wouldn't do taxiing for anything, though there are those who do it continuously. The speedometers are soldered in (unlike that on his present lorry) so that one can't fiddle the mileage, and taxi fares are based only on mileage. One is always up against the traffic police for taking on more than the authorized number of passengers—and of course one always does, one can't just leave good money standing on the pavement. Then the owner is run as well as oneself, and disowns one and sacks one. There are a few

K

pickings to be had such as taking the merchant navy to Arab girls and Swahilis, and taking Indians on similar errands, when one can expect 2 Shs. from the girl for one's trouble—or if one is flush and not in need of money one can take it in kind. But the pickings are nothing like as good as on long-distance lorry driving, and the risks of being caught far greater.

No prospects

For the greater part of the African population of Dar es Salaam there can be little prospect of advancement. Those who can look forward to an improving status, pay and standard of living are mainly the educated, for whom prospects are indeed rosy, with the chance of very rapid promotion as Africanization gathers speed in Government and, even more, in the enlightened firms for whom the selection of Africans for such advancement has for long been settled policy. But the educated are few, so few that they are statistically almost invisible: those of school certificate standard form only 0·1 per cent. of the population; those who completed Standard 12 another 0·5 per cent.; those of Standard 10 another 2 per cent., and those who completed the second stage of primary education (Standard 8) another 5 per cent. These all refer to males only, educated females being far rarer still.

The great bulk of the population falls below this level:

Males only

Completed Standard 4	18 per cent.
Standard 1–3 only	15 per cent.
Koranic only	11 per cent.
Nil	48 per cent.

Thus almost half of all males over the age of 6 are entirely without education; their companions are the even more uneducated women, of whom no less than 82 per cent. are entirely uneducated, and only 1 per cent. educated to beyond Standard 4. The pattern is continued with 28 per cent. of school places in 1956 and 23 per cent. in 1957 going empty in the primary schools; in Standard 1 alone in 1957 12 per cent. of places in Dar es Salaam remained unfilled.

There are, it is true, a wide range of jobs open to the uneducated and the almost uneducated: not only the unskilled jobs which form 19 per cent. of the working men's living here, but all those which I have classed as semi-skilled, a further 19 per cent., and most of those which I have classed as skilled, no less than 48 per cent., as well as the smaller numbers of small traders. It is in fact only in the clerical jobs and a few of the truly skilled jobs that education is a prerequisite: but of course it is in precisely these jobs that a worthwhile career lies. The unskilled labourer, the docker, the mason, the office boy, the houseboy, who between them have almost half of all jobs, have no hope of attaining to a higher standard of living other than by a rise in the level of wages, which has in the past merely been the signal for, or the mark of, a rise in the general cost of living which has left them no better off than before. The dockers, it is true, have through their strong trade union and commanding tactical position attained to a rate of pay nearly three times that of the unskilled labourer, but they are of all people the least fitted by temperament, education and tradition to benefit from a rise in wage. They have escaped poverty, but they have not put the additional money into attaining to a permanently better standard of life. This is true of dockers the world over and should not be used generally as an argument against any raising of wages, but the fact itself is indisputable, as the statistics compiled by this survey showed.

With a marked difference in wage, one might have expected the dockers to live in better houses; or to build themselves houses and join the aristocracy of landlords; or have their wives to live with them and bring up children in town as a settled family; or have bicycles, and powered cycles; but they do not. In housing they avoid the very cheapest lodgings, but equally do they avoid anything better than the average; if one judges by whitewash on the walls, and cement on the floors, and water, electricity and private latrines and kitchen, and fireproof roofs, the most that can be said is that the dockers, so much above the average in wage rates, are better accommodated than the unskilled labourer, but well below the general male average, as depicted in the statistical tables. For instance, in the lowest group of rents (up to 10 Shs. per month) are to be found 9 per cent. of dockers, less than the average of male workers, which is 17 per cent.; but in the better rooms (over 15 Shs. per month, they have only 35 per cent., compared with the average of male workers, which is 38 per cent., and nearly all these are concentrated at the 16–20 Shs. per month level. As to the number of rooms used, only 2 per cent. of dockers use more than one room, whereas the average of all male workers is 9 per cent. Only 5 per cent. of dockers own a house, compared with 19 per cent. of all male workers. In amenities the story is the same, 19 per cent. of dockers compared with the average of 22 per cent. having whitewashed walls; 11 per cent. (16 per cent.) a cement floor; nil (2 per cent.) piped water; nil (2 per cent.) electricity; 23 per cent. (38 per cent.) a fireproof roof; 5 per cent. (9 per cent.) a private latrine; and 1 per cent. (8 per cent) a private kitchen; 11 per cent. (12 per cent.) possess a cycle, and none (1 per cent.) a powered cycle.

An interesting point is that in the sample of 99 dockers not a single one was found in any of the Quarters—the better-class housing built by Government, and rented out at non-profit rates. In such Quarters one may get, at rates well below those charged in Swahili houses, whitewashed walls, cement floor, two rooms (a few have three), a private latrine and kitchen, all in permanent materials: one might expect that such accommodation would have attracted a class of person receiving a comparatively large wage enabling him to jump suddenly from the unskilled man's 2 Shs. to 3 Shs. a day, to 7 Shs. 25 cents a shift; but true to the spender-type's aims in coming to town he puts it, not into food or accommodation but into display or into leisure to enjoy the sights and sounds without the necessity to work every day. More than half the dockers are Zaramo or Rufiji, both with the coastal mentality well developed: this mentality is not based on ambition, as is that of many of the up-country tribes, but on the ideal of the old Arab coconut plantation owners, in whose system of priorities leisure and a Hamlet-like freedom of choice ranked high, while effort is a minor consideration. A revealing echo of this appeared recently in the newspaper *Zuhra*, whose editor, in his capacity of Mubashiri Din (a column advising on religious questions), said: 'So if a fool berates you saying "Why do you not bestir yourself and get rich?", reply thus: "And why do you not bestir yourself and have many children?"; that is his answer, for getting rich and having children both come by God's will. Effort of itself builds nothing at all.'

If one lacks education, one may still get on in the world by training. And the best training, almost the only one in countries still as undeveloped as this, is training in one's job. Any man who stays in the job for five or ten years and gives of his best should be able to rise above his original station and acquire one higher and more lucrative. But to do so one must stay that five or ten years. This is a thing very few in fact do in Dar es Salaam. In the docks, again, though it is not possible to prove it with figures, as the records themselves do not show length of service, it is accepted that there is a high proportion of short-term workers. It is a characteristic of the coastal people, and in particular the Zaramo and Rufiji, that they like to return home, if not every year, at least frequently, to see to the rice harvest, to marry or see a wife and to beget the next instalment of the family. If one is an unskilled labourer, one simply goes, and chances it that on one's return there will be a similar job to be found. If a semi-skilled worker such as an office boy, one either has to await a less frequent leave, and after doing so once or twice, abandon the job because the wait is insupportable; or leave the job in the same way as the unskilled labourer and chance another on return. If an artisan, paid weekly as a rule, one can leave at the end of a week, or a month, or a particular job, and most foremen or contractors are willing to give unpaid leave with a promise of the same job on return; but these again seldom work for more than one or two 'tours', and then have a long rest. It is unfortunate that this important question, of continuity of job, was one of the failures of the survey, being misunderstood by many, and it is one which merits further inquiry; but in general it is fairly clear that the turnover is excessive, and continuity in one job or in one kind of job defective. Such examples as the following may be quoted:

A man first worked as a labourer for a year; then for East African Tobacco for 8 months; for Dar es Salaam Bookshop as a messenger for 7 months; for a K.A.R. officer as houseboy for 6 months; for the Ocean Road Hospital as a dresser for 3 years; for the Liverpool Uganda Co. as a messenger for 18 months; for an unnamed European as houseboy for 6 months; for an employee of Messrs. Smith Mackenzie as *dhobi*[1] for 9 months; for an employee of the Public Works

---

[1] *Dhobi*: laundryman who works on the premises.

Department as a houseboy for 6 months; in the Sisters' Mess for a year; for a police officer as a *dhobi* for 4 months; for the European Butchery as a messenger for 18 months; for an unnamed European as a houseboy for 3 months; as mess boy for a police officer for 7 months; as *dhobi* to a Customs officer for a year; as houseboy to an Italian for 5 months; as carpenter to a firm of constructors for 5 months; then began the job he now has, of a self-employed tailor.

Such a career must raise the suspicion that the man himself lacked the determination to persevere; particularly as he is an intelligent man who has achieved a position of some standing in his own village. On the other hand there can be quoted the case of a man who was taken on as a chainman in the Lands and Surveys in 1926 and on his retirement twenty-five years later was still—a chainman. A case such as this raises the opposite suspicion that such admirable perseverance in the same job —whatever the quality of work—was not met by sufficient imagination on the part of his employers to turn it into something worthwhile. Both qualities are required.

Both examples point another moral; that where there is an abundance of poor-quality labour, at low rates of pay, there is no incentive either for the labourer to improve his output or the employer to improve the quality of his staff; one of the most valuable results of the minimum wage was that it drove a number of unnecessary men out of employment—a harsh human fact but economically speaking a tonic to both worker and employer, forcing the latter to prune staffs, consider schedules, tighten up supervision and begin to make a real effort to get value for money; where this happened the moral effect on the remaining workers of having enough to do was equally advantageous. The process is still in its very early stages and has a long way yet to go, but the further it goes the more incentive there will be to keep a man, and to train him; and to the man himself to stay and to make use of his opportunities.

The first example is illuminating also in the light it throws on the very low level of skill which a man needs to break into the 'skilled' trades. This man appears to have found it possible to sell his services in the skills of medicine, domestic help, laundering, carpentry and tailoring.

Although so many subsist, or at least eke out earnings, by trade, there is no section of the economy where there is a blanker wall before the African than in trade; he operates only in the smallest—though not the least lucrative—types of trade. In this survey, among 1,785 gainfully employed persons only 7 could be classed as 'large trader', in which class come the owners of any shop, however small, or any transport vehicle, even one. Small traders there were in plenty, pedlars of hot coffee, tea-stall holders, sellers of fruit in season, of roast meat, fish, coconuts, firewood, charcoal, onions, or palm-wine, water-carriers, pedlars of milk, old bottles, flattened kerosene cans for roofing, old clothes, and peanuts. Some hawk around the streets, some have set stalls or beats, some simply set their wares outside the house to tempt the passer-by. These trades bring in a satisfactory return: the rate of return from the sale of oranges has already been mentioned, a profit of some 50 per cent. and a turnover in a morning being common form; it is the same with coconuts; fish is even more rewarding—an example was quoted me of two baskets of fish being bought from the boats in Bagamoyo (for they come from considerable distances) for 14 Shs. each; the purchaser rather unfairly was going by bus anyway so did not count in his fare, but noted that the baskets cost him 2 Shs. each, in the bus, making a total outlay of 32 Shs.; on arrival at the Kariakoo market the baskets were auctioned publicly in the usual manner and fetched 20 Shs. and 24 Shs. respectively. Fish traders can thus make good profits whether as in this case they buy from the place of origin, or as in others if one of the fishermen is deputed to sell, or whether as often happens other middlemen intervene, or women who buy either from fishermen or middle men for frying and selling retail—the most profitable of all and the foundation of several houses now going up in Magomeni.

Palm-wine tapping is also a trade yielding good results: one may hire for tapping some ten coconut palms at 2 Shs. each a month; they are tapped twice daily, morning and evening, and from these ten trees he may get a four-gallon tinful of 30 bottles of the wine (*tembo*) which he sells for 30 cents a bottle to the tembo bar (where it is retailed for 50 cents a bottle). So for the price of 20 Shs. a month he can, if he works each day for the required two or three hours, get a return of

270 Shs. Water-carrying is more arduous and less quick in its returns: a man without capital starts by carrying one four-gallon tin, on his head, buying the water at the Municipal kiosk at one cent for the four gallons, and selling at 10 or 15 cents a tin according to the area; later he graduates to the *mzenga* or Chinaman's pole on which two tins are hung, whereupon his profits are up from 9–14 cents a journey (few journeys are more than 100 yards) to 18–28 cents a journey; this trade depends on the social convention which obtains in the centre of town that it is 'not done' to send your wife to get water, partly snobbery, but more due to the bad behaviour of the young men who hang around the kiosks as water-carriers, and to the old custom of purdah; further out, in Temeke and Kinondoni, most wives fetch their own, but many of the Quarters wives prefer to pay to have it brought to the door. The retailing of firewood is a very common and fairly rewarding trade, mostly in the hands of women, who buy the waste wood from the many sawmills and builders' yards and furniture makers all over town, and particularly in Gerezani and the Industrial Estate, at a shilling a headload; this they chop up into kindling and sell at the door at 6 cents a bundle. A headload splits into roughly 30 bundles, giving a profit of some 70–80 per cent. but with a walk of up to a mile and a turnover of little more than one or two headloads a day. The cooking and sale of beans is on much the same small scale.

These are good profit-making enterprises, but in contrast to the Mahri Arab pedlars of cloths, who hawk their wares on deferred-payment terms round every street and backwater in town, but within a matter of months have worked off their capital loan and set themselves up in something bigger, and within a few years own their own shops, the African small trader seems always to be at the same level of trading, seldom to build on these profits anything bigger.

There are several reasons for this, of which one is lack of ambition to make money by sacrificing leisure. This inertia is, however, by no means the whole story: another important reason is that whereas the Arab is by nature and tradition and upbringing a saver, always ploughing back into the business whatever he can squeeze from profits and save by cutting his own expenditure down to a level few Africans would tolerate, most of those Africans who enter petty trade in Dar es Salaam are of the opposite coastal tradition, by nature and upbringing spenders, always putting capital into current consumption; by this means they prevent themselves from keeping up, let alone accumulating, their trading capital. The third and conclusive reason why so very few Africans in Dar es Salaam have broken through to the 'large trader' class, is the very heavy system of taxation: this taxation is levied not by Government but by their relations—a most efficient system both in assessment and in collection, which effectively transfers wealth as it is made directly from producer to consumer, without the expense of administration and wastage so common in other income tax systems. Any African who lifts himself above his fellows is immediately conspicuous, and the object not only of envy, which is dangerous, but of a swarm of what they themselves call 'locusts'; even the man who is on a fixed wage, and perhaps a low one at that, is visited on payday by his less fortunate relations; he cannot by custom refuse to give if he has, and if a man is a shop-keeper he cannot reasonably deny that he has in plenty. The fact that his shelves are filled with goods—though that may all be borrowed capital—will to his relations be proof that he can afford to give them their requirements on extended credit and that he will not expect the bill to be paid. The extent of this borrowing is reflected in the astonishing figures obtained on income by the Statistical Department's domestic budget survey, when borrowing yielded an increment of income of no less than 7 per cent. spread fairly equally over all wage-groups surveyed.

There is a net borrowing in each month of the survey and in every sample, so that it must be tacitly understood that many of these loans never get repaid. And the losers are those who have done better than average, among whom would come any who attempted to emulate the Indians and Arabs and set up in trade. One of the very few African shop-owners comes from Mwanza, 800 miles away: when asked why he had come to Dar es Salaam he explained that to conduct his shop on business lines he must outdistance his relatives, which he has successfully done.

INTERLUDE

(Actual person, assumed name)

Hasan Selemani

Hasan is a youngish man in his thirties, of some dignity and personality, though perhaps inclined to give himself more airs than his elders would allow him. He normally wears for strolling round, especially in the evenings or when nobody who matters will see him, a rather dirty check shirt and black shorts; but when he is 'on parade', that is going to work, or to the market or to town, he wears a pair of long khaki trousers and a clean white shirt with long sleeves, a pair of *chupplis*, and a coastal hat of embroidered calico.

He lives in Buguruni where he built in 1950, and has his own house, a low-roofed three-roomer, whitewashed and with painted doors and lintels, all in a little need of redoing. There are two lodgers, both young men like himself, each with one room and paying 10 Shs. a month to him. They share the kitchen at the back, and the pit latrine, both in the courtyard surrounded by thatch walls at the back.

He was born near Kitunda, that is beyond Mbezi to the north, in a bit of bush where houses are scattered and few. Some of his family are still there, but both parents are dead. When he was old enough to look after himself he moved to Kibada, across the ferry, where he cultivated a bit, and sold mangoes and other fruit in the town. In 1937 he failed to pay poll tax and, being caught, helped to lay the foundations of what is now the Kipawa paupers' camp, as his tax labour.[1] Apart from that lapse he has never been in for any offence, but has had several long gaps in his employment. He worked for the military in Dar es Salaam during part of the war; once he was a Public Works Department daily paid labourer on the roads; several times he had periods of up to a tour with various Europeans as laundryman and houseboy; for some nine months now he has had no paid employment. The 20 Shs. coming from his rent is enough to keep the wolf from the door, at any rate to the extent that it is possible for him to wait for a 'good' job rather than work as a labourer. All the same at tax time life is nervous, and he jumps when there is a knock at the door, especially as the rent does not then come in: how, he says, could I insist on the rent when they have to pay their tax; both his tenants are at the moment two months in arrears; but he is sure that they will pay in the end,

---

[1] At that time tax could be paid in the form of a month's labour on public works.

provided that he keeps reminding them. Sometimes he does a little desultory trading in oranges or mangoes or coconuts.

Even at his present rather uncertain stage of finances he always has breakfast, tea and a bun, patronizing one or other of the *hotelis* near to his house. Here he eats at a table with several others, whoever may be there, though he knows most of them as fellow-villagers.

. . . . . .

I had not seen him for a month or so, and he is a little changed, more spruce, more confident, more of the gentleman-of-means manner. He has had a death in the family, which meant a whip-round among fellow-tribesmen and relatives both here and in the home village a few miles out on the Kawe road; whether he made something on balance out of the funeral, or whether it meant that he came into a bit of property I do not know. Anyhow he has taken out a 20 Shs. licence to be a trader at the Shark Market, and he buys tables and chairs from local artisans, cash down, and sells them on the never-never in the Shark Market, making a margin for himself. He says it is a good living. It will be interesting to see how long he goes on with it, profit or no profit, before becoming bored.

Debt

One of the most striking things which appear from the domestic budget survey now being completed by the East African Statistical Department in Dar es Salaam is the reliance which is apparently placed on income from net borrowing; in this survey groups were taken from the lowest range of wages up to the comparatively high wage of 150 Shs. and over, and in almost every case a steady income from net borrowing was shown to form a significant proportion of the total income. Who the net lenders are remains a mystery, but if the figures are reliable then the money must come from the better-paid workers in Dar es Salaam itself, since remittances from home are separately entered in the table and can be distinguished. One is tempted to suspect that the figures of net borrowing are in fact not reliable, but derive from the subject telling the enumerator each day that he has bought this and that (which in fact he has not), and then being forced to explain how he got the money to do so by claiming to have borrowed it. Against this there is the consistency found both in the amounts borrowed and in the range of articles bought; food for instance keeps a very steady average spread over the various items bought, and clothes are in all cases a very small item; moreover the same phenomenon has been found in similar surveys in other countries.

Another explanation of the very surprising rate of net borrowing is the varied paydays: for instance dockers are usually paid daily (there are a growing number on monthly terms, but the daily payday is still the more popular), while artisans tend to be paid weekly, on Saturdays (though on a card basis, the payments being in advance of salary, up to the amount earned), many others fortnightly (in advance of salary) and others again monthly with a single payday. The proportions are as follows:

	Paid (per cent.)			
	Daily	Weekly	Fortnightly	Monthly
All workers	19	4	22	54

This shows that somebody is being paid at almost any date when somebody else is going short: the result, inevitably, is that A whose payday is far off borrows from B who has been paid today, both intending that the debt shall be repaid at the next payday; in practice it often happens that by then another financial crisis has arisen, a relative has died, or tax has caught up with him, or he has been pickpocketed, and he has to be excused payment, which is understood to be merely postponed, but in many cases is tacitly forgotten on both sides. Net repayment even when it occurs is a very long business, as the borrower tends to repay only to reborrow at once a large part of the loan.

Another explanation is the widespread indebtedness to employers, whether with the employer's funds or with the private funds of one of the employer's officers, as in an office or firm. Advances of salary to cover some emergency such as a marriage, or to buy a bicycle or rebuild a house are extremely common, and these are usually for amounts which would in any case take many months to repay, even if repayment were not delayed by intervening emergencies of a similar kind. Often a crisis occurs when dismissal is imminent and a large part of the debt is outstanding, and in such cases there is usually nothing for it but for the lender to 'forgive' the loan.

Alternatively the borrower seeks yet another loan, and when that is refused he leaves the job—one of the most common causes of disputes between employer and employed—with the result that he is left with his final pay-off severely curtailed by repayment of all outstanding loans: however, he then has the advantage that in a new job it is by most considered reasonable to make a considerable advance of future salary to enable a new employee to pay off old debts and move his lodging to nearer to his work. And so the process renews itself.

Indebtedness to one's landlord, though it cannot enter into the domestic budget figures (which refer only to amounts actually paid or received and not to debts piling up), is also considerable. Indeed one of the main objections to living in Quarters is that one is given only the one month's grace and then in default of payment comes eviction; whereas when lodging with Africans there is, as in all their dealing with each other, infinite elasticity; it works both ways, to be sure, and it may often be the landlord who in a weak moment is borrowing from a flush tenant, but in the nature of things it is more often the landlord who is put to the test of having to badger his tenants to pay their rent; a large number of people are at any time behind with the rent, and although it seems to be the general opinion that such debts get paid in the end it must often happen that the load of debt accumulates until the landlord is forced to 'forgive' the outstanding rent and ask the tenant to leave; several examples of this were encountered in the survey, and usually the landlord is put in an invidious position, for if he has recourse to the courts he has to pay a fee, with little chance of recovering it from the defendant, and the common reaction of the courtholder is to ask him to give the tenant further time—one more chance, so that he has to go through the whole process again. In many cases 'forgiveness' of the outstanding rent is handed to the tenant as a kind of bribe to get him out. Where an attempt is made to catch up with the arrears it is again a long-drawn-out process, five shillings this month, nothing the next, and so on, always with the possibility of another domestic crisis intervening to set the reckoning awry again.

Credit at shops is not perhaps so common, except among the steadier workers. Almost all shops being in the hands of unsentimental Arabs and Indians, who take a businesslike view of loans and credit, it is normally only the better paid, those with known jobs and a regular income, who are allowed to take their groceries on credit; the great majority of those interviewed took no credit in shops, and bought with cash or not at all. Where credit is given it is often a snare and delusion, as few have the foresight or the application to keep a careful account, and arguing avails nothing with the shopkeeper when a large bill is presented at the end of the month. Often there is no money to pay it, and a cycle or article of clothing changes hands. In a number of cases, usually among the older, more permanent residents, any surplus cash—for instance the proceeds of the sale of a crop, or dowry received—is deposited with a shopkeeper, and acts as surety for the monthly credit: when an account is made it is often found that the capital amount has dwindled away to nothing. Other cases are where an Arab shopkeeper has advanced the money to put down a cement floor and bring the house up to a standard at which he is prepared to live in it and have his shop, on condition that this advance is recouped from the rent due: the monthly credit to the landlord for groceries now enters as a third factor in the reckoning, and together with constant small loans is found to have outstripped the rent due, until in time the Arab becomes the owner of the house. Where one party to a financial transaction is businesslike and set on making money, and the other unbusinesslike and set on spending it, such a result is only a matter of time. The same has happened with almost all the coconut plantations, the rice fields and other freehold land in Dar es Salaam: the influx of capital is welcome and the material benefits received considerable, particularly in the sphere of housing; the price paid is loss of control.

Another form of borrowing which does not enter into the high figure of net direct borrowing appearing in the domestic budget survey is that of pawning: this is entered separately and forms a relatively small proportion of the extra-official income.

The addiction to pawning is, however, widespread, though many of those interviewed appeared not to use the pawnshops at all. To many it is used to tide over those awkward five or six days to the end of the month, or in the middle of the month for those who are given an advance at mid-month; the pledge is recovered with regularity on payday and often folded away to do the same duty in a fortnight's time, so that it has its known value and the transaction is quick and almost automatic. One argument was heard where the Indian owner of the pawnshop changed this 'normal' value and gave one lower: the owner of the pair of trousers complained bitterly that he had 'always' got five shillings for this pair.

A few use the pawnshops as a source of small capital, sometimes for trade: for instance the man who pawned a coat for eight shillings, and redeemed it the next day, paying the minimum charge of 30 cents; he explained that he had invested the money in fruit, sold it for twelve shillings, and now wanted his coat back. This is said to be very uncommon; more often the capital is required for one of those constantly recurring domestic crises, a marriage, sickness or death, and a gold ornament is pawned for a substantial sum, twenty or forty shillings, which is left unredeemed for the full period of a year which is allowed by law. (For smaller amounts, up to 15 Shs., the period of grace is six months, to which is customarily added a further week, before the pawnbroker is entitled to sell the pledge.)

There are eighteen pawnshops in Dar es Salaam, a number controlled whether deliberately or not by Municipal licensing; all are Ismaili Khojas, many related both to each other and to pawnbrokers in Zanzibar. It is a closed circle, owing to the licensing system, and when one dies the shop is taken over by one of his relatives; there is no possibility of fresh competition. It does not seem, however, that this position has so far been abused. Within this closed circle there is a certain amount of specialization: for instance one will go in mainly for the pledging of gold ornaments, on the ground that the number of articles is small and, therefore, both storing and accounting are simplified; another specializes in primus stoves (while accepting a variety of other pledges as well), another in under 15 Shs. loans, where the turnover is greatest but the storage and accounting are a problem great in proportion. One specializes in bicycles. In addition most of the regular users of the pawnshops have their favourite shop, where they return week after week or month after month, since to be well known to the pawnbroker is half the battle.

Owing to this specialization the extent of the trade cannot be accurately gauged from a sample taken from two of the eighteen shops, but as one was a low-pledge shop and the other a high-pledge shop it may be surmised that together their trade may not be too far off the general mean. In the low-pledge shop studied, there had been granted in a full year's consecutive operations (September 1955 to August 1956) 25,626 loans of 15 Shs. or under; in the other shop visited, loans of under and over 15 Shs. are not distinguished, but it is perhaps possible to estimate from their overall figure that some 17,000 small loans were granted in a full year; if these two shops are representative it would mean that, say, a third of a million small loans were granted each year in all Dar es Salaam; an estimate with so many guesses in it should not of course be pressed.

The small loans are almost all to Africans; of the larger loans perhaps a majority are to Indians, including Goans, and Arabs, often for substantial amounts, such as £40, on the security of gold and jewellery; the arithmetical mean of 410 consecutive large loans in the shop investigated was 48 Shs., but the spread was very wide. In this range of loans there is also some competition from the goldsmiths, who will always buy back a gold ornament at the price of the unworked gold; this apparently hard bargain appears to be accepted practice among all goldsmiths and their customers, and has been so for many years: in one instance encountered a messenger, on 100 Shs. per month, had had made for his wife a gold filigree necklace for 115 Shs. Five months later he needed money, for building as he said, and took the necklace back to the same goldsmith who had made it, and was offered 70 Shs. for it; after first examining the receipt to prove its genuineness and his obligation to buy back, and then weighing it for its gold content, the price for buying back was fixed at the ruling price of gold less 5 Shs. a tola, the added value of the workmanship being forfeit. With such a large loss in view anyone who can find a private buyer does so, though to do so is not easy, first because few have so much ready cash, and secondly because few would be so foolish as to buy as gold what they have no guarantee for. So in most cases a man who is content with a loan of a good deal less than the full value of the ornament will

3. Swahili-type houses, unimproved versions.

take it to the pawnshop, to be redeemed later, on payment of 3 per cent. a month on the amount advanced. Some pawn their gold ornaments not for the sake of a loan, taking in fact only a nominal loan, but merely for safe-keeping, since they are then the pawnbroker's responsibility.

The number of these larger loans is steadly increasing, if the experience of one shop can be relied on, where the annual total rose from 110 in 1947 to 1,320 in 1952. Trade fell off in 1955 because the pawnbroker was touring Europe with his family, but picked up again to 1,495 in 1956.

To return to the bulk trade, small loans of up to 15 Shs.: in a sample of 3,000 consecutive entries the mean value of the loans granted was 3 Shs. 94 cents: these loans were granted on a variety of everyday items, *khangas*, *kanzus*, shirts, shorts, trousers, vests, and so on; one shop had a whole room stacked to the roof with shoes, on which there is a set value of 5 Shs. a pair for any pair in good condition; another shop had rows of shelves of primus stoves, most still retaining that gleaming shine which even those who let their clothes remain unwashed insist on in their stoves. The storage of these articles of the small-loan trade is a problem in that, as with buses, bars and dance halls, the trade is subject to a violent monthly cycle: on about the fourth of each month the pawnshops begin to fill up as the salaries received at the beginning of the month begin to come to an end (most of them having been applied to liquidate advances, debts and rent owing, and to have a bit of a splash while the going is good); from the 4th to the 13th there is a steady rise in the number of pledges as more and more run out of money; then there is a recovery as a large number receive fortnightly pay or the 'subsistence' advance at mid-month which most prefer; then on about the 20th the queue begins again in earnest, reinforced by the monthly paid, until at the 23rd or so the nadir is reached: this is the true *siku za mwambo*, the 'tight-stretched days'; thereafter it is possible to borrow on the strength of the near approach of payday, and the queues at the pawnshops are relieved. At payday long queues may be seen at every pawnshop, this time with money in hand, and the pledges are redeemed. Figure 1 shows this monthly cycle vividly.

It is often supposed that most articles pawned find their way

L

eventually into the hands of the pawnbroker, when the pledger is unable to find the money for redemption. But investigation at one shop of half a year's dealing (November to April) showed that only 5·3 per cent. of all small pledges (and 3 per cent. of large pledges) were forfeit, a proportion which, considering the clientele, is not unreasonable. Many instances were found where a man who had 'missed the bus' by a week or so was given that extra grace; and many purchase additional time by merely paying the interest due to date, leaving the pledge in pawn. Although complaints are sometimes heard of people losing track of the passage of time and having their pledges sold up through carelessness, no evidence was found that the strict rules of the law were being evaded or abused: many of the forfeit pledges are resold by public auction on the expiry of the period of grace, and often bought by the pawnbroker himself for resale through his own shop: he undoubtedly sells a number direct without going through the auction as the law requires, but this does not seem to bring any disadvantage to the other parties concerned. It is sometimes said that the Zanzibar rule should be introduced here, that the pawnbroker must seek out the pledger at the address he gave before selling, but the experience of this survey in attempting to track the addresses given by people shows that this is a quite impracticable suggestion.

In addition to the monthly cycle of shortage of cash the pawnshop records show also an annual cycle. Fig. 3 shows how the number of pledges reach a peak in March, when a number of licences fall due, and many pay their tax, having started the year high in January and February when other licences fall due; and in the aftermath of Christmas; the number falls away in Ramadhan but with a rise just before, when people stock up with food, and just after when 'Id al Fitr[1] calls for new clothes and presents all round, with many relations coming into town for the festivities. Pledges fall away heavily during June and July, the months of the rice harvest, not only here but all along the coast to Rufiji, when a large capital sum accrues to very many families, and those who are not sent parcels of food by their wives or relatives at home often go there themselves and perhaps recover some of the loans made

---

[1] The festival which ends the fasting month of Ramadhan.

by them on the reciprocal visits. In November there is a last upsurge of pawning, due probably to the expense of the planting season, equipping wives with new clothes and presents so that they can go home to help with the home cultivation, buying seed, paying the fee for the hire of the small rice-fields in Dar es Salaam, and all the other expenses of a new agricultural season: these charts show how important a part the crop year still plays in the economy of people in town; confirmation can be obtained, as far as the fields in and around town are concerned, by a walk round the streets in July, where almost every house in the more outlying parts, and a large proportion even in Kariakoo, has a mat spread out and newly harvested rice drying in the sun.

An interesting and unexplained phenomenon in the pawnshops is the period during which pledges lie awaiting redemption; if, as is generally supposed, the main use of pawnshops is to tide a man over for the few days between *siku ya mwambo* and *siku ya mshiko* (payday) then one would expect this to be reflected in the period before redemption, which should be one of ten days or so; but in fact the mean period (taken from the first three entries in each day for eight months, 600 entries) is almost exactly two months for pledges on which loans of under 15 Shs. were granted. This may perhaps be explained as the mean of two opposite tendencies, the short loan and the long, six-month loan; certainly the individual figures show a wide spread, from one or two days to the full distance, but equally they do not show a preponderance of the tiding-over type of loan.

INTERLUDE

City slang

Dar has a language building, formed from the racy speech of its most numerous component, the young bachelors. As with bachelors everywhere their thoughts run on the fair sex; as they are mostly uneducated, untrained, unskilled, and therefore low-paid, and still young enough to wish to enjoy all the delights which the town offers, their language runs also to emphasis on being broke, terms for inducing a small loan, on the hunger that succeeds a spree.

Some of these slang terms are derived from other languages, particularly of course English, and to a lesser extent ki-Zaramo, the language of a third of the population; more often they are true slang, ordinary words whose meaning has become twisted and esoteric, in the circle of 'city folk', the sophisticates of the courtyard rooms and shanty villages, the smart ones who know their way around; the slang of the bars and *tembo* shops, the teashops and the verandas where schools of young men while the hours away with *bao* or cards.

On the subject of the fair sex some of the less rude expressions may be cited: the semi-political phrase, '*alani taabu tu, shati ninalo siruali sina*',[1] has been diverted to use by a woman thus: '*alani taabu, bwana ninaye akili hana*', to mean, I have a husband (or lover) but he does not satisfy me and he won't notice if I go off with somebody else. Used as a greeting and invitation together this is said to be effective.

The Suez dispute gave rise to the wolf-call '*nalia na mfereji mkuu wa Suez*',[2] latterly this in turn has been brought up to date with '*nalia na bonde la Kilombero*'.[3]

'*Kibiriti ngoma*'[4] describes a loose woman; she is probably referred to as a '*koo*',[5] and described as an '*mtoto shoo*',[6] '*wa kisura*'.[7] To attract her one must show himself a real '*mwana-haramu*',[8] dressing as a cowboy in a '*koti la kigai*',[9] with '*uchinjo*'[10] tight trousers, or perhaps '*siruali ya njiwa*',[11] with '*kilipa*'[12] thick-soled shoes, and '*gaistait*'[13] or cowboy's tie. One must be generous with presents, lest she say one has '*Mkono wa ganzi*',[14] even if it means that in the end '*akukaushe*',[15] she squeezes you dry.

Always it comes back to money; if you have a '*donge*'[16] in hand, that is, a handful of '*wazee*',[17] Kingi George',[18] particularly after the '*mshiko*',[19] well away from its opposite, the '*siku za mwambo*'[20] when your stomach is stretched tight, you can '*kata maji*'[21] and seek the '*mtindi*'[22] till you are '*ndi*'[23] and go '*magabugabu*',[24] or get taken by

---

[1] V-sign, nothing but trouble, I have a shirt but no trousers.
[2] I yearn for the great Suez Canal.
[3] I yearn for the Kilombero valley.
[4] Dance-flame.
[5] Dame.
[6] Show-girl.
[7] Pin-up.
[8] Son-of-sin.
[9] A guy's coat.
[10] Knife-edge.
[11] Ring-necked dove trousers.
[12] Crêpe-soled shoes.
[13] (United) States guy.
[14] Pins and needles in the hand (meanness).
[15] Dries out.
[16] Lump (coin).
[17] Old men (coins with heads on them).
[18] Shillings with King George's head.
[19] Day of grabbing—payday.
[20] Days of stretching.
[21] Cut water (drink).
[22] Buttermilk (alcoholic liquor).
[23] Out (unconscious).
[24] Staggering (onomatopoeic).

the '*karandinga*'[1] or '*mpira*'.[2] But if not, then '*unawaka*',[3] '*unatota*',[3] '*unawambwa*',[3] '*unabanwa*',[3] maybe '*unaluzu kabisa*',[4] unless you can get a friend '*kukusakia*[5] *na kupigapiga*',[6] perhaps you have a friend who is rich, '*muki*',[7] '*mfindi*',[8] a real '*mwamba*'[9] who won't ever want '*kukuvunga*',[10] unless you have used '*unazi*'[11] or '*yahe*'.[12]

Racy speech in Swahili borrows a large number of words from English. As Swahili is written phonetically, and some of the borrowings are mispronounced, their origin is not always immediately apparent. The reader may like to amuse himself with working out the meaning of the following:

1. Cheameni
2. Yuthi Ligi
3. Nailoni
4. Kamisheni
5. Fadhahausi
6. Gita
7. Boni
8. Spekta
9. Lokap
10. Fasti gelasi
11. Hedikota
12. Broo
13. Tapureta
14. Poketi mane
15. Ovataimu
16. Soka nokauti
17. Pareto
18. Saresha
19. Spidi
20. Pijo

Key

1. Chairman
2. Youth League
3. Nylon
4. Commission
5. Landlord (father-house)
6. Guitar
7. Native (born)
8. Inspector
9. Lock-up
10. First class
11. Headquarter
12. Brother (bro.)
13. Typewriter
14. Pocket-money
15. Overtime
16. Soccer knockout
17. Pyrethrum
18. Soil erosion *or* Salaries revision
19. Gear (speed)
20. Peugeot

[1] Police van.
[2] Rubber wheels (police car).
[3] You burn, drown, are stretched, crushed (synonyms for being short of cash).
[4] You lose out altogether.
[5] Hunt for you (for money for a loan).
[6] Pat his pockets (to look for a loan for you).
[7] Mukhi (Indian dignitary), synonym for rich.
[8] Mufindi (place of tea plantations), synonym for rich.
[9] Rock.
[10] To do you down.
[11] Deceit.
[12] Deceit (from Arabic *ya akhi*: O my brother).

Overcrowding

The accommodation in town may be divided into three main classes: rented rooms built by private enterprise; rented rooms built by Government (locally known as Quarters); and rooms privately built for the owner's own residence. The last class is extremely small, and is to be found almost exclusively in the rural areas of the town; even in the houses classed in this survey as Rural (that is, in an area of scattered homesteads with fields interspersed) there were still 30 per cent. of all households paying rent for their accommodation; in the Swahili and Village houses three-quarters of all households live in rented accommodation.

It is in this respect that Dar es Salaam differs so radically from the other capital towns in East and Central Africa. In Kampala and Nairobi there are very few African-owned houses in the Municipal area: in the areas of Dar es Salaam covered by this survey more than 12,000 were listed. Indeed, until the Ilala Quarters were built after the war there was no Government- or Municipal-owned housing in the town; and even now, after a large programme of building since the war with British funds supplied through the Colonial Development and Welfare Fund, only 15 per cent. of all households live in Quarters; as these flats are mostly of two living-rooms, compared to the six or more of the Swahili house, the proportion of the population housed by the Quarters is even smaller: 6 per cent. At the time of the survey there were, apart from 16 rooms built for the bus company, no Company Quarters.

The programme of building Quarters was begun at a time of grave housing shortage, when shanties were springing up on every vacant or apparently vacant plot in town; its object was partly to provide alternative accommodation—or at any rate to prevent further shanties appearing—and partly by renting them out at non-profit rents to hold down the tendency of rents in time of shortage to rise inordinately. Another object, which is not at the moment relevant, was to provide a type of better-class accommodation which was not then available for the rising clerical and artisan groups.

The question early came up whether this Government-built and rented accommodation should be subsidized: it was decided, both on principal and by expediency, the numbers to

be housed being so large, that it should not be subsidized
beyond the provision of the land, water points, and a few main
access roads; but within this limitation rents were set as low
as possible without making a loss, counting in the cost of
building, maintenance and administration. As a result, the
Quarters have offered a much better bargain to the house-
hunter than rooms at an equal rent in a Swahili (African-
owned) house; in particular they have appealed to the man
who wanted to live on his own with his family, and to have
some of the modern amenities such as cement floor, whitewash
and fireproof roof; they have not appealed to the traditional
Coastal man who is not so interested in privacy as in company
and who prefers to live with others of his kind in the traditional
areas and housing of Dar es Salaam.

As far as rents go a flat in the Quarters is charged for as a
unit, whether it be one room (and a private kitchen and latrine)
or two or three. These flats are of three main types: the first
to be built were ambitious and relatively expensive detached
bungalows in Ilala, miniatures of the Government bungalows
which stretch for miles along the northern shore; they were
intended for the better-paid artisan and clerk, and their rents
were set a good deal higher than the town average, but well
below the rent of the then few rooms in the Swahili houses
which offered comparable standards; the greatest draw of those
bungalows is now their central position and to a certain extent
the prestige of living in the 'West End'; turnover is slow and in
the larger, three-room bungalows is so slow that there is a
three-year waiting list. A high proportion of applicants would
prefer to live in the Ilala Quarters and accept a Quarter in
Magomeni or Temeke only in default of getting their first
choice.

The second type of Quarters was built with a different object,
to relieve the strain on the labouring class of the high rents
brought about by a shortage of housing; they were, therefore,
built to the cheapest specification consonant with what were
then considered minimum standards; there are 644 flats, mostly
two-room (plus a private kitchen and latrine), built in terraces,
with little privacy of sound, as the internal walls are built only
to a little more than head height, but at very low rents, though
still with no subsidy except for the provision of the land and

access road and water kiosks; rents in these Quarters compare very favourably indeed with those obtaining in the comparable Swahili rooms.

Last there were built at Temeke 256 flats of an intermediate type, mostly semi-detached villas with two living-rooms in each half; these were built by contract and turned out considerably more expensive than the Ilala and Magomeni flats built by a Government unit, with the result that they are not quite such good value for money, and being at present a long way from town are the least sought after.

These are still the only Quarters for renting to the general public; since the survey there have been built 200 flats for occupation by employees of the East African Breweries,[1] and at the time of the survey there were also Police Lines, and a small Sisal Estate Lines which were all classed as Quarters.

It has already been explained that in fixing rents for the Government-built Quarters, which are administered by the Municipality, the criterion was historical cost (less that of land, roads and water kiosks at intervals of roughly a hundred yards). Such being the criterion there can be no quarrel with the amount charged except to challenge the efficiency of the building unit: but the experience of building the Temeke Quarters by open contract proved that the Government unit is by a considerable margin the cheaper.

Apart, therefore, from providing some better-type accommodation for the beginnings of a middle class, and some minimal accommodation for the labouring class, the Quarters also serve as a measuring rod with which to measure rents in the African-owned Swahili houses, the great majority.

The big blocks of free-style housing, Swahili houses, which have been opened up, and continue to be opened up for private building by Africans, form the other arm of the pincer movement designed to squeeze out the housing shortage, and in the process to squeeze rents down to a 'reasonable' amount.

The theory behind this part of the operation is that since some 6,000 Africans were added, net, to the population every year, on average since 1948, the building problem is of such a size that the capital funds required to build Quarters would be

---

[1] Since given up because the employees struck demanding increased cash wages in lieu of free accommodation and certain items of food.

beyond the resources of Government and would take a larger proportion of the available Colonial Development and Welfare Fund than would be justified; further, that a town composed of a majority of Quarters would expose the Municipality to all the dangers of 'controlled' housing: regulation and enforcement of regulation; the loss of a comparatively stable landlord class with a stake in the town; and the discontent of the tenant 'entitled' to ever-rising standards of accommodation without the intervention of economic laws.

Perhaps these dangers should be enlarged upon, as their avoidance is sometimes taken for granted in Dar es Salaam: here one is sometimes puzzled by references in surveys of towns in Central Africa or in Nairobi to 'permitted number of occupants' and to 'illegal occupants'; for in Rhodesian towns where all accommodation is provided by Municipality or Company, for a specific labour force, there is a constant battle of wits between the authority and 'illegal occupants' who are always drifting in, overfilling the accommodation which did not have them in mind. Checking and getting rid of these people is a process which gives rise to endless friction and in some cases hardship. In Dar es Salaam on the other hand there are no regulations governing the numbers of persons who may be housed in a room, or a 'bed-space', either in Quarters or in Swahili houses: the regulation is left to the law of supply and demand.

Secondly the large landlord class—more than 8,000 Africans —owning one or more houses inside the Municipality is a factor of the greatest importance in the building of a stable urban nucleus: this class is entirely absent in, for instance, Kampala, where African house-owners inside the Municipality are a negligible quantity, and in Nairobi only in two areas, both regarded as a kind of slum, are African-owned houses to be seen in any quantity, though efforts are being made to enlarge the scope of tenant-purchase schemes. One result of this large house-owning class is alone of prime importance: that when the town expands outwards, as it has done twice in recent years, and more land has to be requisitioned from rural Africans, it is for Africans that it is taken, not as in Kampala for an alien population; and all occupants of the land requisitioned have a first refusal of a plot in the newly demarcated area of development. The importance of this in avoiding the discontent referred to in the Royal Commission Report[1] should not be forgotten.

Thirdly, and hardly less important, is the avoidance of all the unreal, yet bitter, arguments about what is 'decent' accommodation, what is or is not 'fit for human beings'. When the economic laws are in abeyance, as they are when Government is building and renting out subsidized accommodation, there is no reason from then on why each man should not be given the very highest type of accommodation known in the country, regardless of his own preferences, previous standards or priorities of demand.

A single example will suffice: in Nairobi and Kampala considerable heat has been generated in Government-built accommodation (where the tenant, being subsidized, was insulated from considerations of cost) over the question of latrines; it was said (and the agitation reached such heights that it is now accepted doctrine) that to share a latrine with other families was below the minimum standard of 'decent' living, and unacceptable. In Dar es Salaam's whole range of Swahili houses, where live persons from the lowest-paid in the labouring class to the highest-paid, and where each house-owner is entirely free to build as he pleases, except that he must have at least one pit latrine, only a small fraction (8·4 per cent. of all households) have in fact decided that it is below a minimal standard of decent living to share a latrine between six or more families, and so far from it being unacceptable to Africans these days it is in fact accepted by the vast majority, to whom it appears a question of very marginal importance: the reason for this difference is of course that in the Swahili house, with entire freedom to build as one pleases, both the landlord, and the house-hunting tenant, look to the best economic return on their money, after putting their desires in a real and undistorted order of personal preference. All that is required in this particular case is to ensure that the alternative, of a Quarter with a private latrine, is available for those few who do in fact put it high in their system of priorities.

In Dar es Salaam, the greatest possible freedom is given to the house-builder to build as he thinks best. Building regulations,

[1] East Africa Royal Commission 1953–5 report, Cmd. 9475, page 222, para. 71.

overcrowding laws and so on have never been made to apply
to houses built by Africans for Africans in non-permanent
materials; only when a more ambitious stone or brick house is
built is it compulsory to observe the same standards as other
houses in the town of the same type. There may, therefore, be
seen examples of every size and shape of house from the rice-
field one-room shelter, through the Rural two–three-room
family hut, low and owner-built of free materials exactly as is
the rural hut the other side of the Municipal boundary and
on beyond throughout the Territory; through the relics of the
shanty days of 1946–8 when a sudden influx of new population
out-distanced new building; to the true Swahili house in all its
forms: plain mud and wattle with coconut-thatch roof, earth
floor and unimproved exterior, but high and roomy in contrast
to the shanties; the next stage where stones are set in the mud
of the outside walls, and the whole plastered over; then one or
two cement floors in the front rooms; an iron roof; whitewash
on the inside walls; the clearing away of the courtyard rooms;
setting up of stone pillars on the veranda; whitewashing or
painting the outside; blocking in the foundations with a *kiuno*
or girdle of stone; setting barred windows: in its final form the
house, good for anything from 20 to 50 years' life, is indistinguishable from a fully stone-built house at twice its own
cost, and the steps of improvement can be taken as and when
money is available over the whole period of the house's life.
It is often said that housing must be regulated or it will go
steadily downhill, ending in a slum town of shanties: this is so
only in the circumstances in which it happened in 1946–8,
a severe shortage of building land. Where, as now, land is
unlimited and provided that plots can be demarcated and
distributed quickly enough, so that there is no shortage, houses
will continue to be built rapidly, and to good standards, so
long as there is an economic demand for rented accommodation.
The proof of this is to be seen even in the old shanty villages,
such as Keko Magurumbasi and Toroli, where the only action
taken by the authorities was to freeze all new building but to
allow 'repairs' to existing structures. Apart from a certain
amount of new building which has gone on unobserved (to
the normal Swahili standards) there has been an enormous
amount of improvement of shanty dwellings, converting them

into normal Swahili six-room houses with high roofs and big rooms. The same is going on apace in Buguruni, where the land is freehold, and new building similarly frozen; the shanties are disappearing as their owners improve them by a series of 'repairs' up to a standard which removes them from the shanty class.

The current danger is in fact not of too low a standard of building, but of too high: accommodation has been short for so long, and rents are as a result so high, that all who build a house think in terms of the full Swahili house with at least five rentable rooms (leaving one for the owner's family); as the shortage is overtaken (and with a declining annual increase in the population and accelerating increase in new building this will not take long) more people should be thinking of building solely for their own use and that of their visiting relations; or else more owners should acquire the habit of spreading their families out over more than one room: but so far there is little sign of either.

At the top of the salary scale, where a few persons are getting good pay as they enter the incipient managerial class, there are signs of a complete break away from the gradually improving standard of what a good house is, and a jump into really first-class housing, architect-designed and with all modern amenities. The first examples have begun to go up, and where the Joneses have trod others will surely follow. At a lower level the African Urban Housing Loans Fund has enabled a small number to build houses costing about twice as much as the normal Swahili house; these have been built almost exactly on the traditional Swahili pattern, but in permanent materials, or partly so. Not all are good value for the money, but they do—more than the first-class houses referred to above—offer something for the rest to aim at. It is unfortunate that the process of obtaining a loan was so protracted that only a very small number had at the time of the survey actually been granted.

Rents

The rents of the Quarters are based on historical cost of the building, with the addition of a margin to cover maintenance and administration costs, but without profit. In the Swahili houses, to use historical cost as a basis would, apart from being an entirely impossible task, be unfair, since the costs of building, as of everything else, have risen fast with the post-war inflation, which is continuing. E. C. Baker, in his survey done in 1939 in Dar es Salaam, gave some prices of materials and worked out the cost at that time of a typical house, and the rise in the cost of materials, and of labour, can thus be seen from a comparison with typical prices today.

The whole cost, using the same data, of a house with cement floors in all the six main rooms, and an iron roof, comes out nowadays at £330 compared to the £110 found by Baker in 1939; while the cost of an unimproved type of house, full size, would be £180 compared to £60 in 1939.

These costs refer to a Swahili house of the full normal size, that is, six main rooms each about 10 ft. by 12 ft., with a 6 ft. passage running down the middle, the height at least 8 ft. to the ceiling.

Rents have of course not remained static against the general rise in the cost of living, including the materials required for repairs. They have, therefore, lost all connexion with the historical costs of the older houses: for instance a house of unimproved type, which cost before the war £60, would now be drawing in 15 Shs. per month for each main room if situated in any of the central areas, or 75 per cent, per annum gross on the capital, assuming five rooms rented and one owner-occupied, less any repairs done. In fact repairs are seldom done on a regular basis, and houses are either left until the roof falls in or the foundations rot and it has to be rebuilt afresh (the histories of several houses showed a rebuilding rate of something like once in every 20–30 years); alternatively, and more commonly nowadays, there is a steady improvement, rather than repair, going on all the time, whenever money becomes available; a good rice crop on the Rufiji will be reflected in a crop of iron roofs in Magomeni; a cashew harvest in Kilwa brings a number of houses up into the cement-floored class; the landing of a regular job may so improve one's credit with the artisan that he begins whitewashing in advance of payment; houses may be seen in every stage of piecemeal improvement; and the same goes for construction, a landlord installing his tenants room by room as soon as he can get a roof on. Almost a third of all houses in some parts of Dar es Salaam have some building going on inside them, and the streets are dotted as far as the eye can see with piles of sand, rubble and earth, to testify to the ant-like processes going on within. With the typical house being thus built and then improved, over a period of years, with little spurts at certain seasons of the year and often long periods when no progress is made, the compilation of cost statistics is very difficult; except for those who for some special reason, such as a gratuity or compensation for the demolition of a requisitioned house, have the money ready to build all at once, few can remember what they have paid for their house, or even all the many steps which brought it to its present state.

There are now not many in town who can build their house themselves, except those who are content with the Rural low two- or three-room hut; all the Swahili houses are now built professionally, usually by a series of contracts; there are a few Africans who will contract to build a whole house, and examples have been found in Magomeni (where the biggest block of new building has been going on during 1957) where a landlord—or more often a landlady—has found a contractor to build her house for a single lump sum, usually around £250–£300. This type of operation was facilitated by the clearing of the ancient Kisutu area, one of the oldest parts of Dar es Salaam, formed around the nucleus of the Upanga Shomvi village, to make way for the encroachment of large modern concrete building by the expanding Commercial Area. The owners of these old houses, some of good Swahili type but many of unimproved pattern, received generous terms of compensation (a liberally assessed modern value plus 50 per cent. for disturbance) and a first refusal on a plot in Magomeni, with encouragement to move out *en bloc*. Many have used the compensation to build large Swahili houses of good quality, and some have found that the sum given in compensation for one old house is enough to start work with some confidence on two modern houses.

Where the cost of a new house being built today is likely to be spread over several years the best that can be done to get some idea of costs is to record what each has spent (so far as they can remember) and try to form an eclectic view of costs. Tables were compiled in this way from information supplied by house-owners at Magomeni and Temeke (the latter has been a slow area for building due to uncertainty over getting tenants, and the spread is, therefore, greater), both of those who have finished building and of those who are temporarily stuck half-way.

These modern costs give some idea of a more rational criterion for judging rents: that of replacement cost. Using this basis one may take the cost, first of an unimproved, or 'basic' house, of full size but with plain mud and wattle walls, thatch roof, earth floors and no ceilings, and with a fenced courtyard, outside kitchen and pit latrine. Such a house has been taken to cost nowadays £180; say, with the addition of three sleeping-rooms in the courtyard, such as is normal, £200. Such a house, in Kariakoo, Ilala or Magomeni, may expect to be filled with tenants, those in the main rooms paying 15 Shs. per month and those in the courtyard rooms 10 Shs.; assuming that the owner lives in one room himself—and he usually does, or if an absentee landlord puts in one room his agent living rent-free—the gross income from the main house is 75 Shs. per month and that from the courtyard 30 Shs. per month, making an annual taking of £63 gross; from this one must deduct the ground rent, 60 Shs. per annum, and the cost of any repairs done: here there is a difficulty, since as explained above it is not the practice to do repairs in any normal sense, so that money spent on the house is very difficult to disentangle into 'repairs' and 'improvements'; perhaps the only certain repair he will have to do is to replace the thatch once every three years, at a cost of £15; the survey's inquiries did not indicate a rate of repairs, other than rethatching, of as much as £10 per annum and in some cases no repairs were done over a period of several years. Perhaps a fair estimate would be a total of £15 per annum to deduct from the gross takings: that leaves £48 per annum or 24 per cent. per annum on the capital.

Such 'unimproved' houses are still in a majority: plain mud walls are used in 78 per cent. of all Swahili houses (90 per cent. in Temeke, but 69 per cent. in Kariakoo); earth floors by 82 per cent. (98 per cent. in Magomeni before the new building started, 69 per cent. in Kariakoo); thatched roofs by 57 per cent. (86 per cent. in Kinondoni/Msasani, 46 per cent. in Kariakoo).

Although these unimproved houses are still in a clear majority, they are falling off rapidly as a proportion of the new building which is going on at present; to some extent this has been the result of official encouragement, in that priority in the allocation of new plots at Magomeni was given to those who undertook to build with iron roofs; partly, however, it is the outcome of generally rising standards both of ambition on the part of the landlord and of demand on the part of the tenant: the fading away of the housing shortage is having, not the direct effect of bringing rents down, but the indirect one of making landlords provide better accommodation for the same traditional rents. This effect has not yet become apparent in the most sought-after areas, such as Kariakoo, but is evident in the newly built parts of Magomeni, and even more in the parts of Temeke where tenants are hard to get.

With this newer type of house now being built, at a cost of £300–£350, with cement floors, walls whitewashed (but still mud and wattle, with plaster), ceilings and iron roofs, rents of 20 Shs. or 25 Shs. can be obtained, or even 30 Shs. in Kariakoo; if 25 Shs. is taken as a typical example, and it is again assumed that the owner lives in one of the main rooms himself, the gross takings from the main house are £75 per annum, and the normal three courtyard rooms will bring in, say, another £25 per annum, making £100 gross in all. Such a house will take more keeping up at ground level, the whitewash will require renewing perhaps twice a year, for the better type of tenant who will rent it; but on the other hand there should be no expenditure on the iron roof for many years; a deduction of £15 for upkeep and ground rent (60 Shs. per annum) should, therefore, be ample, leaving a net taking of £85 per annum or 24–28 per cent on the capital.

Around 25 per cent. per annum is a pretty attractive return on one's capital where little or no risk is involved, and it is the attraction of this sum which has been building houses in Dar es Salaam at the high rate of recent years, limited only by the speed with which plots can be demarcated. From the prospective owner's point of view rents are still satisfactory, and they act as a spur to the building of accommodation faster than the growth of the population; here lies the snag for the future, for there must come a time when the provision of an excess of accommodation brings rent down to an unattractive level;

4. A Swahili-type house; one of the improved versions.

prospective house-owners may then remember the reverse side of the coin, the arrears of rent, the monthly struggle to collect it, the bad debts, and perhaps turn to more secure investments requiring less energy and involving less ill will; if there is then a general revulsion against this form of investment it may not be possible to rely on private building to supply the needs of the African population; the time may then come for large-scale Municipal housing.

There is still the third and most relevant basis for considering the level of rents: its proportion of the income of the tenant. Here one is once again up against the problem of ignorance of the incomes themselves; is one to trust the domestic budget survey figures of the East African Statistics Department and take as a rule of thumb that the income of a given group is some 6 per cent. above its basic wage? Is one to remember or ignore the 7 per cent. per month figure of net borrowing and arrears of rent? Possibly the clearest, though crudest, way of tabling the evidence is to ignore both, and take what are easily checked and easily ascertainable: the rent payable and the basic wage-rate; even if the resulting ratio is out by a substantial margin it provides an unambiguous figure which can be compared with similar figures elsewhere and at other times.

A further approximation has to be made before using the figures of the survey: rents are here expresssed in groups of 5 Shs. at a time, e.g. 11–15 Shs.; for the purposes of this ratio the upper figure is taken; similarly in using the wage-groups, e.g. 76–90 Shs., the upper figure is taken. A final approximation is that for the 'under 60 Shs. per month' wage-group the figure 50 Shs. has been taken as being, as far as inquiries show, the modal figure for this group, and for the 'over 210 Shs.' wage-group the figure 250 Shs. has been taken for the same reason. All cases of rent-payers who were also wage-earners were then taken, just under 1,000 cases, and the rent paid by each expressed as a percentage of his wage. The table on page 162 was obtained.

The Quarters figures are put beside those for the Swahili houses for interest's sake, but the sample is very small (36) and the high proportion of 'over 250 Shs.' makes it unreliable: for instance many of the group having a 17 per cent. ratio are those in 28 Shs. per month two-room flats, some of whom may be getting well over the arbitrary figure of 250 Shs.

M

Rent as percentage of wage	Tenants in Swahili houses (per cent.)	Tenants in Quarters (per cent.)
4	1	
5–6	3	
7–8	9	16
9–10	12	11
11–12	13	30
13–14	6	16
15–16	3	2
17–18	18	11
19–20	9	7
21–22	6	—
23–24	—	4
25–26	8	2
27–28	1	100
29–30	6	
31–32	—	
33–34	2	
41–42	3	
	100	

We may for the moment ignore the 'over 210 Shs.' wage-group, since with all the accommodation in town to choose from it is unlikely that they are in hardship. At the other end of the sample, however, is the rather nebulous group getting (in August 1956) under 60 Shs. per month. Of this group many were houseboys to Indians, Arabs or Africans and were given free food, which in effect lifted them out of the group; even of those who did not get free food 28 per cent. were domestic workers, mostly houseboys in individual households, and again mostly to Indians, Arabs and Africans; another large group were unskilled labourers. Much of the hardship of high rents is to be found in these two lowest groups under and up to 60 Shs. per month: it is worth considering, therefore, what the position of rents would be if these groups were to be entirely liquidated —by the painless method of a rise in their wages. The table of rents as a percentage of wage would now read (deleting also the 'over 210 Shs.' per month group):

Rent as percentage of wage	Swahili (per cent.)
4	1
5–6	2
7–8	11
9–10	15
11–12	18
13–14	8
15–16	2
17–18	18
19–20	11
21–22	8
25–26	6
27–28	1
33–34	1
	100

These ratios are undoubtedly still too high. It may be thought that any ratio over 20 per cent. is *prima facie* high, and if this be accepted, nearly a fifth of the rent-paying wage-earners are seen to be beyond this limit.

One curious aspect of the problem is what one might call the immobility of rents; one would expect that as a man's salary rose so would the rents paid, remaining a set proportion of his income. To some extent this is true, inasmuch as only those in the upper income brackets rent the very expensive rooms; and to a lesser degree it is true that the better paid are less frequently to be found in the very cheapest rooms; but the astonishing fact remains that the most common rent—15 Shs. per month—is the most common in *every wage-group*, including those getting as basic wage over 210 Shs. per month; similarly the next commonest rent, 20 Shs., is the next commonest, by a long way, in every wage-group.

As to the level of rents in the different types of house, it is to be expected that the Rural houses will have the lowest rents of all, and in fact no rent of more than 15 Shs. per annum was encountered among them.

It may be asked where the capital for all this building has

come from in the past ten years, and whence it can continue to come if the pace of building is not to slacken.

In the first place, in the days of great shortage immediately after the war, there was a pent-up demand, not only for housing, but for an outlet for the large amounts of accumulated cash: the wartime drives to increase agricultural production, the rising crop prices, and finally the gratuities to demobilized askaris and others engaged in civilian war jobs, provided the funds for the first great surge of building. At that time, too, building standards were not markedly different from pre-war and had not reached the more ambitious levels observable today, while the prices of materials and labour had begun their long inflationary rise but were still on the lower slopes; many of the lucky ones, therefore, built houses on relatively easy terms, with ready money, in the expectation of a most attractive margin of profit from the armies of new immigrants camped in overcrowded shanties and in the courtyard rooms of the old town.

After the first start there have been several further spurts, due to the clearing of the shanties and the older areas such as Kisutu, where generous compensation was paid at rates which have enabled a new house or even two to be put up to replace the old.

Since then the building boom has been sustained by the hope of a good margin of profit from the rents, which assumes that there is still a large margin of unsatisfied demand for rented accommodation: the first crack in this façade of confidence appeared when the new suburb of Temeke was opened up, nearly 2,000 plots for Swahili houses alone; there was the usual rush for plots, many putting in for two or more, and a number of speculators obtained plots with no very great thought for the capital to build, rather hoping for a resale of the plot to an unlucky applicant and a quick profit-taking. When the first houses began to be completed, and the owners tried to get tenants at the same sort of rents as obtained in the central parts of town, they found there was a limit to the demand for housing: Temeke was considered too far out from the places of employment, requiring a long walk, and from the places also of enjoyment, and from old friends; it would have been popular enough to attract tenants only if rents had been lowered. In default of such a lowering, at least for a time, many houses remained empty and the building of very many others came to a standstill as confidence in building rented accommodation as a form of investment ebbed away. The fortunes of Temeke are being gradually repaired as time and the dock expansion bring the town out to meet it, and as it acquires more amenities and thus has more to offer to the man who cannot afford to go too often into town; the steady increase in the population as the years pass is also helping demand to build up again. But though Temeke will undoubtedly fill up and prosper, it was a warning to many, particularly to the speculators in plots, that the market had its limitations. In 1956–7 Magomeni was similarly opened up to new Swahili building, and there was the same rush for plots; here there was not the difficulty of distance from town, for Magomeni is well situated close to Kariakoo and to Upanga where the construction boom has been providing employment for many of the new immigrants.

Magomeni has also its attractions for the younger element, for it has a life of its own and more than its fair share of bars, clubs and call-girls. Here again the compensation given to those whose houses were being demolished in Kisutu gave an initial impetus to the building, particularly as much of the Haya trade moved bodily from the doomed 'old Kisutu' to 'new Kisutu' in Magomeni, and the wealth accumulated by the trade showed itself in more worthy building standards. So far there has been no sign of a faltering in the rush, and the waiting list in November 1957 remained at 2,394 (1,850 for Magomeni alone) which, although it may be suspected of containing a large number of duplications and some who would, if put to the test, not now wish to invest in building, remains a formidable figure.

In sorting out the applicants for these Magomeni plots preference was to be given to those who had the cash ready, to avoid the difficulties experienced at Temeke where many tried to build beyond their financial strength and where to this day hundreds of unfinished houses are tying up capital which could have been better employed in a more concentrated manner. Preference was also given to those who undertook to build with a fireproof roof, and to those with wives and children, thus bringing to the forefront of the queue a mixture of the financially strong, those with higher building standards and those with greater need. When a little over 500 plots had been so allocated a tabulation was made of the sort of person who had been successful; as explained above the criteria for getting a plot included ability to provide the capital, but there were also other considerations, so that this sample cannot be taken simply as an indication of the source of building capital; for instance the successful applicants claimed to have between them almost a wife apiece and almost two children apiece, far above the town average (only 63 per cent. of all males aged over 16 are married while less than half of all married women have a child with them in Dar es Salaam, and less than a quarter have more than one).

The biggest group by far were skilled tradesmen, more than a third of all successful applicants; a long way behind came people in a small way of business, small traders and hawkers, and assistants to shopkeepers; they totalled 18 per cent., and close behind them at 15 per cent. came the self-employed persons, such as cultivators, and those who gave no occupation, many of whom were old people living from the rents of other houses; after this group came the 11 per cent. of clerks and teachers, and also at 11 per cent. those in jobs with some responsibility or experience, such as watchmen, askaris, and gang-leaders; next at 3 per cent. came big business, shop-keepers with the odd transporter, auctioneer and timber merchant; next were the semi-skilled, at 2 per cent.: winchmen, supported by a herdsman, porter, grasscutter and sweeper; behind them, surprisingly enough, came the rising middle class of better paid and better educated: the Assistant Labour Officers and Probation Officers, and a saleswoman who was the highest-paid person on the list: they totalled 2 per cent.; and finally two small contingents, the property owners (landlords, plantation owners), and Administration (Jumbes, Assessors), at 1 per cent. each.

So much for the classes; but this division gives a rather mis-leading impression; individual jobs within the classes show themselves in a different order: for instance although the class of clerks and teachers totals only 11 per cent. of the whole, the clerks by themselves form the highest individual group, with 10 per cent. of the whole; next in the individual list come people who describe themselves as 'traders', and immediately behind come the 'hawkers', who are in practice little different, so that this group should lead the field with 18 per cent.; then come the first of the skilled group, the drivers, 8 per cent. of all successful applicants; next the cultivators (here shows a part of the influx of capital for building from the surrounding District of Kiserawe, and of other parts as far as Rufiji) at 6 per cent.; behind them are the masons with 5 per cent., bracketed with the messengers and office boys (many of whom, though on low salaries, are of very long standing and have opportunities for making money not strictly part of their duties); the 'unemployed' (many of them old people with their own houses) are also 5 per cent.; and so the list tails off, including by its end 59 different jobs. Most of the applicants were at the time living close by—38 per cent. in Kariakoo and 25 per cent. in old Magomeni. A further 15 per cent. were living in Ilala.

When it is said that some of the capital is coming in from outside, from the profits on crops in Ruvu and Rufiji, and the Southern Province, little confirmation is forthcoming from this sample, only 5 per cent. of whom were at the time of application living outside Dar es Salaam; however, this cannot be pressed, since a man naturally comes to Dar es Salaam to make his application in person (few have much faith in a written application sent through the 'usual channels', without personal guidance through the various obstacles which are set up in any office and particularly in one which has something to grant or withhold which is in general demand) and he gives as his address that of the relative or friend with whom he is staying. What this sample does disprove is the statement often heard in Temeke that all that the new Magomeni is doing is to empty Temeke: in fact only 3 per cent. of this sample came from Temeke.

A more direct light on the source of the money is given by the proportion who are already the owners of other houses: no less than 30 per cent., together with a further 7 per cent. who admitted to having close relatives who were house-owners; it is often said that it is the first house which is difficult to build, but thereafter the rents and profits from the first will enable one to continue building others indefinitely; of this group 11 per cent.

had more than one house already. Again it is sometimes said that all that is happening is that those who have houses are being enabled to build more houses, and that the general population are no better off; when, however, it is remembered that there are over 12,000 African-owned houses in Dar es Salaam, the numbers of those who own more than one are seen to be very small, and although tenants are in a large majority, three-quarters of the population, the ownership of houses is well spread, only 2 per cent. of all households owning more than one house, and only half of 1 per cent. owning more than two. There is at present very little demand for houses for occupation by the owner only: when that comes it will be time to give a bigger share to the smaller man; so long as people insist on building the big renting tenements it must be the bigger man who gets the bigger share.

It is commonly believed that many of these new houses are being put up by women: this again is difficult to prove or disprove, since many people apply in the name of their wife or daughter, some in order to get in several applications under different names and thus, as they think, increase their chances of success; sometimes an official has been known to put his houses in the name of female relatives in a far-sighted desire to avoid their confiscation if anything should go wrong in the future. Bearing this in mind, the 19 per cent. of all successful applications which were made in a woman's name should not be taken too literally; it does, however, indicate that building by women is a significant part of the whole: many are believed to be the owners of houses in Kisutu, recently compensated. Kisutu, one of the first settlements of Dar es Salaam, became in about 1908 almost a Manyema village when they were 'town-planned' out of the New Africa Hotel-Askari Statue-Splendid Hotel area and resettled along what is now Bagamoyo Street, right up to the Msimbazi Creek. Many of the Manyema are now of ripe age, and women predominate among these older ones; they support themselves not only from their rents but by some of the more lucrative small trades, particularly that of fried fish, which is reputed to have built more than one house in Magomeni. This predominance of women in the old Kisutu is confirmed by the rent register which recorded (at 1 January 1956) 51 out of 113 houses in Kisutu as registered in a woman's name. The same effect is predictable if any of the old areas is cleared, such as Chang'ombe kwa Wanubi, but not in such areas as Keko or Buguruni which grew up without control.

The older parts of Dar es Salaam naturally have a longer history of house-building, and a sample of 59 house-owners in Kariakoo and Ilala, therefore, showed a high proportion of owners who had inherited their houses: no less than 16, mainly women, who had inherited them from deceased husband, or parents or brothers. The remainder of the women owners (7) had built their houses from what they had made from cooking and selling cakes, fritters, beans and coconut-ice; and one from 'what she saved from her husbands'.

Of the men there were two big groups: those who built from the savings of artisan jobs (10): mechanics, masons, dockers, painters, telephone operators, sailors, and a general handyman. The other main group (also of 10) was of those who built from the proceeds of their self-employment: butchers, charcoal sellers, a fisherman, a cassava- and soup-seller, a snuff-seller, a beer brewer, a shopkeeper and one who engaged in 'trade'.

Smaller groups were those who saved from public service: in the Government Press, the Police, the Municipality, and the District Office; from domestic service: two to Indians, one to a European; and from windfalls: two gratuities and one who was compensated for the clearance of his old house.

Again and again one comes back to the question of the demand for more housing: it is a leading factor in the production of capital for new housing, since on it depends the probability or otherwise of getting a good return on that capital through rents; it is one of the main reasons for embarking on a programme of the provision of more building land, and of Government building of Quarters; and it is a prime factor in wages since rent forms at its present level so high a proportion of a man's expenditure. It is, therefore, important to know how genuine this demand is; how far there is, by present standards, overcrowding in these areas.

Before any attempt is made to decide at what point of density overcrowding begins it is expedient to survey the facts, particularly as such wide publicity has been given, in the report of the Royal Commission,[1] to statistics of overcrowding,

[1] Op. cit., p. 211.

which, though referring to East Africa, are plainly based almost exclusively on Kampala and Nairobi: indeed, the only specific reference to Tanganyika overcrowding is to an estimate that 'in Dar es Salaam it has been calculated that the average number of persons living in a room 16 ft. by 20 ft. is eight and that in some rooms it is as much as twelve'. I have not been able to trace the author of this astonishing calculation or the basis on which he made it, but it certainly bears no relation to anything to be observed today. For this survey, 640 houses were chosen, spaced at intervals throughout the mainly African occupied areas by the method of selecting every twentieth house from the rent registers (or from new lists compiled for the purpose of the survey, where no register existed), and it was possible to compile statistical tables of average density for each subdivision of each suburb, and for all types of housing. This density refers not to room but to house, except that where Quarters are concerned it refers to a flat, whether of one room, two rooms or three rooms. Where Swahili houses are concerned the average house had something over six rooms. In rural houses the average is between two and three rooms, while in the Village areas the majority are of three rooms, with a considerable sprinkling of six-room houses. In some cases, where the number of rooms was counted, the average density per room could also be calculated.

These tables[1] make it clear that there is a very general average of about two souls in each sleeping-room through all types of accommodation: in the Swahili house this gives an average of about 12 a house except in the less built-up parts, Magomeni (at that time), and Temeke and Kinondoni, with a slightly higher average total in Ilala where the average number of rooms is not brought down (as it is in Kariakoo) by the Indian-occupied houses which seldom have courtyard rooms; an apparently high figure in Keko kwa Birali is also due to the fact that this area, though classed as Village, is composed almost entirely of large Swahili-type houses. The majority of the Quarters (80 per cent.) are two-room flats (ignoring for this purpose the veranda, kitchen and latrine), so that here also the average per sleeping-room is well under two, except in Ilala where most of the Quarters were at that

---

[1] Which are not included in this edition.

time (August 1956) fully detached bungalows with full privacy, so that a couple with two or three children living in two rooms were not relatively worse off than the rest.

As to whether this figure of two souls a room is increasing or decreasing it is not possible on present evidence to give a full answer. E. C. Baker in his survey in 1931, brought up to date in 1939, gave an estimate based on a count of 133 houses in 'four representative areas in the town' of 8·8 souls per house, of whom 4·03 were men, 3·27 women and 1·5 children. At that time only Kisutu, Kariakoo and Ilala existed, but many of the shacks in old Kisutu which have since disappeared must have been still there, and may have formed part of his survey. From that time (1939) population density increased to its worst (though unmeasured) point in 1946-8, and has now returned to the present figure of about 12 souls to the Swahili house in the central area. A measurement of the more recent trend of density—though not necessarily of the density itself—can be found from a comparison of a count made in 1950 by employees of the Medical Officer of Health in certain streets of Kariakoo which were then being considered for demolition in order to provide open spaces in the future town plan; they were not selected as being particularly crowded, or empty, or in ill repair, but simply because their deletion would have made for a more spacious layout, with room for new schools, mosques and so on; the original figures for these houses have, by a happy chance rare in the story of government archives, survived, and it was possible in the present survey to re-count six years later the same houses. They are not strictly representative of all Kariakoo, still less of the whole town, but they give a fair—though not random—sample of the type of mixed street in Kariakoo where the population contains a proportion of Indians and Arabs as well as Africans.

In all Kariakoo it is reckoned from this survey that there are 6,000 Indians (12 per cent.) and nearly 2,000 Arabs (4 per cent.), whereas in the streets of the comparative count the two together formed 27 per cent. of the whole population in 1956.

From this re-count it is clear that the density in these streets has decreased as between 1950 and 1956: the decrease is traceable to a big fall in the number of adults per room, lessened by an increase in the number of children. The decrease for Africans was from 2·0 souls per room to 1·84. The decrease from 13·7 souls per house to 12·25 is not strictly comparable as some of the old Swahili houses have since been converted to three-story concrete buldings: the only safe comparison is that of souls per sleeping-room.

The comparative tables reveal that there has been some decrease in the number of courtyard rooms (a sign of an increased standard of living since these are of poorer quality and let at lower rents than the rooms in the main house). The excess of males over females, common to all races, was much reduced for all except Arabs, and the ratio of children to adult females rose, slightly for Africans, and greatly for Indians, who attained a rate nearly four times that of the Africans. The proportion of Asians rose, but by a greater amount in population than in the living-space which they occupied, so that they continued to be more crowded than Africans.

The opportunity was taken to obtain further information, for which no 1939 figures were available on which to base a comparison: this showed 4 rooms out of 5 rented to tenants; and 75 per cent. having a fireproof roof, 41 per cent. having electricity and cement floors, and 29 per cent. having piped water—showing the order of preference for such amenities. These proportions are not of course valid except for Kariakoo—the 'West End' of the areas surveyed.

Four types of housing have been studied in this survey: Swahili, Quarters, Village and Rural; the last are scarcely relevant, since it is only by accident that they are in a town, and if the Molohan proposals are put into effect these rural areas of the Municipality may be excised and the anomaly disappear. That leaves three very different types, over each of which, and the proportion between them, Government has the power to exert effective influence. It has funds which may be applied to increasing the number of plots (whether serviced by all-weather streets, water points and street lights or not) for building by private individuals; or to increasing the number of Quarters (complete with at least one road to a quality good enough to attract a bus route, and water points, but so far not street lights); and it can decree, and has in the past decreed, the tearing down of the Village houses in a slum-clearance scheme, and resettling the occupants elsewhere. What are the advantages and disadvantages of each course, and of various proportions of all three?

To answer this we need to know what type of person has a preference for each type of house. The type of person who wants a plot to build his own Swahili house, and the demand for it, have already been indicated. Figures are also available to indicate what sort of person wants a flat in the Quarters. These figures are not entirely parallel, for the Swahili applicants were those who had been successful in their applications, and some bias had entered in that preference had been given to those with the money ready, with the intent to build to a good standard, and with families. The applicants for Quarters on the other hand are those still waiting for flats, and no priorities enter into it at this stage. The following information is abstracted from the tabulated applications for Quarters.

But first some explanation is necessary: in the first place there are really three quite different types of Quarters provided —the detached bungalow type of Ilala; the semi-detached villa type of Temeke; and the terrace of Magomeni. Both the type of accommodation and the central position make Ilala by far the most sought after: 57 per cent. of all applicants asked for Quarters in Ilala; Temeke on the other hand, though of a good type of accommodation, is so far away, requiring either a bicycle or 15 Shs. per month in bus fares to get to work, that it was the least popular, getting only 8 per cent. of the applicants; Magomeni, being central and cheap, got the remaining 35 per cent.

In the population as a whole 91 per cent. of all households live in a single room; there are a few Quarters for the type of single person or childless couple, who really prefer a single room; and it is interesting that among the outstanding applicants for Quarters 16 per cent. asked for a single room; but the bulk (60 per cent.) prefer two and with Temeke hardly in the running because of its distance and also comparatively high rents it is the Ilala 2-room Quarter which is the most popular, followed by the Magomeni 2-room flat, with the Ilala 3-room bungalow third.

The occupants of, and the applicants for, Quarters are recognizable types: in the first place they have to be better off than the mass of the population, not only because preference is given to those with a wage not under 150 Shs. per month but also because the Municipality insists (as the landlords of Swahili houses do not) on payment of rent on the nail, so that the more thriftless are gradually weeded out. Secondly, and most noticeably characteristic, the occupants of Quarters are predominantly Christian: of present occupants 57 per cent. are Christian, compared to 12 per cent. Christians in the population as a whole; and of waiting applicants no less than 62 per cent. have Christian names; this does not necessarily mean that *all* Christians, or even the majority, wish to live in Quarters, for of the Christian community 63 per cent. now live in Swahili houses, 14 per cent. in Village and 3 per cent. in Rural: some are no doubt waiting to get a Quarter, but there are whole blocks, such as the Mission Quarter of Kariakoo, where it has for long been traditional for Christians to live: the Mission Quarter, even so, houses only a fourth of the Christians of Kariakoo, many others (particularly the Haya, who are perhaps a special case) preferring the Gerezani section of Kariakoo, south of Kichwele Street.

The third characteristic of the occupants of the Quarters is that they are drawn mainly from the clerical (38 per cent.) and artisan classes ('skilled' 45 per cent.), whereas in the population as a whole although the 'skilled' class are a slightly higher proportion (48 per cent.) the clerks and shop assistants are only 6 per cent. Among the waiting applicants for Quarters the proportions are a little lower (clerical 34 per cent., 'skilled' 38 per cent.) but still showing a marked preference by clerks for this type of accommodation. The few with responsible jobs show the same preference.

Remembering that three types of accommodation are offered by the three areas of Quarters it is not surprising that the higher the salary and type of job of the applicant, the more marked his preference for Ilala; and conversely the lower his salary and the status of his job, the more he prefers Magomeni, where the cheapest type of accommodation is. The few that favour Temeke are in the higher groups.

When it comes to the number of rooms applied for, it is only those with responsible jobs and comparatively high salaries who ask for three-roomed bungalows; in the groups with the lowest pay among the applicants there is shown a preference for single rooms. It is also noticeable that Muslims have a greater proportion of their number in the group which prefers single rooms.

To some extent it is true to say that more married people prefer Quarters: for of the present occupants only 16 per cent. of all households were of single persons, while for the population as a whole the figure is 31 per cent.; but among the waiting applicants the figure has risen to 22 per cent.

Bearing in mind the characteristics of the present occupants of the Quarters, and the type of person who is still waiting for one, to what extent should the building of Quarters be given a priority over opening up more plots for the private building of Swahili houses?

In the first place there is a large unsatisfied demand for both: the waiting list for Quarters at 27 December 1956 (when these applications were analysed) was exactly 1,100, and at the end of November 1957 it was roughly 1,200. Meanwhile there was a waiting list for the 900 Swahili plots being allocated in 1957/8 of 2,394. In both lists there are no doubt a number of duplications and of 'dead men'. It takes a long time to get to the head of the list in either: in the Quarters the average waiting time varied, according to the type of flat, from 1 to 7 months in Temeke, 12 to 18 months in Magomeni, and 26 to 52 months in Ilala. (The very high figure for Ilala 3-room bungalows is due both to there being very few of them and to the fact that the present occupants are permanent retired persons and, therefore, such bungalows seldom fall vacant.)

When considering the Quarters and Swahili houses as alternatives there are several factors to be borne in mind: although Quarters are not subsidized beyond the provision of the land, access road and water points, the rents charged, being non-profit-making, are well below those of Swahili houses in the open market; this fact naturally increases the popularity of the Quarters. Thus of all the 1,240 units of Quarters available when the survey was made, 44 per cent. were in the 10 Shs. per month range per room, 3 per cent. in the 12 Shs. range, 48 per cent. in the 14 Shs. range and 5 per cent. in the 16 Shs. range, which is below the general level of rents for Swahili houses. The latter were found by the survey to be in these proportions: 12 per cent. below 11 Shs. per month; 44 per cent.

at 11–15 Shs.; 34 per cent. at 16–20 Shs.; 9 per cent. at 21–30 Shs.; and less than 1 per cent. at more than that. The disparity is in fact much greater, since the Swahili houses contain a high proportion of houses with mud floors and walls and thatched roofs, while all Quarters, whatever their other shortcomings, have cement floors and solid walls, tiled roofs, private kitchens and private latrines. Their rooms on the other hand are much smaller than the rooms in the Swahili houses.

The first factor, then, is that the provision by Government of non-profit-making capital enables Quarters to be rented at well below market rates: it was indeed one of the objects of the Magomeni terraces to provide cheap flats for the lower-paid workers; the same effect could eventually be obtained by allowing enough building of Swahili houses to bring rents down.

The second is that the preference of Christians for Quarters expresses a desire by a certain type of person who appears to be found mainly in the more responsible, the clerical, and artisan classes of job, for more privacy than is to be had in the Swahili house, for a kind of house where he can raise his standards both of furniture and of hygiene, and for a spread into two rooms when a family begins to grow or get older: such a spread in a rented Swahili house would be an expensive business.

A third is that the Ilala bungalow type of Quarter has provided something to which there is no alternative elsewhere in the town: the small detached houses of Buguruni and Tandika perhaps come nearest to it, but they are not of the same high standard of building. The Indian and Arab solution of renting a complete half of a Swahili house, which is then 'semi-detached' by giving it a separate access gate, and its own kitchen and latrine and either the whole, or none, of the courtyard, has not been followed so far by many Africans: it would not be surprising, however, if more did so in the future as the formerly Indian-rented houses in Kariakoo, many of which are of a good standard, are vacated by tenants who move to Upanga; while Indians normally pay 150 Shs. to 200 Shs. per month for a three-room half-house of this sort, rents would almost certainly drop to the African equivalent, which in the few cases found was 90 Shs. for the three rooms, kitchen and latrine (it will be noticed how favourably the rent of a three-room Quarter, 48 Shs. per month, compares with this). As an

5. An Arab shop in a Swahili-type house.

alternative it would be desirable if some of the prospective builders of Swahili houses forwent the prospect of renting out a large Swahili house and built, only for themselves, a three-room house of good quality: but so far there is no sign of many wishing to do so, since the renting boom has not yet been proved to be over.

Perhaps the most important factor on the other side is the desirability of increasing the number of house-owners in the town; the Quarters provide a good standard of accommodation at a very reasonable rent; they provide the rising class of company salesmen, Government employees in responsible positions, and others reaching out for a better standard of living, with a means of putting some of their ideas into their standard of accommodation; but they do not at present offer any hope to such people of owning their own houses. It was originally intended that some of the Quarters should be taken at enhanced rents which would over a period pay for the house, so that it became the property of the tenant; but this scheme has never been in operation, since nobody was found who did not prefer to pay a lower rent now and forgo the prospect of ownership. So for the moment it is a straight argument between ownership and tenantship; and in favour of the latter is only the presence of a career-man class who do not wish to invest in a house, and would be unwise to do so.

The material advantages of owning a house at the present time are obvious: once the house is up its maintenance is a far lower charge on a man's income than rent of equivalent accommodation would be; this margin will be a constantly narrowing one, as standards of housing—and therefore the cost—and the prices of building materials and wages go up, while the provision of ample plots for building may be expected to complete the overtaking of the housing shortage and so bring down rents. Added to the advantage, at present, of having accommodation at cost below that of renting it, is that housing is—again at present—an investment bringing in a return sufficient for a retired man to live on: for the sort of man who is used to an 'unimproved' Swahili house, of which he lets five of the six main rooms at 15 Shs. per month and perhaps two of the courtyard rooms at 10 Shs. per month, is able to support himself in a quiet retired life at 95 Shs. per month (above the

N

minimum wage); while the man who is used to something better and whose house, with cement floors and an iron roof, reflects this, can expect 120 Shs. per month in his retirement— not princely, but more than what half the wage-earners of the town now get. Again, the provision of ample building plots will flood the market and tend to bring rents down (or force land-lords to provide better amenities for the same rent), while a continued downward curve in the rate of the population increase may lead to a slump in housing. Meanwhile, however, the rentable house remains a very good investment.

But it is perhaps the immaterial benefits to be had from the accumulation of a class of house-owners within the Munici-pality which are the more important: in this respect Dar es Salaam is unique among the capitals of East and Central Africa; for in this survey there were counted more than 12,000 African-owned houses within the Municipality; the reason is not far to seek: whereas in, for instance, Kampala, severe building standards made it virtually impossible for Africans to build houses inside the Municipality, such strict rules have never been enforced in Dar es Salaam, although the law[1] does provide powers to control building and living standards to a fairly strict degree. In practice prosecutions for overcrowding are undertaken only when such overcrowding is a real danger to health; they have been very few: as a result it has been possible for Africans to own houses in the heart of town as well as on its outskirts.

An analysis by tribe of house-owners shows, as one would expect, that those families which first settled in Dar es Salaam have a disproportionate share in house ownership: the Makonde, Manyema, and Yao are in this class (but not, to any great extent, the Shirazi, who have never taken much part in town life, keeping themselves to themselves in their cut-off fishing villages). It is interesting that the Zaramo, some of whom have been in Dar es Salaam as long as anybody, and many of whom must regard a town house in Dar es Salaam as a desirable investment close at hand, have significantly less than one would expect; this is particularly noticeable since their share of the population, which was over half in 1948, is falling.

Over half (57 per cent.) of the house-owners were in work in

[1] Dar es Salaam Overcrowding Rules, GN 270 of 1946.

August 1956; the skilled and clerical had about their fair share of owned houses, the unskilled rather less—but not perhaps as much less as one would expect; the small band of cultivators living on the outskirts had, naturally enough, six times their share; and the semi-skilled, for no ascertainable reason, had more than their share, being 28 per cent. of all house-owners, but only 19 per cent. of the whole population. In education the house-owners fell midway between the 'whole population' figures for males and females, reflecting the number of female owners among them; thus while in the whole population 48 per cent. of males and 82 per cent. of females had had no education at all, among house-owners 63 per cent. were uneducated; while at the other end of the scale the 2 per cent. of house-owners who had passed Standard 10 or over was greater than the less than 1 per cent. found in the whole population.

From this the 'typical house-owner' emerges as a Coastal man gone urban, of the earliest immigrant tribes, uneducated (partly because he is of the older generation, as propertied people tend to be, and partly because he originates from the Coastal Spender class). He is probably an artisan, or a messenger, watchman or other 'semi-skilled' man. We shall consider him again when discussing 'settledness' and the formation of public opinion.

INTERLUDE

Buguruni

First thing in the morning, some are drinking tea, two or three gathered round a pot; a docker has a teaset, pot, cups and tray of the same design, and he and his friend eat buns as well as drink tea for breakfast; he is on the night shift. Women are washing their pots and scraping them with sand outside the houses, while they talk with each other. Already the Arab shops are open and a good business is being done, small quantities of sugar, onions, packets of tea.

A little later the bakers' vans arrive and go round the shops. Also a man carries loaves round from house to house where the van cannot go. He is paid by the baker, by the month, and carries the loaves in an openwork basket. Later people are seen having the midday meal, tea and dry bread; this may be their breakfast if they were late rising, or it may be lunch. Many here are in regular work, and have two snacks a day in addition to the evening meal.

At one house are two women, visiting; they are dressed in the new clothes they got at 'Id al Fitr and are very smart; most wear *buibui* on the outside of *khanga* or dress (*gauni*); many have brightly coloured plastic-covered shoes or sandals; there is a mixture of tribes, showing in the different hair-dos and tribal markings, even an occasional split lip with core of wood in it.

At one house a *mwalimu* holds his class of Koran teaching, consisting of teaching one child to say a passage by heart, who then leads the others, each with his Koran open at the place but unable to read or understand a word of the Arabic written there. Passage by passage the obligatory parts of the Koran are committed to memory.

One of the original inhabitants of this village, who built his house here in 1921 when there were only half a dozen there, strolls in dignified aloofness, a white ring of beard in the Arab style to hint at his antecedents. He has now three houses, and retains enough trees, mangoes, coconuts and cashew nuts to bring him in a small income to supplement the rent from his lodgers; his out-goings are small, as his sons are now all self-supporting and few of his relatives are alive to need his support—although if alive they would not hesitate to ask for a little assistance now and again and he would not feel that he was being battened on, rather would accept that he who had much owed this to those who had less; for the outside world he feels no obligations. Now he is a man of substance with the graveyard of the early settlers by his house, and the respect of the later-comer to enjoy.

In the shade of a low-hanging eave lies in a deck-chair a young man, hat well over eyes, a cigarette drooping from his lips. He scarcely bats an eyelid as a stranger approaches. But he, and the others lounging at the corner, do not slide away, they stand their ground, swaggering slightly, without saying anything. The women disappear behind doors, peeping out. Some, however, are too busy, one doing another's hair, and they try not to notice the stranger, but when addressed smile pleasantly and speak without embarrassment. The man who was standing a little way off and apparently lost in contemplation of the sky moves closer to listen, and soon joins in. An old woman weaving a mat pays no attention till spoken to, then replies with spirit and personality, ready with a joke to cap a joke.

There are many small chores going on: some women have bought lengths of wood and are chopping them up for firewood, laying them in a trough in the sandy soil and splitting them with an axe lengthwise; others, women mostly, but one man too, have fish sizzling in a pan over a charcoal brazier made from a tar barrel, to be sold either to one of the Arab shops or to the men direct when they come home from work; others again have bought a sack of charcoal and laid it out in small heaps for sale; tiny children carry bowls of hot cooked beans from house to house; a larger child carries a basket with a conical cover, full of cooked food: they are visiting.

Some of the rooms are still dark, and inside someone who was up all night slumbers on, answering grumpily to the cry of '*hodi*'.[1] On many doors is the legend 'Cry *hodi* thrice, then go'. The doors are a whole reference table, first a big number painted on five years ago when first the village was plotted; then a date, the mark of the rat-catchers; then a yellow line, the mark of the anti-yellow-fever residual-sprayers; sometimes a further number, where the house is a test one for a mosquito count; somewhere each day is seen the mosquito man with his spray slung over his back, but just now he is on other work as the light aircraft is doing his spraying for him. 'No good' they say of this latest development. Nobody now looks up as it passes within 500 feet, nor for the larger airliners constantly passing overhead.

People are still cleaning up, women or men, sweeping up the dead leaves around their homesteads, brushing out the compound, and then throwing the household refuse on a pile behind the house, where chickens peck and scratch it over, followed by their newly hatched brood (large ones, as the mango trees give good protection from hawks).

As the stranger passes men exchange questions in ki-Zaramo, 'Why is he here?' 'Is it all right?' Meanwhile he has reached another house and has addressed the inmate; there is a moment of anxiety while they exchange greetings, then when it appears that all he wants is the yellow-fever card with the house's number on it there is an almost audible sigh of relief, and it is brought out hastily.

One tiny child accosts another: 'Where did you get that tin?' (which he is using as a drum).

'I found it in the bush.'

'No, you didn't.'

'Yes, it was just thrown away.'

'Then come to Salum and see if he agrees.'

'I'll give it to him later.'

On the house nearby are bits of iron, asbestos, packing-cases, which have all been found thrown away and have come to rest where they are appreciated.

All the time through the trees comes the hum of the Metal Box factory, and the occasional hoot of the diesel train. A goods train lumbers slowly out along the Central Line, a long way to go till the wagons are next inspected. Beside the tracks, feet away as it passes, are some huts thrown together with bits of old iron and sacking, almost supported by the maize that surrounds them; here a man

---

[1] '*Hodi*': 'anyone there?'

moves off wearing a woollen dressing-gown and old trilby hat.

Out of a door pops a girl's head, the face powdered as though for the 'Id, a bold look in the eye, and below, a flowered dress and coloured sandals. The head pops back again and the sacking curtain falls back into place.

Across the rails, almost as close on the other side, is a neat little house, freshly whitewashed, and the edges picked out in blue, with red window-sills. Inside are curtains of white calico, gathered into a knot at the bottom, and over each glassless window a criss-cross of expanded metal. The owner is by trade a mason, and here on private land he has found the place he likes, close to the rail and road, the rice-swamp and the vegetable garden, the *tembo* club and the Arab shop; yet far from the offices and inspectors, the schools and the police patrols; once he lived at Makaburi further in towards town and also by the tracks, but he was moved out of there, and out to Buguruni, and here he has settled with many of his old friends. Yet he likes to go in to town, first for his work, which has been regular now for some months, and also to see his other friends who are scattered all over town, some in Kariakoo, where he can fit in a visit with a shopping expedition to the market, others in Temeke whither many moved from Makaburi—but there is nothing but his friends to see. He likes Buguruni because it contains his friends, and yet the great majority of its inhabitants he does not know, many he has never seen; many are on evening shifts, and keep odd hours; some come and go for no well-known reason; many are birds of passage, working in the Metal Box or another of the factories across the rail, for one, two, or three months and then away. Even of his lodgers he often learns little more than their first names, and they are often changing; sometimes they fail to pay the rent, but not often, for with his well-set-up house he can now expect a better class of lodger, who with steady work is able to pay the 15 Shs. which he charges for a room. And he in his turn, with the better income coming in, regularly each month now that the expense of building is over, has become a man to be respected, a householder, a Muslim who is to be seen with the solid men at the Friday mosque, a man who has learned to mix an Arabic guttural with his greetings and shows now no trace of his country birth—not that he is in any way ashamed of it, or of his relations who visit him from time to time, bringing welcome gifts of rice and fruit. He does not go to dances, but is to be seen most evenings with others like him, in the coffee-shop at the corner, silent or quietly exchanging desultory conversation. Though the young men these days have no manners and swagger around the public streets and bars, he has enough presence to berate one who offends him, and have no stream of dock-labour abuse hurled back, though the man may be getting twice his daily wage, or nearly.

Administration[1]

As an authoritative study of the administration of Dar es Salaam has recently been made,[2] this survey will touch on only one or two points of interest.

The many changes in the administration of Dar es Salaam have been caused by the basic difficulty that towns are not here an indigenous African development: that the bigger and more urban a town becomes, the more the African element tends to be submerged by the mainly non-African purposes—in this case large-scale trade, business, and the port—for which the town exists.

When the town is still small, as are many of the up-country towns today, the system of their administration needs to differ little from that outside: a Liwali or Akida or Jumbe may be appointed under the District Commissioner as the executive of the Central Government, and under him there will be subordinates, who if not traditionally part of the structure of the surrounding tribe will at any rate have been chosen at least partly for their acceptability to the African population of the town.

As the town grows, and these Jumbes and elders have been accepted as more or less traditional, the system resembles more that outside, with the District Commissioner as chairman of the town council (a mainly non-African body reflecting the business interest on which the town itself is founded), being also the executive of Central Government acting through his Liwali and headmen, much as he would act, outside, through the Chief and his subchiefs; in law there is a difference, at this stage not important, in that the Chief is a Native Authority, with defined powers to make rules and orders and to preserve good order and government, whereas inside the township there is no Native Authority, its place theoretically being taken by the Township Council. In addition the District Commissioner is the one who is charged with preserving and upholding African interests.

[1] There have been many radical changes since this section was written: it describes the system as it was in 1957.
[2] *Detribalisation*, by M. J. B. Molohan, C.M.G., M.B.E., Government Printer, Dar es Salaam, 1957.

So long as the District Commissioner is the chairman of the Council and also the executive of Central Government and the representative of African interests, he is able to 'marry' these opposing roles. When the next stage of the evolution of local government is reached, and the township becomes an autonomous Municipality over which Government's only control is the provision—and therefore the threat of withholding—of annual grants, the three functions of the District Commissioner are separated: the chairman of the Municipality becomes the Mayor, elected by the members—themselves nominated—of the Municipal Council; his executive is the Town Clerk and his officers, all owing their allegiance solely to the Municipal Council: this council reflects, as it should, the predominant interests of the town, which are those of trade, business and the port; on it, therefore, the African representatives form a minority.

When the Municipality was formed, in 1949, the second function of the District Commissioner, that of representative of the African population, was taken by a Native Affairs Officer, who was an official of the Municipality, serving under the Town Clerk. The third function, that of executive of the Central Government, with a responsibility for law and order, was not catered for, it being considered that this could be left in the hands, firstly of the Police, and secondly of the Secretariat. The disturbances of 1950 showed that the absence of a more definite focus of authority in this respect could be dangerous, and it was decided to bring back the District Commissioner.

Thus evolved the recent system, whereby the District Commissioner replaced the Municipal Native Affairs Officer, being made responsible for all African affairs; and also was the representative of the Central Government in its function of preserving law and order. In both he was subordinate to the Provincial Commissioner for the Eastern Province, who resides at Morogoro, 126 miles away.

To take first the capacity as representative of African interests: the District Commissioner was chairman of each Ward Council; each such council was elected annually by (in theory) all adult males resident in that ward, or suburb. In 1957 village councils were instituted, and primary elections were to these bodies, each of which then supplied a fixed number of delegates to the Ward Council, which thus became indirectly elected. The village councils were presided over by the Wakili of the Ward, with an Assistant District Officer present whenever available; once elected, the ward councillors chose two of their own number to serve on a higher all-African council known as the Council of Forty, or more usually the 'Liwali's Council', together with others nominated to represent special interests; of this also the District Commissioner was Chairman. The Liwali's Council did not elect from among its number the six African members of the Municipal Council, but on the other hand these six (who it will be remembered were nominated) attended the Liwali's Council meetings in order to keep in touch. None of these councils over which the District Commissioner presided had any financial or executive powers; they were purely vents for expressing opinions. No member of the Municipal executive normally attended, though very occasionally the Engineer or Medical Officer of Health might be invited.

It will be seen from this that the hand that held the purse and that wrote 'yes' or 'no' to any suggestion was entirely unconnected to the ear that was applied to the ground; in township days when the same person heard complaints and said 'yes' or 'no', not only was the whole procedure much shortened, but there was a feeling that complaints were in fact getting through, that grievances were effectively taken to the point where they could be dealt with. But when a District Commissioner without any power to sway the decision of the Town Clerk acted simply as a go-between, hearing the complaints and reporting back, then reporting from the Municipality to the ward council, the feeling, however unjustified, was born and grew that these complaints were not in fact being heard. The councillors felt frustrated and their confidence in the District Commissioner and in the council system itself slowly but surely evaporated.

As a result of the Molohan report further changes were recommended: Dar es Salaam was to become an extra-Provincial District of which the mainly African areas would be under a District Commissioner, whose duties were confined to African affairs, with an enlarged staff; above him, and co-ordinating African and non-African affairs as an executive of

Central Government, was to be a Deputy Provincial Commissioner who, it was envisaged, would eventually be responsible not only for these affairs within the Municipality, but also for those of the peri-urban areas, with the help of another Administrative Officer resident outside. In this suggestion the weak weld, between the Municipal executive and the African affairs section, would now appear at the level of the District Commissioner who is to be at one and the same time the subordinate of the Deputy Provincial Commissioner (and thus an executive of Central Government) and of the Town Clerk. These proposals have not all been accepted, but certain of the detailed suggestions have been put into effect.

The most valuable part of the reforms then undertaken was a strengthening of the administrative staff and their transfer to a place nearer to the African centre of town. Previously the *Boma*[1] had been in Acacia Avenue,[2] a good shopping centre but a long way from the mainly African parts, which tend, like so much of Tanganyika, to lie west of Kassum's. The movements of the *Boma* are indeed symptomatic of the difficulties of administering Dar es Salaam, for going back in time it, or its sub-office, had been, before Acacia Avenue, in Kiserawe, Azania Front, Temeke and Nzasa. The result of these changes and of the distance of the offices was that it became a matter of surprise, and the forming of a small crowd, for officers of Government to be seen around in the mainly African parts; they visited them in the course of business, but to an ever-increasing degree that business had to be conducted at a desk, and in any case the affairs of the mainly non-African trade and business of the town took up a large portion of the time. Furthermore it is not in office hours that the African part of the population—or any other part—is to be met, since this is a working town, but between half past four and six in the evening, or after seven. It is, therefore, most important that members of the administrative staff will in future be living in these areas, available (whether on duty or not) to see and be seen, to accustom people to the physical presence of Government, which has not up to now been possible.

There remains the basic difficulty of the divorce between the Town Clerk, who under the Municipal Council and within the

[1] *Boma*: Swahili for District Commissioner's Office.
[2] Now Independence Avenue, (1962).

Estimates can say 'yes' or 'no' to any proposal; and the African population who have their proposals to make. To place a District Commissioner in an invidious position in between to catch the kicks and curses and be unable to influence the one who can give or withhold the remedies, is not a solution. Sooner or later the ward councillors discover that he is redundant, and either by-pass him and take their complaints direct to the Municipal officers, or fall silent and allow their grievances to smoulder until some other agency, perhaps a political one, takes them up.

One might think that the six African members of the Municipal Council would form the required link between governors and governed; but they have two defects: they are not elected, and in fact not representative or closely identified with African interests; and they form so ineffective a bloc in the council that the views they represent carry insufficient weight. It is here that changes might with advantage be made: if the Ward Councils are devices for making heard the views of the general populace, then they should elect their own representatives to the Municipal Council (the requirement of knowing English is not one which has caused any difficulty in Legislative Council, and it need cause none here if Swahili is accepted as a second language for discussion); and those elected representatives should be the Chairmen of the Ward Councils and by their attendance at the Municipal Council they would then provide the direct link that is at present lacking: pressure could be brought at every monthly meeting of the Ward Council directly on the Ward's representative in the Council which allocates funds; he in his turn would both protect himself and use his influence by bringing to such meetings as often as possible at least the senior African officer of the technical department (Health, Engineer's Department, etc.) which is likely to be concerned with the discussion, so that items such as the provision of drainage or lighting might be discussed fully on the spot by those able to do something about them or to explain why nothing can be done.

The other main difficulty is that of the responsibility for law and order. It was on this that the first system, of a Municipal Native Affairs Officer, which is the logical solution, broke down.

It broke down because although 'native affairs' were admitted to come under the Municipality, no responsibility was taken for the preservation of law and order, which was considered by the Municipality to be a function of central Government. In practice Central Government in Dar es Salaam, in the sphere of law and order, is first the Police (at the District level, under an Assistant Commissioner), and in emergency or threat of emergency the Local Government branch of the Secretariat, or even the Chief Secretary's Office.

Now that law and order is the direct responsibility of the Deputy Provincial Commissioner (cutting out at least one ambiguity, whether and to what extent the Provincial Commissioner at Morogoro, 126 miles away, should be consulted rather than the Secretariat officers) there still remains the difficulty that neither he nor any of his officers, whether they be District Officers, Assistant District Officers, the Liwali, or Jumbes, have any executive powers in law. They have not the power to summon anyone before them, still less to make the rules and orders by which in rural areas sanction is applied to the edicts of government at this level: for in the town there is no Native Authority. The lack of these powers used not to be much hindrance, such was the prestige of Government, but with the growth of the town, of politics, and of questioning of all forms of authority, legal sanctions are becoming increasingly necessary.

Ward Councils

The Ward Councils have never had more than a very limited degree of success, whether measured by the attendance at, and interest in them of the elected members, or by the desire of new candidates to be elected, or enthusiasm of the electorate to see that the right men are elected. The reason for this is that they have never been given any financial powers, without which no council can ever be a reality. Whereas in Zanzibar, for instance, the Local Councils were from the first given certain revenues, which they could allocate as they pleased (subject to the approval of their Estimates) to any works which they thought important, and could supplement them (as they almost invariably did) by voluntary subscription, here in Dar es Salaam all the works which the councillors wish to be done are in the hands of the Municipality, and all they themselves can do is to put their desirability to the District Commissioner who conveys this opinion to the Municipality.

Nor have they had any specific duties, except two: while permits for firearms were being given all applications were made to pass through the Ward Council; and similarly applications for the remission of school fees on grounds of poverty were made to pass through the councillor of the village concerned; these two administrative rulings did have some effect in giving the Councils and their councillors some importance —something to give or to withhold. But apart from them they appeared each month only to give their views on what was set before them. After the first few meetings, when they had asked for street lighting, more water points and better roads and drainage, and the reason why they could not have them was explained, they lost interest. The job of councillor was unpaid, and until 1957 there was not even an attendance fee to make it worth the while of the more distant to take a bus in to the central meeting-place.

With little to show for the existence of the Councils, and with the councillors wishing they had not been elected, it was not surprising that the elections were very sparsely attended; in 1956 the estimated attendance of electors was:

		Eligible voting population
Kariakoo	81	10,800
Ilala	98	10,300
Magomeni	194	7,200
Temeke	925	10,400
Kinondoni ⎱ Msasani ⎰	116	2,900

The comparatively good attendance at Temeke was due partly to a personal effort by the Wakili, and partly to the holding of a series of local meetings (of which this is the total attendance) so that people from the outlying villages did not have far to go and some parochial interest was aroused.

In January 1957, when the system changed, and primary elections were to Village Councils, subdivisions of a Ward

Council, there were very many more electoral meetings; a greater effort also was made to give the election full publicity. Even so the attendance at meetings in the built-up areas was extremely small.

In some areas there was so little interest shown that in 1956 all councillors for the area—for instance all the Quarters— had to be nominated; and in 1957, in Kigogo, so little had been understood of the purpose and nature of the councillors, despite the publicity given to them, that an unemployed labourer whom nobody knew put himself up (thinking that it was a paid job), and he then nominated others from those who happened to be standing by, all of whom were elected forthwith by the casual crowd. It was only when they began afterwards to ask what these councils were all about that they took the position seriously, and then most of the 'candidates' decided not to attend any meetings, and to try to back out.

In other areas there were the first glimmerings of interest; in Temeke in 1957 there was sufficient interest for two factions to appear, a faction of the 'young men' (mostly those politically inclined) who revolted against the traditional hold of the 'elders' on the selection of such people; there were meetings and consultations, and the elders agreed not to put forward anybody as candidate who was not acceptable to the young men's faction: this was indeed a big step forward towards getting elected the men acceptable to the greatest number.

In the Village and Rural areas tradition held sway; the candidates were put forward by the traditional elders (those descended from the first settlers), and accepted as a matter of course by those who bothered to attend and 'elect' the candidates.

In Msasani both methods were to be seen: the recent arrivals, many of them from up-country tribes, who live in Mikorosheni turned up to the elections and proceeded to choose those who were willing to stand; but the people from the old fishing village on the foreshore who reckon little to the 'new men' of Mikorosheni, refused to be rushed, and went away to make their choice in the old traditional way, after consulting (i.e. getting the nominations of) the traditional elders, the descendants of the first families. Being rather opposed to the whole business, and disliking outside interference in 'their' village at the best of times, they did not bother to report what they had decided until asked more than once, but the final choice was in fact persons chosen by the traditional elders.

In some areas the easy way out was taken by the electors, who asked what the last year's councillors had done wrong, and when it was explained that they had done nothing wrong they re-elected them without further ado.

A breakdown by tribe of all those elected in the past three years shows that ward councillors are not chosen on grounds of tribe, nor has each tribe a quota, but that nevertheless electors do tend to vote for people they know best, who are often (particularly in the less built-up areas) people of their own tribe; in such areas as Kariakoo there is much cross-voting for people of repute throughout the area. But there are in Dar es Salaam very few people indeed who are well known to more than a fairly small group. An experiment was tried in this survey of asking people for a list of the twenty Africans most prominent in the town, and hardly any person so asked was able to name a full twenty, most falling silent after the first two or three.

INTERLUDE
Kariakoo: some Asians

A slap-up house, divided between an Indian, and his brother in the same three rooms, who, with their wife each have fifteen children. At the time there seemed to be no crush, as all the children were outside playing with the neighbours' children; the other half is rented by a Hadhrami Arab, from Hajr, who came here in 1916, and bore all his five children here; he has a young-looking wife, like all the rest of the family dressed in Western fashion, and she rather over-made-up, though I am sure she was quite respectable; his grown son, speaking good English, has a wife newly wed, from Zanzibar, in a dress, but no make-up; all go barefoot indoors; both sides of the house complain bitterly of the landlord, another Arab, a butcher, who does no repairs and charges 140 Shs. a month for each set of three rooms, with latrine and kitchen attached.

An even better house, with an Anglia drawn up outside, and an African polishing it, belongs to a Comorian who speaks excellent English; he has made a European-type garden out in the street, a gateway of creepers and a hedge of cannas, all fronting an open cement 'stoep'.

One or two of the houses in the same street (no street has any sort of homogeneity) are owned by very old women, usually the head of the family, but sometimes having a husband; these houses are usually in poor repair, have no cement floors, and have two or three courtyard rooms, no water or electricity, and thatch or kerosene-tin roofs. Often the courtyard at the back is full of girls; in such a house one may find an Arab tenant, but never an Indian; the only really poor Indians, that is, who are content to live in a cementless room seem to be those in Kisutu, some of whom are there for reasons other than economic.

Indians are of every kind: there was the young man, fluent and inaccurate in both English and Swahili, who served with the R.A.F. throughout the war, and is a member of the R.A.F. Association; he is waiting for his name to come out at the top of the list for an Upanga house, which he has applied for on the owner-tenant terms, over 16 years; using the other half of their rented house was one of another generation, difficult to understand in any language, but particularly so in English, who was for thirty years and more an artisan in the Public Works Department. He lives in a clean but not too well-furnished room, with lino on the floor, and a sufficiency of furniture but no more.

Next to a particularly hovel-like old house is a three-story Indian house, divided into three flats, the owner an old Bohora who speaks little or no English; the son speaks well, but both are so fluent and so anxious to please that it is difficult to get a straight answer out of them.

In a rather down-town area lives an old Indian woman, rather dirty, and surrounded by children both Indian and Swahili; she is trying to recover a football that she lent to one of the boys, which is rapidly disappearing over the horizon pursued by some hefty Indian boys; one of the smaller girls speaks a word or two of English, taught by an elder sister; the old woman turns out to be the mother of two very well-to-do tennis-playing merchants of Kigoma; she has been given the family house in Dar, not by any means an extravagant one, and she looks after most of the children. She is on good terms with the African opposite, who is leader of the Wanyiramba and was a town Jumbe; she is minding one of his babies.

How many Indians are there in this house, one asks. This side six, and the other side no Indians, but five Banyanis (Hindus); Indians and Swahilis alike make this distinction, meaning by Indian a Muslim of India or Pakistan. A tenant is a Comorian; one asks, innocently, of a Swahili which column the Comorian should go in, Swahili, Arab or Indian, and he says without hesitation: Swahili. The word *chotara* (half-caste) I have so far met used mainly to denote an Arab/Manyema or Arab/Swahili cross, but it is also used of an Arab/Indian and Indian/Swahili. There are a few European half-castes too.

A well-dressed Chinese girl waits for a bus on the Kilwa road, high-heeled shoes, parasol, print frock, make-up. Her father, a Cantonese, lives up-country but she stays with her mother in Keko kwa Akida, while her young brother and sister go to St. Joseph's convent school. She also went there, and speaks English, though they use Cantonese at home. The parental house is a bit of a hovel, perched over the edge of the creek, but they have a car, used for her father's business, which is market-gardening.

Decline of elders

Before the last war, when Dar es Salaam was a much smaller and more compact town, both geographically and socially, the administrative structure relied heavily on the elders to convey information and explanations of Government to the people, and the complaints and difficulties of the people to Government. Head of this structure, under the District Commissioner, was the Liwali, with under him a Wakili and Jumbes, at times one Jumbe for each street, and it was their responsibility to bring forward complaints and to transmit downwards instructions and explanations of policy. Many of them did little or nothing, and it was felt better to concentrate the money available for their salaries into the pay of far fewer, two to four for each suburb, who would then be adequately paid and expected to do a full-time job. It was then intended that the Ward Councillors, each of whom was elected to represent an area of two or three streets, would take the place oi the Jumbes who had been abolished, as far as their function of keeping contact between Government and governed was concerned; while the paid Jumbes would become more the spokesmen and executives of Government. Many of the abolished Jumbes were found jobs as court assessors, but a number retired into private life.

Before the war there were also a number of tribal elders, recognized by Government, who were consulted on the affairs of their tribe, and were understood to have the backing of their tribal associations; any letters addressed c/o the Boma or the Liwali's court were handed to the relevant tribal elder for delivery. Some of these elders have since died and have not been replaced, and the only two of prominence who remain are Wakili Saidi Chaurembo, representative of the Zaramo,

o

Ndengereko and Rufiji, and Juma Sultani, representative of the Nyamwezi, Sukuma and Sumbwa. When one asks by whom the deceased elders have in practice been replaced one gets a confused answer, and it is clear that in most cases they have had no successors: this is symptomatic of the decline in the influence of the elders as a class, and their replacement either by more formal instruments of government or representation, such as Assistant District Officers on the one hand and Ward Councillors on the other, or in some ways by the agencies of political parties, which can claim both to organize and to represent without incurring the stigma of being conservative or pro-authority. In the general atmosphere of change and uncertainty which has been growing since the war, and which has quickened enormously in the last two years, it is the influence of these elders which has taken the brunt of the change. As older men they inclined naturally to conservatism, and as persons in authority they inclined naturally to the support of the government of the day; in both ways they have become the object of attack by the forces of change. This has progressed to the stage where, as described above, the younger men could refuse to accept the nominations of the elders for candidature, and were able to force a compromise by which no candidates were put up (by the elders) who were not acceptable to the younger men.

Older men must come to the fore in any society, by reason of their greater experience; in a virtually uneducated society such as Dar es Salaam the fact that the older men are also the most uneducated is no great handicap, and in many parts of Dar es Salaam, particularly the more rural or village areas, they still to this day decide who will be elected to a Ward Council, whatever the outward form of public election may be. Some of the older men, too, have seen the signs of the times and have themselves taken to politics, thus avoiding at least one of the objections to them, that they were wedded to authority. But others are too far committed in support of Government over many years to change now, and they, seeing their influence whittled gradually away, and the authority they have served uncertain whether to back them or abandon them, are in some cases in a state of great perturbation, verging on bitterness.

These are, however, few in number, for there are not many so committed. Far more reflect accurately—as representatives should—the changing sympathies of the people at large; as the general population of the town has taken to politics, and to one particular brand of it, most of the elders, the house-owners, the ward councillors, many even of the Jumbes, have followed suit. It would be surprising if they did not, for they are not full-time officials, but part of, and a reflection of, the population as a whole.

Transfer of information

Dar es Salaam is a poor conductor of news. There are things of immediate importance to the inhabitants which appear to take days to reach from suburb to suburb. When for instance Government is holding Ward Council elections and puts on a programme of explanation with all the means at its disposal: cinema van, radio talks, newspaper articles, and explanations to the Ward Councils, not only is the resulting turn-out poor in the extreme (which could be due to other considerations) but considerable numbers appear not even to have heard about it. This applies also to the political parties: for instance in Kinondoni, where more than 700 persons claim to be literate in Swahili, a Tanganyika African National Union notice which had been inadvertently posted upside down attracted so little interest (in a strongly pro-T.A.N.U. area) that it remained so for several weeks. An attempt was made in this survey to measure this non-conductivity; a talk was given over the radio, and broadcast twice on the two evenings before the survey 'census' started; meanwhile an explanation of the purposes of the survey had been made to all Ward Councils; and all the houses to be surveyed in Kariakoo, Ilala, Buguruni and the rural areas had been visited and at least one occupant told of the survey and the reasons for it. An article had been prepared for the local Swahili daily, *Mwangaza*, but unfortunately it came out too late to be of any use. However, disregarding the news-paper article, those concerned could have heard about the survey through radio, Jumbe or councillor, a friend or relative, another, or not at all; when the questionnaire was put to each person he or she was asked how he *first* heard of it: the answer was that 62 per cent. had never heard of the survey till the moment of being asked the questions; 6 per cent. had heard through the radio, 3 per cent. through their Jumbe or ward councillor; 10 per cent. had heard through a friend or relative, and the larger number of 18 per cent. who had heard through 'another' showed to what a small extent those who had had the survey patiently explained to them bothered to retail this explanation to the others in the house!

The radio and the newspaper are without doubt powerful media for the dissemination of news, even in a town where 59 per cent. of men and 88 per cent. of women are illiterate and where the majority of radios are in Arab shops (and as often as not tuned to Sana' or Cairo in Arabic rather than to a Swahili programme which Africans could follow). There are loudspeakers in the Kariakoo market, and a number of people do listen, while there are small groups, usually of better-dressed young men, listening to radios in shops, and the Quarters and parts of Kariakoo are a forest of aerials. Similarly sales of *Mwangaza* (which achieves most of its sales in Dar es Salaam), *Zuhra* and *Mwafrika* show the avidity with which even dull material is read, often by half-literate labourers who have to spell out each word; the attendances at night-school confirm this craving for the written word, and the survey met many instances where a man answered Nil to the 'education' question but claimed, and was able to prove, literacy in Swahili, self-achieved. And yet, with all this desire for knowledge, the processes of news-spreading are slow.

As has been described earlier, the main method by which a man keeps himself in touch with others in the town is by constant visiting of relatives; although he may come to stay with a brother, once he has his own job he will launch out into a room of his own, which may be in any part of town, not necessarily even in the same suburb; but he will continue to visit that brother, and also all his other relatives all over town; this criss-cross of mutual visiting is the main method of spreading news; it is more effective in the long run than a pamphlet; for each man and woman (for the women visit each other as much at least as the men) has a complex of relations and the process is continuous and self-multiplying, like chain letters. But it is slow: for each visit will take the best part of an evening, and the next will not be until the next day, or even until two days later. It is also an ideal method of spreading distorted rumours, for each will embellish the story a little in the telling.

Another mart for news is the club, whether it be a formal club such as a football or jazz-band club (and these meet often for social reasons) or merely a 'school' for *bao* or snakes and ladders, dominoes or other game at which a dozen or so will foregather fairly regularly to play, stake and lose a little, and hear the latest; gangs at work, or men waiting for a porter's job at a street corner, the benches where one gets a cup of tea and a bun in the morning or a plate of something in the evening in company with up to a dozen others; the beer market or the palm-wine bar; the women washing dishes and clothes together in the courtyards or chattering to pass the time until their menfolk return: all are media for the spreading of news. All keep word moving, but in an unorganized way, conducive to rumour and divergence, not to the propagation of a single line: such a single line would be put across only by radio or newspaper; and here there is a political barrier in that both radio and *Mwangaza*—the daily paper with much the biggest circulation—have been used so much as vehicles for Government's views that they are now distrusted as such; for instance the news soon after Ghana's independence of the dispatch of troops to a tribal rising was dismissed here as Government propaganda, partly because it came in *Mwangaza*. It is a familiar dilemma, that to be interesting and find favour a paper must be 'agin the government', while if it becomes too critical government has no incentive to subsidize it. The starting up, since the survey began, of two anti-government papers, *Zuhra* which specializes in slangy tone and *Mwafrika* which is a soberer (and much duller) paper, both strongly in support of T.A.N.U., have to a large extent taken the place of the mass meeting as a means of getting an identical message over to a large number of people.

As explained above, neither *Zuhra* nor *Mwafrika* was being published at the time of the basic questionnaire, in August 1956, and the choice of papers was, therefore, restricted to the Government daily (*Mwangaza*), weekly (*Baragumu*) and monthly (*Mambo Leo*), and one or two papers from Kenya: in Dar es Salaam, where all Government papers are obtainable and the news is very similar in all three (some say the articles are copied almost word for word, but this is an exaggeration), people tend to buy one or other but not two or three. 88 per cent. of those questioned stated a preference for *Mwangaza*. Only 2 per cent. claimed to read the English-language daily *Tanganyika Standard*.

There has been little attempt on Government's part to improve its means of communication with the Dar es Salaam population as such: such papers as *Mwangaza* have become more and more directed at Tanganyika as a whole (with half an eye even on Zanzibar), and purely local news is excluded. For the same reason it is aimed at the more literate sections of the community, not at the large numbers, which Dar es Salaam holds, of semi-literate, who can appreciate simple, direct statements, pictures, or comic strips, but not the long involved sentences translated from Reuter's which convey so much of world news. A comparison of an issue of *Mwangaza* with one of *Zuhra* points the moral: the former will have its front page taken up with speeches by world statesmen, directly translated in all their circumlocution. An extract taken at random reads, re-translated back to English (21 February 1957):

'The correspondent of the BBC, London, stated that he believed that the consultations held between President Eisenhower and Mr. Dulles and the American Government representative at the United Nations concerned America's policy over Israel which formed part of the discussions between President Eisenhower and Congress leaders held yesterday in Washington.'

This is of course all good stuff, and the staple diet of readers of *The Times*. It is arguable that it is also what the more sophisticated readers of *Mwangaza*—the teachers and clerks—require, and the 2 per cent. of Dar es Salaam males who have been educated beyond the second stage (Standard 8) of primary schooling. But there remains a need for something more suited to the appetites and aptitudes of the 41 per cent. who are merely literate in Swahili. This need is at the present being filled by *Zuhra*, and to some extent by *Mwafrika* (the dullness of whose presentation is offset by the exciting fact that it is anti-government). *Zuhra* does not print translations from the news: instead the editor gets one point which he wishes to put over, and he plugs it straight, hard and without qualification, in the simplest terms which alone the semi-literate can understand. What is required, if the printed word is to be a means of Government communicating with its public, is something aimed exclusively at Dar es Salaam, in the simplest, most direct terms (not scorning the comic strip, and the head-line style of writing such as puts across the views of the *Daily Mirror*). On paper there is no end to the small improvements that could be made, with posters, play-teams such as are being used by the Health Education section, and leaflets: in practice there is nobody with the undivided attention required for what is a full-time job; the Public Relations Department have here only a headquarters office, which, though it happens to be situated in Dar es Salaam, is concerned with this town no more than with every other corner of Tanganyika. There is no information officer for Dar es Salaam itself; even the Public Relations Officer for the Eastern Province is stationed, not in Dar es Salaam but in Morogoro. This gap yawns the more because it is precisely in Dar es Salaam that the normal means of communication (through a traditional hierarchy of chiefs, subchiefs and headmen, *barazas*[1] and the like) are lacking, and government, like anyone else, must address the individual direct, through his own eyes or ears.

The influence of foreign radio and newspapers is impossible to measure. The survey, which in its question on newspapers allowed an answer 'other', found few who claimed to be readers of papers outside the list of better-known Swahili publications; the Indians to be sure to read papers in their own language rather more than those listed, and some of those from Kenya and Bukoba read their home District papers. But there was no evidence that foreign newspapers have much currency here.

Foreign radio is another matter. Radio Cairo, Delhi, and Moscow are all easily received here, both in Swahili and in English: while Sana' and Cairo are easily heard in Arabic. The majority of sets being owned by Arab shopkeepers, they at least are able to listen to these stations, and such controversial news as the Omani-Muscati dispute reached here almost exclusively in the Omani version; until recently there were few Yemenis here and the pro-Yemen versions of news are fairly

[1] *Baraza*: a traditional form of open public meeting.

sceptically received by the Hadhrami coast Arabs who form
the bulk of the so-called 'Shihiri' population and who keep in
close touch with the truth by letters from relatives. Delhi, with
its strong anti-colonial slant, has its listeners, but much the
most popular of the foreign radios is that of Cairo: not only
because it is anti-colonial and anti-British and anti-Western,
but because its presentation is hard-hitting, unequivocal and
makes no attempt to be fair. Fairness, presenting both sides
of every question, with due qualification of every statement,
gains few audiences among the uneducated or the ignorant.
Moscow and the BBC may be guessed—for no figures are
available on the question—to bring up the rear of 'listenership',
both being interminably dull. Both live again, however, in the
columns of the newspapers, Moscow in the pages of *Zuhra*,
which usually quotes Moscow radio in its leading article, and
the BBC in *Mwangaza*.

Interest in world affairs is spasmodic: an affair like Suez
was as eagerly taken up by the Dar es Salaam public as by the
world at large, and phrases derived from that conflict passed into
the wolf-calls of street-corner boys; the Omani-Muscati affair
—again be it noticed one of peculiar interest to Cairo—was
closely followed. Sputnik-watching was a sport of Dar es
Salaam as much as of other parts (though many were appre-
hensive of Divine reaction to such interference with the laws of
nature). But apart from such outstanding events there is little
public among the bulk of the populace for a steady following
of the world news, the incessant comings and goings of the heads
of governments, the interminable conferences, the endless
scrums and kickings for touch of the international game. And
it is here that the semi-literate public of Dar es Salaam is ill-
served, for *Mwangaza*, with its till recently large circulation,
purveys a steady daily view of just these comings and goings,
none of which are of interest in themselves, but only as a move
in a game, which unless closely followed is meaningless. What
the Dar es Salaam public wants is the occasional headline
when the world news is spectacular, and otherwise a stream of
purely parochial news: of local personalities, local football,
dances and controversies.

An entertainment

The show is advertised by poster, handbill, and in the local
Swahili press, featuring a picture of King Kong, the conjurer, and
promising real *nachi* dances. Tickets are 5, 3 and 2 Shs. and the
hall is hired. It is due to start at 9 p.m. but at once proves the
genuineness of the fare provided by starting 40 minutes late, which
bothers nobody. At ten past nine there is only a small crowd of a
dozen or so waiting outside the doors while chairs are set out. At a
quarter past a few rows are full and the Alwatn Egyptian-type band
starts up, its choir of female voices, heavily swathed in black
buibuis, partly hidden in the wings but occasionally audible. The
band has a nucleus of Arab fiddlers and a row of very respectable
old gentlemen in a variety of clothing, sitting in the front row and
playing guitars, banjoes, drums, castanets and the other instruments
which go to make up that combination of plonking and trailing
which marks Egyptian off from other music. The leader of the
band, and a few others, wear European suits, in the long-coated
Egyptian style, loose-fitting; the front row vary, according to age,
from long trousers covered by a *kanzu* and surmounted by coat,
topped with *tarbush*, to long white trousers and a deep red shirt. The
main singer for tonight, a young man of rich parentage, who has
been unable to settle down in other walks of life, has the confident
and slightly fruity air of dance-band singers throughout the world.
He is of pure African blood by the look of him, and the full lips
combine well with the indolent sensuosity of the songs and the
suggestive shakes and tremolos of the music.

The band plays several numbers, as time passes and the rows
behind fill up. There is always something to look at. Two boys in
ragged trousers and shirts, one with socks in alternate rings of
crushed strawberry and grey, with holes in the heels, remove a large
black pen from the stage and carry it away. Others cart below stage
blocks of ceiling board. At times people singly or in pairs mount
the stage, survey the audience with what seems a cynical eye, and
dismount again, puffing at their cigarettes. The crowd of young men
who were hanging round the doors at last give up hope of getting in
free and go round instead to the window to get a priority peep
through the curtains. The conjurer, who five minutes after the
advertised time was last seen getting a taxi to go off somewhere else,
returns.

By now only the first few rows, the 5 Shs. seats, have vacant
places. In them there is a trio of two men and a woman, one a
Seychellois mechanic, with his wife and probably her brother,

whose very crinkly hair might be Italian or even Arab. A well-dressed Indian woman sits alone at the end of the row, with a small baby on her lap. An Indian family, the parents prosperously curved, the daughter almost gaunt, sit behind an Arab trio, the two young men and young woman all dressed in European fashion, one of the young men wearing a motor-cycling wind-jacket. There is an Arab boy with them with that bright look and inborn confidence.

A little further back, in the 3 Shs. seats, there is a mixture of Indians, Arabs and Africans. The last are there with their ladies, some wrapped to the nosetip in *buibuis*, others free. The men are in white suits and good shoes. There is one Arab in the traditional *futah*, coat, and the modern tradition: leather shoes and heavy woollen stockings, turban redressing the balance.

Back in the body of the hall, which is packed, dress is normal, as seen in the streets, *buibuis* are the almost invariable rule, and there is more evidence of having come on from the bar.

All this while the band had been playing intermittently, ignored by the audience as would be the orchestra in a restaurant. Hardly a handclap greeted the end of each item. At length the conjurer, a locally born Indian, appeared and began the programme, doing one or two tricks, which were quietly received. It was not until the first *nachi* dance came on that any great enthusiasm was shown, and this was obviously what at least the 2 Shs. had come for. The first 'girl' (they are actually 'queers' dressed in women's clothing, Africans from coastal tribes) was discovered by the drawing of the curtains (one side by string, the other, which had gone wrong, by hand) in a kneeling posture, fixing the gallery with one of the largest smiles in the trade. From the wig of woolly hair in '*shoo*' style, the scarlet cheeks, kohled eyes, powdered skin—a light shade of greenish yellow—satin falsies, bare midriff, long skirt (but not long enough to hide the pair of navy blue men's socks in which all three 'girls' danced) she was all that the seeker after forbidden pleasures in the bad city could want. The three 'girls' came on at intervals, interspersed with band solos and bouts of conjuring, each dance based on Indian originals, but with a liberal admixture of Port Said belly work, and not a little pure Africa. The front row of the band kept their wooden faces securely in place, and were this not their living one would have supposed that they were puritan disapprovers. The singer's full lips curled slightly and his eyes brightened. The scene shifters were frankly fascinated. The body of the hall gradually woke up. Next time the conjurer came on he was assailed with good-natured heckling, to which he replied in kind. His next few tricks ended in applause and a babble of speculation which drowned the first notes of the band. From half past ten onwards the show was a success: the noise increased; the outer doors and windows banged as those outside fought for a better view through the chinks. Drinks were brought in, cokes for the Indians, and some beer at the back. By the last dance before the interval appreciation was at its height. This dance began with the most feminine of the three 'girls,' who specialized in hip swaying with a long flowing movement; she was soon joined by a second, who went in more for slight, jerky but unmistakable movements; after a few minutes of the kind of dance which they had both been doing all evening, they brought out their set piece, a dance where each in turn sank on to a chair and palpitated in a manner leaving nothing whatever to the imagination, while the other heaved and undulated standing on the other chair above. The audience made full amends for their earlier apathy, and rose as one man with cries of appreciation, several young men jostling each other to approach the stage and throw coins to the performers, one getting a particular cheer by tossing one slap on to the affected part. The interval came, at eleven o'clock, in a welter of excited talk reminiscent of the break-up of a close cup final crowd, with a rush for the bar.

. . . . . .

The other day in Ilala in a *tembo* bar a man turned up who could play a mouth-organ with his nose. The first people to notice him were astonished and called to others to look. Many left their drink and surrounded him, and everyone was laughing with amazement to see him do it. He didn't mind a bit being thronged about, and went on playing. He never put a note wrong and played all sorts of tunes. People gave him several glasses of *tembo* and money. At intervals he would ask 'Shall I play you another?' And people would reply 'Yes, maestro, just go on, we like it.' He was invited to come again and give more pleasure to the customers, and he said 'Thank you very much'.

Idle hands

The lack of normal means of communication, of administrative 'structure' below the paid level of officials, is paralleled by the absence of routine occupation for a large part of the population; Dar es Salaam is indeed a working town, in that few never work; but to a large degree it is a resting town, in that few work all six days of the week, or all 26 days in the month. The crude figures of unemployment given earlier are only half the story: they do not show the thousands who have taken a day off to trade, or merely to rest, or to visit a relative, or to go to their home in the Kiserawe District. It is not easy to measure the extent of this under-employment, for most have short memories for days worked. A small sample was taken from casual labourers, who stand at street corners and take such loading jobs as are going: a popular job with many, for it involves no registration, no clocking in, no gang-leaders, and no questions asked if one does no work for a period and then returns; the average days worked in the previous month appeared to be between two and ten, but although answers were given willingly enough few were found who could in fact remember as far back as a month and make an estimate of how many days they had worked; a more reliable guide is perhaps the figures produced by the dock agencies, which show that dockers work on the average roughly every other day: this figure too cannot be pressed since the registration card without which it should not be possible for a worker to get in to a dock gang has a ready hire value, and the figures recorded by registration must, therefore, be taken as a maximum.

It would be pure guesswork to put a figure to the overall under-employment: but if to the crude 'unemployment' figure of 18 per cent. one adds what is believed to be a substantial margin for under-employment, a resulting figure of a quarter or even more of the working-age males as being on any given day temporarily free from the necessity for working to earn a living is not in conflict with one's own observation. While it is not usually profitable for an observer to seek out in office hours those whom he wishes to interview, he will in his round encounter, certainly not an empty town, where only women remain, but one where, though most are gone, every house contains one or two males, and in places, as at street corners round a board of *bao*, or in the shade of a big tree around a barber, or in the lee of a house, there are groups of five or ten gathered and passing the day. In the further parts of town these unoccupied persons have usually come to rest, having found themselves company for the morning; in the central areas they tend more to keep moving, lounging along the streets seeing what goes on, usually in pairs, or singly; nearer the commercial area or the busier parts of Kariakoo they merge imperceptibly into the groups of those who actually are on the look-out for a casual job, but who while waiting for one to turn up chat with each other and watch the passers-by.

'There was the usual crowd at the corner of Ring Street and Bagamoyo Street, waiting for odd jobs as porters and other casual labourers. Suddenly the bored line of young men sitting against the wall in the shade was galvanized to action as a big lorry drew up and the driver shouted the number of men he wanted. They scrambled to be among the first to jump on, and one in his excitement fell to the ground. For thirty yards up and down the street the baying sound of Africans who have seen an excitement went up, though the lorry was stationary and there was in fact no danger.

'Further down Ring Street, and on a different occasion, an African employee was being dismissed by an Indian woman, who ran a shop on her own; he argued, and she called him a thief; he demanded the job back, and at once at the sound of raised voices a crowd of thirty or so gathered round, pressing so close that the Indian woman drew a police whistle from her pocket and blew it. Nothing happened for a moment. The shopkeepers, other Indians, all along the street heard it and watched, but none came to her aid. As she went on blowing the whistle the African at the heart of the matter slipped away. "All I did was to ask her for my job," he said, "and the silly old woman starts blowing police whistles." The crowd remained close around her door, long after the man she was quarrelling with had gone away, and after five minutes a police car stopped and dispersed the crowd. "She was a lone woman", said one of the Indian shopkeepers in the dispassionate tone of the born neutralist.'

The ease with which one may live in town without an income makes it possible for those without work to remain long after they should have given up hope of getting employment, and returned whence they came; but so long as there is a relative who will give food and shelter (and so long as one has the remains of the little sum of money one brought to town from the country, and a few clothes to sell) it is possible to hang about, seeing much that is desirable and with a mounting temptation to take it by stealth. It is people such as these who fall into bad ways, not because they are criminals by intention but because they see the opportunity and have not the upbringing, the strict morality or the discipline to resist the temptation.

When one such is caught, he is taken before the Courts. Here the Probation service comes into the scene. Each one is assessed as a good or bad risk, and put on probation or sentenced accordingly. The bad risks are those who have settled on a life of crime, with several convictions; the good risks are those who have no previous convictions or only one or two, on minor charges. The records of the Probation service are able to distinguish these two classes, and it is worth while to examine what is the difference between them.

For obvious reasons the sample chosen for study was not from the most recent cases; but it is not thought that the type of person has changed much in the last two or three years. Of a sample of those who were considered good risks for probation—who will now be referred to as the 'Foolish'—88 per cent. were charged with various degrees of theft; a further 15 per cent. were tax defaulters, who it was felt would get steady work and pay up once they felt an eye on them; a few were charged with such crimes as (technically) receiving, assault, false documents or filching from a house (technically housebreaking). The great majority (81 per cent.) were first offenders, with a further 13 per cent. having only one previous conviction. In all, the sample contained 111 cases.

Another sample was taken of those who were *not* considered good risks—these will be referred to as the 'Bad'; 51 per cent. were recidivists, and only 10 per cent. were bound over, 41 per cent. were sentenced to up to six months, 41 per cent. to more. The total of this sample was just under 900.

Comparing the two samples, there was little to choose as regards age: the Bad divided neatly into 51 per cent. aged 25 or over and 49 per cent. under 25; the Foolish were the opposite; of the latter 6 per cent. were less than 16 years old.

The Foolish were slightly more Muslim than the population at large; 92 per cent. as compared with 87 per cent.: this ties in with the fact that they were mostly from the Coastal tribes, which are solidly Muslim. Their Districts of origin were analysed and it was found that those who had been brought up in Dar es Salaam produced far less than their share of both the Foolish and the Bad; these come more from the nearby Districts, particularly Kiserawe, but proportionately even more from Morogoro and Rufiji. And these Districts specialize in the Foolish rather than the Bad. The tribal breakdown confirms this picture, for while emphasizing the part played by the Rufiji, it shows that the Kiserawe-born Zaramo and the Dar es Salaam-born Zaramo taken together have on the average less than their share of the Foolish: the fault lies not in the tribe but in the circumstances of their coming to Dar es Salaam; it is the country-bred who fall into bad ways, not the town-bred. The Ndengereko too appear to have established an alibi, leaving the whole blame to fall on the Rufiji.

When the length of residence in town is studied, although the various sets of figures cannot be exactly correlated, a comparison can be made, from which it appears that while both the Foolish and the Bad draw the bulk of their recruits from those of long residence, those of short residence provided, in proportion to their members, far more than their share.

As to the proneness of the single man to crime, or to 'foolish-ness', whereas the 16–45 age-groups of men in the whole population counted 39 per cent. single, the Foolish and the Bad both reckoned 64 per cent. (of those probationers who were married rather more than half had their wives in Dar es Salaam).

Few of the Foolish or the Bad had parents with them in Dar es Salaam (4 per cent. and 10 per cent. respectively); just under half the fathers were alive but out of town. But 53 per cent. of the Foolish actually lived with wives, children or other relatives, and two-thirds of the Bad had relatives in Dar es Salaam.

There was no noticeable concentration of the Foolish or the Bad in any one area of town; the proportion living in each tallied well with the figures for the whole population. No less than 9 per cent. owned their own house, most small huts in the Rural areas; the high proportion of 39 per cent. paid no rent, 23 per cent. being housed free by a relative; rather more than the average were in the cheaper rooms (with a rent of less than 10 Shs. per month) and none paid a rent higher than 20 Shs. per month.

As to whether they were drifters from one job to another, to a greater extent than their fellows, it is hard to say; a quarter of them had an average of under six months a job, half averaged between six months and three years a job, and a fifth averaged more than three years; indeed to have served for many years in the same job seems to be no guarantee that a man will not succumb to the sudden temptation, often for trifling gain.

Not all were in the lower groups of wages, for one or two got up to 185 Shs. per month; 12 per cent. had no paid work or employment. A number were self-employed, but the Foolish included a fair cross-section of the whole range of employment, though naturally the greater number were to be found where the temptation was strongest and the chances of being found out least—among dockers, watchmen, drivers and turnboys, and houseboys. The biggest group of all were unskilled labourers, who usually fell from grace while loading or unloading a lorry, from which they acquired some item of the cargo; the comparatively high pay of dockers did not save them from the temptation of the greater opportunities they have for pilfering.

The rather depressing conclusion to be drawn from these figures is that there is comparatively little difference in the circumstances and background of the three classes—the recidivists, the first offenders, and the general public. There is a small bias towards crime of those with rather less pay, less work, less family responsibility and less continuity; but it is a small one. Many with far less promising backgrounds fall into no error, and conversely many of the recidivists have little to blame their backgrounds for. The Probation Officer who deals with each as an individual finds the key in the personality of his charge, but much illumination in his circumstances. The author of this survey, hoping to derive understanding from a sample too large to know individually, had to admit himself baffled.

INTERLUDE

Keko Magurumbasi

Even in the morning Magurumbasi is a-humming with life, with enough young men sitting around to make six or seven good football teams. The truth of the saying that houses here are only used for sleeping or sheltering from the rain is shown by the number of people, young men, women, couples presumed to be married, old men and women, and children, who are reclining outside the houses in the sandy soil, playing *bao*, playing cards, eating, drinking tea, playing with the hobby-wheels which small children make (decorated with balloons, bells, 'wireless aerials', bits of silver paper or what not) or just talking lazily in the warmth of the early morning sun. The 'main street', which is full of Arab shops, is blocked with hawkers selling oranges, vegetables, charcoal, firewood, anything that one can get in the Kariakoo market; and throughout the morning, particularly towards noon, this street is thronged with shoppers. In the compounds there are yet more people, of all ages and of both sexes, clothes being washed and hung on the ubiquitous clothes-line of heavy-gauge railway wire (which also goes to make the hobby-wheels' handles). There are a number with sore legs, but all have clean bandages on them, unlike their brothers up-country, as a sign that they go to a dispensary for treatment. Much in evidence are the municipal sanitary labourers, many of whom live right here in Magurumbasi, who go round the houses collecting rubbish into baskets and burying it in the ground in little pits all over the place, an effective and sensibly simple way of doing it which obviates the need for motor transport. All these villages suffer from paper litter rather than vegetable waste, so that there is no great danger to health, particularly here where the sandy soil dries out quickly and there is almost no grass or bushes.

In the middle of Magurumbasi is a little mud and wattle Lutheran church, no bigger and no better than the surrounding huts. Many of the inhabitants are Luguru or Nyasa, and there are many Christian names among those of the house-owners. Even so most people have difficulty in pronouncing them, let alone remembering them.

Despite the very sandy soil lorries go through at least the main streets, and taxis are to be seen frequently; but much of Magurumbasi is not navigable, a mass of twisty lanes with no control over where each house is built, each of the few wide streets in danger of having a house built right across the middle of it. Even at the far end where there is ample space new houses are being built higgledy-piggledy. A new departure in recent years has been the building of houses on artificial terraces on the Gerezani creek banks, usually by Luguru vegetable growers. Some are now almost at the bottom of the creek.

That some women are willing to accept visitors is hinted by one or two names, such as Dalini,[1] and by an inscription on a door, in English: 'I have me the sleeping.'

As elsewhere, bottles seem to have no value and they are used often as doorstops or borders. Usually they are beer bottles. And yet it is said that one can get five cents each for them: why then are they used so prodigally?

[1] *Dalini*: darling.

P

There is a preponderance of the compound or hollow square type of group of huts, or the facing-stalls type where two rows of rooms look out at each other across a narrow passage. All the old huts are low, but many are being replaced now by full-sized Swahili houses.

Amorality

If ethics be a personally accepted set of 'thou shalts' and 'thou shalt nots', a system imposed partly by a religious expectation of reward or retribution; partly by further instruction, based on religion, from parents and the tribal authorities who for these purposes take the place of parents; and partly by the edicts of codified law and the fear of its sanctions; then the change in a man's life from his youth in an up-country tribal community to a life in town might be supposed to loosen these influences to such an extent that he is left with much weakened ethical impulses and inhibitions, a man with less positive morality to oppose to hard choices and the temptations which will confront him.

It is indeed tempting, when the picture of life in town is one of amorality, in marital and extra-marital relations, in scrounging, winning or thieving, to attribute it to a breaking down of his moral code as a result of the changed life in town. But this cannot be taken as self-evident.

Religion

In religion, for instance, Dar es Salaam contains as wide a variety as it does of tribes and tribal customs; when asked his religion hardly a man or woman (a bare 0·2 per cent.) admitted to anything but Islam or Christianity. And yet if the truth were told the great majority would be classed as 'irreligious'. This is true, except for a minority, of the small Christian element (13 per cent.), as it is true of the Muslims who form the bulk of the population. The outward observances of religion are strikingly absent in Dar es Salaam: it is rare indeed to see an African Muslim praying his daily prayers, though attendances at Friday mosque are full enough; in Ramadhan people may be seen anywhere eating and drinking publicly during the daylight hours, and very many more do so in the semi-privacy of the Swahili houses, making little effort to conceal it. The consumption of alcoholic drink by Muslims is almost universal, and so well accepted that it is not considered, except by the few who claim to hold to the strict observance of religion, to need excusing. Marriages contracted with full Islamic rites are a minority. Alms are in abeyance. The lack of such observances cannot of course provide proof that the inward religious awe and true belief of which they should be the outward and visible sign are also absent; but in the case of Islam some are mandatory and an essential part of religion, without which a man cannot be a true believer. And it does not take long for an observer to come to the conclusion that outward appearances are not deceptive, and they reflect a real lack of religious feeling.

But is this the result of town life? Are daily prayers, the fast in Ramadhan and the forswearing of intoxicants, the giving of alms, the rule in the country Districts outside, from which so many of the inhabitants of Dar es Salaam come? The answer is that they are not. A stricter observance of the laws of Islam is indeed to be encountered, on the Rufiji and in Uzaramo and Bagamoyo, more often than in Dar es Salaam, by the older men in particular; Friday prayers are more assiduously attended, and absence from them would be considered more surprising in a man of standing; more (again of the older generation particularly) would refuse all intoxicants; and in some areas there might even be a sufficient number who would observe Ramadhan to make it socially impossible for others to flout it; but the majority is still fundamentally irreligious. The fear of divine retribution plays no part in the decisions they make; the hope of divine reward is no effective incentive to do those things which they ought to have done. For this majority religion as a test by which they make their daily choice of alternatives is already a weak force before ever they go to town.

Add to this irreligious majority those who come from pagan areas where the religion is the tribal one of their ancestors: these on arrival in town call themselves Muslims—some few call themselves Christians—in order to conform, not to be conspicuous in a society where Islam is supreme and where to 'have no religion', as people put it, is the mark of the uncivilized. Some go so far as to be circumcized and to be formally admitted to Islam: most merely use a Muslim name instead of a tribal one; some have two names, a Christian and a Muslim, to cover all eventualities. Such people, still adhering in most cases

to the ancestral religion, take easily to the social aspects of
Islam, or Christianity, but are unaffected by its religious side;
their ethics are founded still on tribal teaching and the fear of
ancestral displeasure. Both are in town absent: no single tribe
has any organized teaching of the tribal lore, or holds the
initiation ceremonies at which it is taught; many forms of
ancestral worship require a particular locality, and the physical
presence of the outward signs of the ancestral spirit: these too
are absent in town, except in some rural parts on the outskirts
where miniature huts may occasionally be seen. Most feel that
when living far from the seat of their ancestral spirits they are
beyond their reach; those whose homes are reasonably near
may go back when in trouble and perform the necessary rites
in the proper place, returning when they are done; many more
send money home for the performance of rites required to cast
out sickness or other misfortune in one of their family; their
beliefs are intact in so far as they affect those of their family still
at home, but where they affect their own lives in town the
spirits of their own ancestors are felt to be powerless.

There are other spirits, however, local ones, deriving from
the Zaramo spirit world, which are consulted and propitiated
even by people from distant tribes as being the 'owners' of this
land; these are readily believed to possess the power to affect
men's lives even in town.

In addition there is the tolerated magic which has grown
up under Islam and with a semblance of being part of it.
There are a number of 'Sheikhs' who, without any diminution
of their claim to be true believers, yet make a profitable trade
from the sale of magic formulae, charms and talismans, which
they copy from books of such formulae, wherein is set out a
remedy for every occasion, employing texts from the Koran,
from well-known prayers and quotations from holy men, with
an admixture of invocations to intermediaries, half spirit, half
saint, to give the charm magic force. These charms are in much
demand, as is shown by the substantial fees exacted, up to
60 Shs., and are applied to the needs of the modern town man,
to getting a job or avoiding dismissal, attracting the affection
of a girl-friend or another man's wife, or distracting the atten-
tions of a rival.

The Muslim and the pagan are inextricably mixed up in

town: some Christians also mix freely in the Swahili and the Village houses, but for the most part Christians feel themselves so much a class apart, with their higher education, their different taboos, their strict canons of divorce, that they prefer to be physically separated; unlike the pagans, who have conformed at any rate to the outward appearances of the Muslim majority, they have stood out and reacted against it; in many ways this voluntary segregation has high-lighted the differences between the two religions, and has put the Christians on their mettle; they have a reputation for more stable marriages, and often give the 'immorality' of the coastal women as a reason for wishing to live in self-contained or semi-detached flats, in a mainly Christian area; their religious beliefs are, therefore, for many, strengthened in town; in particular those for whom their religion has meant anything spiritual in their home country, and who have been in close touch with their particular Mission, come to Dar es Salaam with an introduction to a local Mission and surveillance, divine and human, under which they had previously lived.

Some tribes are almost exclusively Muslim: such are the Zaramo, Rufiji, Ndengereko and Ngindo comprising over half of the population of Dar es Salaam; these tribes can muster hardly 1 per cent. of Christians; others are scarcely less overwhelmingly Muslim: Yao, Matumbi and Manyema all have less than a tenth of their number Christians. At the other end of the scale some of the smaller tribal communities, such as Chagga and Haya, are solidly Christian; but of the major Dar es Salaam tribes the 'most Christian' are those like the Nyasa, Luguru, Ngoni, Pogoro and Nyamwezi, which are about a third Christian. In total the African population of Dar es Salaam adds up to an overwhelmingly Muslim community, 86 per cent. of men and 90 per cent. of women professing Islam.

In discussing the effect of religion on a townsman's morality only one aspect has so far been touched: the purely spiritual; but the hold of Islam in East Africa is not here: it is not, as it were, a religious religion as transplanted to this land, so very different in climate, and life, from the Arabia from which it came.

The belief in the One God which is the vital central thought of Islam was never entirely accepted by its Bantu African

converts, whose Divinity was an impersonal, disinterested
Fortune, and whose life was influenced more closely by individual ancestral spirits, about whose propitiation Islam was
silent. If Allah, or God, has been accepted it is as a new belief,
not the striking of a chord with its own echoes back into a
man's traditional assumptions.

So Islam had its main impact at other levels: outwardly it
has its signs, in circumcision, clothes and observances. The two
first were easily accepted, as the outward signs of any materially
successful civilization are imitated by those who hope to
achieve some part of its material success; the last, the observances, have been faced with more of a struggle.

Islam for the Arabs who brought it to these shores demanded,
and still demands, a strict régime of training which helps to
keep man morally fit to counter the great hardships and
difficulties under which he lives; the daily prayers, some before
dawn, are an inescapable timetable which force him to be up
betimes, and thereafter to organize his day within the framework of the prayers; Ramadhan is an annual exercise in a state
of training still harsher than his normal life; abstinence from
intoxicants deprives him of a consolation in his hardships
which might degenerate into an escape; but such rules of
training hardly apply in the lush coastal country where food
can be had not only every year but every month with little
difficulty, where to undergo a fast is no necessary preparation
for survival; and where it is not necessary to toil day-long under
an unremitting programme in order to scrape a living. So the
observational side of Islam has never taken such firm hold as to
force the unwilling to conform. In town the breaches are so
frequent as to be the rule: they are more numerous than in
country districts but are only an extension of a laxity already
prevalent. This extension is due partly to the dilution of Islam
by pagans-in-*kanzus*, partly to the greater temptations of town,
and partly to diminution of the awe of elders and authority in
general.

With the purely religious and the observational aspects of
Islam removed, what remained? What was the attraction which
not only gave it its original converts when it was unopposed by
the competition of any other major religion, but gives it today
in the coastal areas such a vitality that Christianity, with all its

advantages of superior organization and wealth, and the prestige of the ruling cadre, of its possession, in a modern education, of the key to material success, has made in these areas little or no impression? For it is not by any means for lack of trying that the Missions of the coast have been unable to muster as their followers more than 1 per cent. of the tribes forming half Dar es Salaam's population.

Undoubtedly the greatest attraction even today is that it is the religion of the majority; by donning a *kanzu* and skull-cap the veriest up-country bumpkin is automatically received within the family of coastal people; as the *kanzu* covers over with its envelope, adaptable to any shape or size, clothes of rich and poor alike, and shows an equal face to the world, so the word Muslim covers the Shirazi, with his claim to Arab descent and a certain strictness in the doctrines and observances of Islam, and the pagan just down from Nzega with little but his new name, Abdallah, to distinguish him from the untouched pagans at home. To conform and to be accepted are the first needs of a man entering a new society, and Islam exacts the smallest fee and the most easily paid.

Secondly Islam, as practised on the coast, was in complete sympathy with the conservative sentiment of so much of Bantu society, with its accent on the superior wisdom, and, therefore, prior claim to power, of the elders, of the virtue of old customs and old ways, of tradition and continuity, of the importance of the extended family and clan rather than of the individual; it accorded no recognition to the claims of the 'new man', the brash, the bustling, the man who wanted to get on and impose himself on the world; it put its weight behind order and stability in society and in custom and enabled the man without modern education or income or property to be notwithstanding a man of substance and of dignity; in a world where the traditional rural standards of living are now discovered to be poverty, where to have learned by rote a few verses of the Koran is to be characterized as uneducated, and where the ability to seize one's share of the delights of town and so escape from this 'poverty' is linked with a standard of 'education', Islam provides to the many who must fail by the new criteria an alternative set of criteria by the standards of which they have not failed. In times when the power of the elders, still supreme in the Rural areas of town, and still holding its own in some of the Village areas, is much challenged elsewhere by the younger element, Islam is their most effective ally, rejecting the very premisses on which their power is attacked.

Thirdly part of the attraction of Islam as practised on the coast is its undemandingness: where a Christian is expected to obey the edicts of his religion, to forswear adultery and drunkenness, and even in town may be under the supervision of a pastor who will upbraid him for any breach, Islam has no organization for the supervision of private life; though the rules of Islam are in fact stricter than those of Christianity as concerns drink and fasting, and at least as strict on adultery, there is in practice far less enforcement, or attempt at enforcement, for the coastal Muslim. Where Islam is less strict, in allowing easy divorce, this is welcomed, though here again practice often ignores the precept, and even the easier forms of marriage and divorce allowed to Muslims are by-passed. But however inconsistent the thinking, the knowledge that Islam here has no means (or desire to possess the means) for the enforcement of the rules of private life, is an attraction to many who would be wary of joining a more demanding régime.

The mosque, it appears, does not form, through acquiring a core of regular worshippers at the same place, a 'congregation' who might become a community of friends; for few worship regularly—even among those who do worship anywhere regularly—at the same mosque, most going where they happen to be nearest on Friday at that time; nor did more than one or two, even from among the older men, say that their friends were met among such congregations.

This is the appeal of Islam, which has till now remained firm against the encroachments of new ideas; it is hard, however, to see how it can remain firm much longer. The new ideas which now catch the imagination and loyalties of men run directly across much of Islam; political parties, whose leaders are almost exclusively Christian, base their attack on the power of the elders, on their lack of consultation with the more modern, who are in fact the younger, and with their lack of qualification to lead, because they have no modern education; these, the same ideas which are used against the chiefs, cut across the old order of Muslim society as they do that of the old Bantu clan and

tribe. Democracy opposes to the old half-truth of the equality
of rich and poor, or educated and uneducated, the new half-
truth of the equality of old and young: and in a changing
society it is the new class of have-nots which must win, bringing
with them to power their own criteria, even perhaps as power
is concentrated more and more in the hands of the educated,
the moneyed and the adept in modern ways, the attraction
of Islam may wane from the defection of the many to the side
of the new élite.

Meanwhile the 'thou shalts' and the 'thou shalt nots'
enjoined by religion, weak already in the country and weakened
in town by the greater temptations and the release of the
individual from Islam's only supervisory organization—that of
public opinion in his own circle—are not strong enough to form
instinctive impulses and inhibitions which will guide a man's
life in town. If there is any public opinion in town it is that of
one's own associates, who in the case of the majority are not
people of their own extended family—who are regularly
visited but usually scattered over town and not living together
—but persons of a variety of tribes and origins; even if all or
most are Muslim they are a group constantly changing in
composition so that a group ethic has no time to emerge: and
even if one were to emerge it would be unlikely to bear much
resemblance to the stricter edicts of Islam; more likely it would
be a reflection of the easy tolerance of town: 'am I my brother's
keeper?' Peccadilloes are amusing rather than scandalous;
there is no disposition to remonstrate or interfere; a man's
private life is his own business (though paradoxically it is the
subject of endless interested gossip).

Religion has laid the foundations, in the Muslim parts of
the country from which the majority of Dar es Salaam's population come, of the ethics of their lives; it has little reinforcement
through teaching while in town, and only a minority of today's
children go to Koranic school (in most of which teaching is
purely by rote, in some with a minimum of understanding
even by the teacher: an example was encountered where a
Koranic teacher did not even understand the Arabic he was
teaching and was instilling parrotwise a Qasida from a Swahili
transliteration whose meaning he was unable to explain);
pressure is strong from the Muslim elders for opportunities for

children to go to Koranic school in addition to modern school and the difficulty of combining both was undoubtedly in the past a deterrent for a certain class of stricter Muslim from sending their children to school, but they, though the most vocal, are today not representative of the majority who take little care to instil in their children the precepts which should guide their lives.

Many children too come to town early in their lives, some with uncles or other relations, others independently, from not too distant homes. These are entirely free from the parental reinforcement of Islamic precepts, and for them any morality which remains owes little to religion.

Little controlled by a 'built-in' system of ethics derived from religion and reinforced by parental teaching and supervision or that of a close community of those similarly influenced, is the Muslim in town kept to the strait and narrow by the courts? It is true that all cases taken by the Liwali's Court or his subordinate courts are taken by Muslim Law, whatever the tribe or religion of the contestants, and that, therefore, the strict letter of the law backs those who invoke its aid. But such as do invoke it do so mainly on questions of divorce or the custody of children, and no cases were encountered where the courts were used to enforce the edicts of Islam in the conduct of a man's private life, though the occasion is often taken to bestow a moral lecture in passing, and the courts, with their assessors taken largely from among the redundant administrative heads of streets and hamlets (themselves chosen as pillars of stability and worth), represent the old guard of conservatism in strict religion as in other aspects of life. Such lectures, however, affect but a tiny proportion, those who seek the aid of the courts, or against whom their aid is sought. The influence of the courts in strengthening the hold of the Muslim ethic cannot be more than a minor one. The courts of the Resident Magistrates on the other hand, which deal with much of the crime, have a Christian background but an entirely secular outlook. They punish the man who is caught: they cannot hope to influence, other than by fear of such punishment, the man's inhibitions against erring in future. And fear of punishment is effective only in proportion to the chances of being caught.

INTERLUDE

A conversation

Abdallah (we were drinking together and he was talking about his life here in Dar es Salaam): I came to Dar es Salaam in 1946 and my whole life here has been spent as a hotel boy, but the pay is very low; but what I like about the job are the many tips; if a European is in a good mood every time he sends you for something he tips you, and sometimes this amounts to more than your day's pay. On Saturdays sometimes I come off duty with 25 Shs. to 40 Shs. (in tips). In the first place if a European is drinking he couldn't care less about the change. Some of them can't be bothered with coppers, so they say 'This kind of coin is yours', and they take just the notes and silver. So my pay was enough for my rent and I was sometimes able to save.

Andrew: I am looking for a new room. I am fed up with the room I am in; some time ago I invited a friend to stay with me, and now it's four months and he is still hanging on there. So I've come to the conclusion that the best is for me to leave the room to him, as he upsets me: because he has a mistress to sleep with him while I sleep on a bed all by myself. So at nights I have a hell of a time with him lying there so comfortable and me tossing and turning.

Ali: Why don't you get yourself a mistress like him?

Andrew: I haven't yet found my feet: I have no nice clothes or things in the room. This is my first year of work, so I feel it's best to live by myself and not try to do everything that Rome does the first day. Drink takes all my time, let alone whoring. All that would happen would be a dose.

Ali: You're a young man, don't be frightened of a dose, there are hospitals all over the place and you can be cured straight away with an injection, better than the trouble you have, lying there sleepless with desire and ruining your clothes—don't you see how awful it is?

Andrew: Everyone knows what he wants himself, it's not a matter of following others and just doing what everyone else does; you don't know this town, there are swordfish here which can gulp a man down whole. Better to move room than get into all that trouble.

Abdallah: Do you think it's better here to have two or three sharing a room or to have one to yourself?

Kesi: As I see it, it's best to have a room to oneself. You are master of the room: if you want water you get it, and kerosene, and the rent of the room, and the furniture, it is all your business and nobody else's. But if two people share you have to share everything, rent, and if one has a woman both have to, and then you get the trouble that Andrew has so that he is now looking for a room of his own.

Abdallah: I don't deny that a room of one's own has its points, but for myself I think it's not good for a man to live alone because a lot of things can happen; for instance if a man gets a temperature or some sudden illness in the night he won't even have anybody to ask to bring him water, and his door will be locked: that's quite a thing, isn't it? Secondly, granted nobody wants to die, but as an illustration, suppose you are living by yourself and die in your room—and that night you had locked your door: how long do you suppose the corpse would lie inside the room? It might be a week until the neighbours noticed the smell and opened it up. Now if there were two people sharing that room something could be done and you could have been sent to hospital. That's a big advantage, isn't it?

So we all agreed with Abdallah. And we agreed that it is better to live two in a room, or to marry better still, and be shot of quarrels in the house and with the neighbours. So we all tried to persuade Andrew not to move room, but to stay with the same friend whatever he was like, for he might improve; but if he moved to a room of his own he might find things much worse; we advised him to find a sweetheart to live with him, and if he didn't like that, to get married quickly and then everything would be lovely.

Marriage

In one important sphere of town life the courts interfere hardly at all, and the struggle is a straight one between a man's upbringing and his temptations, with the latter offering greater convenience, greater pleasure, but perhaps less ultimate satisfaction. This is the sphere of marital or extra-marital relations.

Hence one of the most noticeable aspects of life in town is the licence with which men and women cohabit, without the formal bonds of marriage and dowry, the uniting of two families, which is obligatory in most tribes up-country. The basic idea of marriage, the granting of 'our daughter' by one family to 'their son', on certain well-understood terms and conditions, must be radically modified where most of the parents are not in Dar es Salaam, and the families may not ever meet each other. In the distant past, when single individuals came to Dar es Salaam from the ends of the Territory, and the

Congo beyond, and little or nothing was known of them beyond what could be observed of the character of the man himself, it was extremely difficult for a stranger in town to find himself a wife from among the daughters of the country: cases did occur, but only in circumstances where the man had by then established himself and could be relied on not to disappear whence he came: in many such cases, the stranger was given land by his father-in-law to cultivate so long as he remained with his wife.

In marriages between the members of neighbouring tribes, such as the Zaramo, Luguru, Ndengereko and Rufiji, the same difficulty did not often occur, since the negotiations could easily take place with the families in their original villages; the ceremonies could be held there and if the worst came to the worst negotiations for a divorce could be conducted between the families in the usual way. Marriage between one of these tribes and a 'stranger' tribe were less common, and usually the stranger had by that time attached himself to all intents and purposes to the tribe into which he wished to marry. In some cases a member of a tribe from outside Dar es Salaam married a girl from Dar es Salaam (for instance a Ndengereko marrying a Manyema) and the children, while retaining the name of the father's tribe, became part of the community of the mother.

Full formal marriages between members of two stranger tribes are not common, and where they occur are usually between educated persons, who met in the course of their schooling, or between persons of long residence in Dar es Salaam. Cases of this sort do not seem to require that the tribes themselves be related, or have similar taboos or customs, though it is generally admitted that extreme dissimilarity must inevitably lead to friction in the home.

All the above refers to formal marriages with the full consent of both sets of parents or guardians, and the sanction of the religious body concerned. Such marriages I believe to be in a minority. Unfortunately I did not find it possible to measure their frequency, for whether two persons living together are so married, or whether they have 'married themselves' without reference to parents and with only an initial gift of clothes and money to take the place of the traditional dowry; or whether they are merely living together for so long as it is mutually convenient and pleasurable, is a question which the interviewer cannot possibly discover except in a quite unrepresentative number of cases. It is in fact a question to which even the other tenants in a Swahili house often never discover the answer; nor are they particularly curious to know. For there is little or no disgrace attached to such unions, which general opinion believes to be very widespread. (To the interviewer it leads to endless confusion, one question being answered to the effect that a man is 'living alone', the next that the total in his 'household' is two.) An attempt was made to measure the incidence of free marriage by asking those 'married' whether they were married by religious rite or by tribal custom, or 'otherwise', but very few rose to the bait; more detailed inquiries of a selection of families revealed little more, and it became clear that no measurement of this rather intimate item of the Dar es Salaam way of life could be achieved on any large scale, using the method of an evenly scattered sample. Indeed one of the most valuable advantages of the 100 per cent. limited-area sample used in Kampala was the ability to discover such intimate details. Although the use of the term for free marriage—in Swahili *kinyumba* or *kimada*—does not in most cases give offence, still most men do not like being asked, particularly in front of anybody else. Women are still more reluctant, which accounts for some of the difference in the figures for single persons, as between males and females in the 16–45 age-group: 39 per cent. as opposed to 11 per cent. (the bulk of the difference is of course accounted for by the excess of men in the town); for most women even when 'living with' a man will say they are married, while a fairly large minority of men will admit, at any rate if pressed, that it is not a formal marriage.

There are gradations of 'marriage' from full formal marriage between families, through formal but personally arranged marriages, to long-term arrangements which differ from a formal marriage only in the absence of dowry and the permission of the parents, and have considerable stability; to alliances of months, weeks or days, for the duration of an infatuation, or until the first quarrel reveals the shallowness of the relationship; these gradations have been well described in the Kampala survey *Townsmen in the Making*,[1] and the variety there described is present also in Dar es Salaam society.

In Dar es Salaam there is the additional reason for a quick turnover, in that it has been traditional for many years on the coast, even in rural districts, for marriages, however formally celebrated, to be unstable, and reshuffles to be frequent. The tendency to frequent divorce and remarriage in some tribes is reflected in the statistics, which show, for instance, that 50 per cent. of Manyema and Nyasa women had been married more than once, and of Yao women 38 per cent., and Mwera 36 per cent. (the mean of all women in Dar es Salaam was 31 per cent.). Similarly whereas 36 per cent. of all women had been 'ever divorced', this proportion went up to 42 per cent. of the Yao, 52 per cent. of Nyasa and 53 per cent. of Manyema. It is notable that these tribes, whose marriages are the least stable, are those which have been longest established in Dar es Salaam. This is true not only of long-established tribes but of long-established individuals: for whereas 55 per cent. of the whole population had lived here for over six years, this proportion rose to 77 per cent. among divorced persons.

There are a number of formal marriages (apart from the Christian ones which are in rather a different category) which have been arranged with the full formalities of presentation of the *barua* or letter of proposal to the parents, with a present to certain relatives, followed at intervals by the other stages of negotiation until the payment of at least an instalment on the bridewealth and the final transfer of the bride. There are for both parties considerable advantages in this, the traditional system: in the first place it is the most respectable, and has the full blessing of the older people, of both families, and of Islam; it may or may not be formalized by a visit to the Liwali and the taking out of a marriage certificate—many of these marriages, perhaps most, take place up-country but even if not employing the means of recognition offered by the state it is nevertheless entirely orthodox and enforceable by Islamic Law; its object is the procreation of children that the name may continue, and the family increase; a subsidiary object, particularly if the marriage takes place up-country, may be to

[1] *Townsmen in the Making*, by A. W. Southall and P. C. W. Gutkind, East African Studies, No. 9, Kampala, Uganda, 1957.

provide a worker for the family fields: this object is of course the less important the more urbanized the Dar es Salaam resident is; hence a large number of the formally married are to be found on the outskirts where it is possible to have cultivation within easy reach. The payment of bridewealth, with its financial penalty for dissolution of the marriage, makes for stability, and in many cases bridewealth follows the rates operative in the tribal area from which both come, so that the small or token amounts which tend to be customary in the more urban marriages are not so common as would be expected; the higher the bridewealth, of course, the higher the penalty for dissolution and the greater the incentive to make it last (conversely, the higher the bridewealth the greater the temptation to evade it by a non-formal marriage). The marriage being between two families, both sets of in-laws have an interest in its survival and will bring their influence to bear and give their assistance in settling quarrels before these get to the stage of being 'grounds for divorce'. Those who prefer the formal marriage will (if Muslim) say that if the marriage is not a success divorce is easy, and requires no protracted or expensive litigation, or even long periods in the public court (such cases are usually heard in chambers by the Liwali, and the litigants need stand in open court only for the pleas and the verdict); divorce cases of whatever tribe are heard according to Islamic Law—which is clear, and to the great majority acceptable; to those to whom it is not acceptable, as cutting across the tribal custom on which the marriage was founded, the usual recourse is to arbitration by elders of that tribe, but as far as has been ascertained such cases are in practice few. Islamic Law is to modern ideas of the equal status of women somewhat harshly in favour of the husband, and occasional complaints are heard on this score, but in fact the majority of cases of divorce are brought to court by the wife, whose repayment of bridewealth is said in many cases to be financed by the 'other man'. Occasional cases occur in which the court refuses a divorce applied for by the wife, on the ground that she had received all the treatment required of her husband by law: but although she may fail in this instance, it is said that she is soon able to make the home insupportable to the husband so that he himself asks for a divorce, which from the man's side is easy to get. The ability to end the marriage without fuss and expense is thus present even in the formal marriage, though admittedly the bridewealth remains a deterrent. The disadvantage of these marriages is the universal one that the spouse grows old and more attractive alternatives are at hand; but here again Islam is accommodating, allowing a man, providing he treats all alike, to have up to four wives; in practice to keep four wives in Dar es Salaam, all an economic liability, and each requiring, if she is not to quarrel with the others, a room of her own, requires a rich man. Notwithstanding, there is a substantial minority who have more than one wife—6 per cent. of all men aged 16 or over (though here again there may be some confusion when a man having a mistress in town and a wife in the country describes them both as his wife). Usually when there is more than one wife the husband contrives to keep them apart by providing rooms in different houses, preferably several streets away from each other; but one case was encountered where a man had both wives in the same room, where there was a bed, and a mattress on the floor, on which the two wives took turns: I was assured that they were on the best of terms, and as far as I could judge this was so.

The most usual reason for not marrying with full formality and bridewealth is that the parents are often simply not available, being at the respective homes out of reach: for only between a quarter and a third of parents live in Dar es Salaam.

Another reason for avoiding formal marriage is the greater expense of the preliminaries, and in particular the bridewealth itself; although many cases were met of much reduced bridewealth this remains a very large capital payment for a man living and working in Dar es Salaam on one of the lower ranges of salary. Every employer knows how often this is the occasion for a loan, or the object of savings.

Some avoid it in town because it can be formalized there only on Muslim lines, which may not always be in conformity with their tribal customs: in such cases it is far more common to wait until he can marry at home.

In many cases men do not marry while on their first 'tour' in town, partly because they have not the money to pay bridewealth—this may indeed in many cases, particularly from the south, be the reason for moving to town—and partly because they prefer to marry a girl from their own village, leave her with their relations and working on their fields at home, and visit her periodically to ensure the growth of the family and supervise the disposition of the profits from her cultivation. Where the man makes almost an annual journey home, as many of the Rufiji and Ndengereko do, such an arrangement may endure and be satisfactory to both partners, continuing over a number of years: a quarter of all males who had been resident in Dar es Salaam for three years or more had paid at least one visit home during that period of a month or more, many of them for this purpose. This preference for leaving a wife at home is based partly on fear that the smooth operators of town may alienate her affections, and partly because, whereas at home his wife is an investment and an economic asset, growing enough food in normal years to feed all his family and assist him, in town she is an economic liability, having no plot of land (only 7 per cent. of all households have one in Dar es Salaam) and very often no small trade: yet requiring a constant succession of new garments, ear-rings, and plastic sandals, if she is to be kept contented and not made to look ridiculous by the other wives in the house. Some do bring in quite large amounts of cash; by cooking beans and selling bowls of them at the door, or buying and splitting up firewood, or frying fish (though this is more often a professional job); many sell small cakes of rice-flour (*vitumbua*) or coconut sweet-meats (*kashati*) and often these are peddled in the street by their small children; a good profit may be made by these small trades, and the husband, particularly if he is working, has no check on the income from them; neither he nor his wife normally disclose their earnings to each other, a fact which must be important both as cause and as symptom of that mutual distrust which marks the failure of a marriage.

It often happens that there is no child to a marriage and there is then a divorce, without rancour, it being well understood that the first object of a marriage is the provision of children to carry on the name of the husband's family. There is even a custom of waiting for the next 'turn of the monsoon' which is said to bring better chances. But eventually a divorce is arranged, and the bridewealth returned: such a return, according to Muslim practice, need not be in full, but the husband may agree to a much reduced repayment (and he must in any case first pay out any outstanding portion of it), or forgive the wife or her parents entirely. Whatever the terms, the woman is then free to remarry without bridewealth, to 'send herself' as the Swahili has it. Even if the divorce has taken place for other reasons—a quarrel or failure of either to fulfil the duties of a spouse—the same right of the woman, once married and divorced, to marry herself off without any further permission from parents or anyone else, obtains. These 'personally arranged' marriages are possibly more numerous in Dar es Salaam than those with full bridewealth: they are equally respectable and equally have the full backing of society and Islamic Law. But at remarriage the woman has full choice of spouse; when marrying for the first time she was in most cases a *mwali*, a maiden in the closest purdah, usually locked in a hut of her own and ostensibly visited by none but her mother or sister bringing food; she was kept thus, often in semi-darkness, for up to two years in a country district, until the day of the wedding itself, when she saw for the first time (provided the supervision had been adequate) the man she was to wed. Even in town this custom persists, and a girl may live permanently for a year or more in a corner of a room, behind a cloth strung across to veil her from the rest of the family in the room: more often she is sent to the country where the full rigour of the system (customary to the Zaramo and others and blessed by Islam) can be enforced. So it is often the case that the woman looks forward eagerly to her first divorce and the chance to 'marry herself' to a man of her own choice. Her market value is enhanced by her independence and ability to choose or reject; she may this time be marrying in the hope of bearing children, or she may have been attracted to the racy town-life of some women and decide to follow their way of living—independent and supported only temporarily by a series of men, free at any time to stay or to go. Many men are pleased to find a wife who has had one marriage already for she has as it were been tried out, and has by now a reputation, whether good or bad, on which she may be judged. He likes the ease of such a marriage, with no preliminaries, and no bridewealth (supplanted by a present to gain the lady's favour); if she does bear him children they are legally his, whereas the children of a mere liaison are by Islamic Law the property of the mother. If there is a disadvantage to this type of marriage it is that by now she is a true town woman (many are the wives from up-country marriages who have had a visit to town and been so taken with its ways that they have become discontented at home, been divorced and come in to live permanently). From now on she is liable to be less easy to please, more liable to demand that water be carried by a servant or hired man, that she be well dressed and fed, that she be taken to cinemas and dances. If the husband tries to treat her as a subservient being, an old-time wife, she who has tasted freedom and independence is unwilling to knuckle down, and will depart, with no bridewealth to make her think twice. Although there is not a very great disparity between the sexes (women are 42 per cent. of the whole) there is sufficient demand to ensure that she will have little difficulty in finding another husband.

If she has done this once or twice she is almost on the verge of the third class of 'marriage'; that in which forms required by law or religion are not gone through. These may be termed 'affairs'. They range from a short affair terminated by a quarrel, or when one partner becomes tired of the other, to some which shade off by the very fact of enduring into a relationship which we should call 'living together' (in Swahili the woman is known jocularly as 'the cook'). In these longer relationships the four commodities which the 'wife' has to offer her man: cooking and washing, pleasure and companionship, have changed places in his list of importance. In the short affair of infatuation pleasure heads the list, and the others may not even be insisted on; but in the longer kind, when they live together, companionship may have crept to the head, the two having grown used to each other and developed that tolerance of each other's faults which is marital affection. Secondly the wife's usefulness as a cook and washer of clothes and dishes has become more important, and she on her part will perform these duties more willingly, having become, in all but name, his wife. Some of these liaisons last a lifetime, others a matter of months or years. They are based on that balance of pleasure and convenience which, if the liaison is to last, must tip over on the side of convenience and affection; if it does not, it remains as the majority do, an affair, subject to constant jealous doubts, and suffering from the tension that is the counterpart of pleasure.

Many enter these affairs casually, after a meeting at a dance, or bar, or a conversation at a water kiosk and a brisk piece of repartee. In the Swahili house, where the courtyard is common ground and the women are washing-up and cooking most of the day, while the menfolk are mostly out working, meetings are easily arranged, and affairs easily started. The man may be merely out for pleasure and have set his fancy on this particular face; he may be working a 'tour' before going home to marry, and be amusing himself meanwhile; he may have a wife cultivating his fields at home, and be filling in the time; or he may, like many, be anxious to try many flowers, and willing to pause for so long as the taste is sweet. If he is married already he will not wish to go through the formalities again in Dar es Salaam; and even if not married (and 39 per cent. of the men in the 16–45 age-group are single) it is cheaper, less tedious, and less of a commitment to form a liaison than to go through a formal marriage. On the woman's side, her price as a mistress is higher than it would be as a wife, for she holds continuously the spoken or unspoken threat that, if presents are not sufficiently frequent and expensive, she will move on to a rival. In her status as a mistress she cannot be forced to do the menial jobs that a wife would have to do (it is for this reason among others that landlords do not like to have single men as tenants, for their girl-friends will not take their share of the sweeping). This threat diminishes if the relationship turns into that of 'living together', for the woman ceases to live with him because he is the highest bidder, and begins to do so because they suit each other: a more dependent status, and a weaker bargaining position, but one of less tension and more content. One might suppose that some of these longer-lived liaisons might be transformed into a formal solemnized marriage, but in fact no instance of this was found: perhaps it is that they occur only between persons steeped in town ideas, to whom the traditional form of marriage is by then irrelevant to their own circumstances—the circumstances of individuals each operating, at any rate as far as the periods of their stay in town are concerned, independently of their families though in close touch and sympathy with them.

For the young man out for a good time, or the grass widower, the short affair offers the quickest return and the least obligation or commitment: like those living together, he and his girl can part at any time, and do as soon as for either the infatuation is over. The inhibiting factor on the man's part is simply that of expense, for this is the most expensive kind of liaison, since it gives the woman the greater advantage; her threat to leave for a rival is at its most potent. Many such women are of independent means in any case; barmaids, ayahs, or the few with wage jobs such as those employed as nurses or in the printing works. Others have no independent means and rely on their boy-friends to support them in a way which will make it worth their while. These liaisons are said not often to lead to children, but if they do the child belongs to the woman unless the man decides to stay with her, and even then he has no claim in law. The supposedly low birthrate of coastal women is generally put down by townsfolk and country people alike as being due to this constant flitting from boy-friend to boy-friend, which is said by them not only to make them less fertile, but also to make them fear the loss of income that having a child would entail, and so use means in which they are said to be expert to ensure that no child is born.

INTERLUDE

Living together

Two women, who seemed not to be married, were behaving expensively: they came into a *tembo* club in Magomeni. Although they were not very pretty their bold manner, singing and dancing around as they pleased, drew the men who were there. Also with the money they had they began to buy beer and *tembo* and spirits.

Suddenly a man came in and took hold of one of them. She refused to leave, as she was getting on well with another young man in the bar. So the man began to use force and tugged furiously at her. They tore each other's clothes and scratched and fought. Many of the customers watched this. The comment was: 'they have been living together as man and mistress for a long time, and they always do this.'

. . . . .

'The other day a friend of mine, who had had a girl in just occasionally and casually, grew fond of her and asked her to be his permanent mistress. She agreed and he gave her a pound to buy some clothes with, to close the deal. She went off and never came back.

'He came to me and told me the story, and I advised him to go and see her and remonstrate. He did, and said "What's all this, you agree to come and live with me and I give you a pound to buy some clothes, and you just beetle off and leave me, what's the matter with you?" But she got on her high horse and said "I'm just not coming to live with you, you gave me a present, and that's the end of it; if you don't like it, report me." So he came back to me and told me what she had said, and I said to him: "Why not? Go and report her to the Police." So he did, and told them that his girl had cheated him by taking a pound off him and going off on her own. They questioned him a bit and then called the girl and put the pressure on her, saying that she could either give back the pound which she had got by false pretences, or she would have to go and live with my friend, by force if necessary. So she went to her aunt, and asked if she could help; the aunt had not the money (the girl had spent it all, of course) and couldn't do anything to help her. So she came back and they went before the Police again, and she said she couldn't find the money. So the Police said she must go and live with my friend; and she did, but it didn't work out, as she really didn't care for him, so after a few days he let her go, saying: "You can go home now, but remember, you are under Police orders to live with me, and if ever I want a girl I'll come and get you, wherever you may be, even if you are living with a man as big as an elephant."'

.   .   .   .   .   .

'A man I know came and was looking for a room to rent. As usual he was asked if he had a wife, as lone men are not welcome in these houses where they may make eyes at other men's wives. He was frank with the landlady and said that he had a girl, but she was not really his wife, they just lived together. The landlady agreed to rent him the room and they lived in it together. After a week she left him, and he was alone again. Soon this was noticed by the landlady, and she asked "Where is your wife?" He said: "I explained when I came that she was not a wife but a mistress, she is a free agent and can go when she pleases, I can't stop her. Now she is gone to her people. If you want me to have a wife in the house, you find me one." The landlady said "All right, I'll do that" and she searched around and found him a girl in Temeke. The girl was a sensible girl and first asked a few questions—will he give me good clothes, Ramadhan is coming on and I need a new outfit. The landlady reassured her and described the man in glowing terms, he was a clerk, a man with a regular job, generous. He had just lost his previous mistress and he had treated her well and she was always well dressed and well done by. So the new girl agreed, but then she remembered, she had a man already this month and she couldn't very well leave him flat just like that. So she promised to come along after the 'Id festival.'

Prostitution

There remains the most casual of the relationships, that of the prostitute. This is of two distinct kinds, the professional who has come to Dar es Salaam, often from a great distance, specifically for this purpose; and the amateur who after a number of affairs has drifted into the professional class, either by inclination or because the cash profits are greater (it must be remembered that a girl-friend does not accumulate much in hard cash—unless she is careful to convert her presents as she goes along—but receives most of her payment in kind, dances, cinemas, taxis, beer and brandy, with presents of clothes and ornaments thrown in, which she must use to keep up her attractions; much of her takings are in the form of a 'good time'; if she wants money in order to save for a house or a husband then the quicker and surer way is to set up as a professional prostitute).

The ex-amateurs are from the same main tribes as form the bulk of the population, with Zaramo predominating; they are collectively referred to as 'Swahili women', in a slightly derogatory sense; the professionals have a higher reputation, reflected in a higher price: they come from the Christian tribes, with the Haya inevitably in a huge preponderance; classed together with the Haya but rather above them are the Ganda (who like the Haya are, if single, often assumed to be prostitutes until the contrary is shown); higher still are the Indians, Arabs and half-castes, whose clientèle includes all races but only the higher income-groups: they are usually well dressed and live in rooms of considerable affluence.

While it is easy enough to discover who is and who is not a prostitute, it is not a question which all are prepared to answer about themselves (though some did so enter it as their profession); a rule of thumb was, therefore, decided on for the purposes of the survey: that where three or more single women in one house each paid her own rent, then all were prostitutes. Signs which can be added as confirmation are a preponderance of Haya, and a habit of cooking on primus stoves in the central passage (for fear of missing customers by being in the back premises when they call); this rule is if anything a cautious one and may have excluded some genuine prostitutes; it is unlikely to have maligned any who were not. For as a rule prostitutes (as opposed to a rather different class whom I shall describe as 'call-girls') band together and rent all the six main rooms in a house, each taking one and being herself responsible for its rent. The rooms in the courtyard may be taken by persons unconcerned in their business, but more often they are occupied by servants and messengers. It is not difficult for such women to rent rooms in this way. Though some landlords do not like to be mixed up with the type of clientèle they bring, often drunk and quarrelsome and noisy, many are prepared to put up with this for the sake of the steady rent—prostitutes having a reputation for paying on the due date—and one well above the average. A room which by its condition and amenities deserves at present rates a rent of 20 Shs. to the general public, will bring in 30 Shs. from a prostitute, not to offset her ill repute, but because she is known to have the means to pay more than others.

The type of house varies naturally according to the grade of prostitute, from the Swahilis of old Magomeni living in plain mud and wattle houses with earth floors and thatched roofs and charging 1 Sh. for a short visit, 2 Shs. for a longer one, and counting among their clientèle the 'payday boys' from Kariakoo or nearer by; through the houses in old Kisutu (now in process of demolition and the removal of their occupants in a body to newly built houses of better quality in new Magomeni) which though often rather low by modern standards usually have cement floors, whitewashed walls, carpenter-made beds with headpieces and let-in coloured tiles, and an easy chair or two. Here live the Haya and the more successful of the ex-amateurs, charging 3 Shs. for a visit and 5 Shs. for a night; their clientèle varying over a wide range: the unskilled labourer on payday taking 'nothing but the best', the better-paid clerks and artisans, and the sailors off ships; anyone who can pay is acceptable.

In a higher economic grade are the most successful, living in substantial houses, where perhaps a steady client, often an Indian or Arab, pays the rent of the room and furnishes it with four-poster bed, pictures, artificial flowers, linoleum and good furniture; here payment is as high as 5 Shs. or even 10 Shs. (for an Indian or half-caste) and although the steady client may try to be jealously possessive other clients are taken. There is perhaps more variety in this class than in any other: one may be an Indian prostitute wearing expensive saris and ornaments, another a Seychelloise or of other mixed blood; another a Manyema from Kigoma or a Swahili with traces of Arab blood; to all any man who can pay the fee, which is high, is acceptable. Often as many as three rooms, a complete semi-detached half-house in a Swahili-type building, are occupied by the one woman; many of the half-castes live in the eastern end of Kariakoo (nearest to the custom, the most lucrative of which comes from the Commercial Area) in the older houses which divide neatly into two-room flats; but others prefer the old Christian area at the other end of Kariakoo, the Mission Quarter. Apart from Kisutu there is no real 'red-light area' and the houses containing the trade are scattered fairly evenly in the more likely positions: naturally the areas nearer the centre are the most popular, but now that Kisutu has moved to 'New Kisutu' in Magomeni the latter area, previously the preserve of the 'Swahili women', has a quota of the more expensive Haya establishments.

There appears to be no organization, let alone exploitation of prostitutes; occasionally there is a 'madame' living in one of the courtyard rooms, usually the landlady, but each tenant is entirely independent and has to pay from her earnings nothing more than the agreed rent, which though higher than normal is not exorbitant.

Cases were met where an established prostitute had introduced a younger girl, who performed the domestic chores while being introduced to the trade, but this appeared to be merely an attempt to help a distant relative rather than a business transaction. Most newcomers to the trade enter through the help of an established friend or relative, though one case was met of an up-country girl, not a Haya, who came first to the Police Traffic Lines to stay for a few days (because, as she said, she had a fairly large sum of money and wished to be safe) and thence found introductions and set up independently.

The end of such a career comes usually when the prostitute has made the amount of money for which she came, and goes home. On her return it appears that she has every chance of making a good and respectable marriage, for she brings with her as a kind of dowry the profits of her trade, usually a sewing-machine, a gramophone and records, a bicycle, good clothes and ornaments, and all the polish of town. Those with whom this question was discussed appeared to have no doubts of their reacceptance into the society which they left, and indeed more than one such make regular visits home where they are said to be much admired as successful women.

Although it is generally assumed that prostitutes take good care not to have children—and they have the reputation of knowing well how to arrange this—the figures show that this is only relatively true; in that the proportion of those who had never borne a child rose from the mean of 33 per cent. to 48 per cent. in the case of prostitutes; but more than half had borne a child, mostly (29 per cent.) a single child, and 10 per cent. had borne four or five children (compared to 12 per cent. in the sample of all married women).

Some of course never leave town: theirs are the new houses springing up in Magomeni, which they often let to others of their trade; when the capital for the first house has been accumulated there is an assurance of a steady income from rents and some now have several houses; some of these older women (and others who have never entered this trade) take younger husbands much in the position of 'kept men', who are kept for companionship and prestige and the advantages of having a man about the house, though they themselves retain strict control of the property.

As these women do not go out to seek their custom, but stay in the passage or veranda of the house talking with those others of the tenants who are disengaged, it is necessary that their address be known, or that they have some link with potential customers. An established prostitute will of course have built up a clientèle from those who have once visited her, and those to whom they recommend her; new clients are most often brought by the taxi-drivers, who serve as scouts, partly in

their own interest, for the sake of the fare and with luck a
charge for waiting time, and partly by a standing arrangement
which is a business transaction, for a commission or tip, or
payment later in kind.

A separate type is the 'call-girl', who does not operate from
her own room, but lives sharing with several other girls, splitting
the rent, and working outside. These too rely heavily on the
taxi-drivers, who take them to their destinations and find them
custom. It is this lucrative trade which ensures that the newest
and biggest taxis are to be found in the more African parts of
town. Besides their taxi-driver scouts these women go out to
look for their custom, in dances, bars and cinemas, and some
even walk certain streets, usually in pursuit of non-African
custom. They are easily recognized by a bold glance and a
lively reply to an inquiry (they have a reputation for a quick
wit and few men, least of all patrolling policemen, care to take
them on in an argument) and their companionship is purchased
by an entrance ticket to a dance, or a bottle of beer and a
cigarette. After the party they can be taken to a room, of
which there are many kept vacant for such an eventuality, both
in the smaller hotels in the Commercial area and elsewhere,
and in Swahili houses in all parts of the town, which can be
hired by the hour.

Finally there are a much smaller number of homosexuals
who operate professionally; some are those who dance as
female impersonators in *nautch* dances: these, like female
prostitutes, pay a rent above the average; in one case the
link with clients was an old woman who lived next door and
employed one as a servant, and ran a Koranic school as a
sideline.

Prostitution is a necessary safety-valve in any big town and
port; in Dar es Salaam it is neither over-abundant, obtrusive,
nor in the circumstances likely to lead large numbers astray.
Where so many have passing unions the prostitutes cannot be
accused of being the primary carriers of disease, indeed the
more successful take pride in patronizing only the best doctors
in town, and a far greater danger to health must be the
amateurs: it is believed that many develop a tolerance of
gonorrhoea and that the incidence is high, though the Government hospitals are not able to measure this incidence.

The reasons for the prevalence of this very widespread amorality or immorality in sexual affairs are not as obvious as might be supposed; it has been suggested that it originates in a 'pioneer-town' atmosphere, where the only women were 'bad women'; but from the very start Dar es Salaam, although having its full quota of free young men, has had also a core of steady marriages, bearing children; it has been suggested that the main cause is an excess of men: but in the relevant age-group, 16–45, the proportion of women is 42 per cent., not a very grave disbalance; another reason put forward is that the men are impermanent and live here only for the day before returning home: this also is only half-true, in that the majority (67 per cent. of men) have been here, off and on, for six years or more; or again, that men live here with a sense of being free from the normal restraints, and with a desire to be free from the responsibilities of married life; this is more particularly true of those who intend to marry or already have married a 'real' wife in their home District, so that here they are merely filling in time.

The question is one on which depends (as pointed out in the Kampala survey) the whole assumption that policy should seek to enable the strict family to become the basis of normal life in the town: is there in fact any desire on the part of the majority for settled family life in town on any conditions? Is it the habit of living in one room of a tenement that gives rise to constant affairs and temporary liaisons? Would private detached dwellings make any difference (the Royal Commission report appears to assume that they would). Do people leave their wives at home only because it is more profitable to leave them where they can produce food and money, rather than bring them to live in town where they will demand an increased standard of living and where the opportunities for earning are limited? Do they leave them at home for fear of losing them in the licentious atmosphere of town? Or do they in fact like the freedom from responsibility, bestowed by such a life coupled with the creation of a family, the growing of food and the earning of a surplus, which regular visits to a wife kept in the home District can ensure?

The origins of the amoral atmosphere and the reasons for its continuance must be a combination of all the above, not all being valid in any one case, their relative strengths varying. But it is at least doubtful whether enough is known on which to base a firm policy of establishing the strict family as the basic unit in town. While town life will always be more lax than country life, it may be that when the town ceases to grow quite so quickly the core of settled families will exert more influence, and will themselves have more of a reputation to lose by laxity; the pattern of the coastal grass widower will probably never be broken, but the numbers of career-men (bringing their families) may form a higher proportion and perhaps take a greater part in town life than they do at present; and women may find other ways of showing their independence. One thing is certain: it is a problem for the Africans themselves.

INTERLUDE

Dawn in Dar es Salaam

The sky is still silvery with the first light, but already the first stream is on the roads, houseboys in their clean clothes walking briskly from Kinondoni to Seaview, from Kariakoo to the Burton Street area. Mingled with them are a few messengers, a fisherman with his paddles over his shoulder, a Prisons askari on his bicycle.

Outside the big blocks of shops and offices the nightwatchmen are brewing themselves a dawn cup of tea and packing up to go. At the station a pair of Police askaris stroll round on patrol; in Kichwele Street another, wrapped in his cloak, hurries to some business or other. Along the Azania Front and Ocean Road families of Indians are going for a pre-dawn walk, parents and children all together in the half-light; many young Indian men are going to bathe in the sea with towels over the shoulders. By six o'clock the town begins to come to life, the commercial area full of hurrying figures, en-*kanzu*'d, in the ragged shirts of the dock labourers, in clean shirts and long trousers, some still pulling up their trousers and tightening belts as they hurry along. The Kariakoo market is dark and deserted, only a few young men who have spent the night there, avoiding the patrolling askaris, sleeping on the concrete stands.

A young man stands at the door of a house, brushing his teeth with a piece of soft wood. At a bus stop a man, and three women huddled in their *buibuis*, await the first bus. Many sit wrapped in a cloth on the *baraza* of a house, talking and watching the people pass.

Swahili Street is dead, not a soul to be seen, but in Mafia Street, Msimbazi and Udoe many are beginning to stir; in Mnazi Mmoja only two taxis are at the stand, but in some of the back streets cars and taxis are drawn up at the side.

At the first dock hooter, just after six, there is still only an awakening, but as it comes light, at ten past six suddenly the whole world is awake: every Arab *duka*,[1] and Indian *duka* too, is ablaze with light, people are already buying food, one *duka*-cum-tea-shop has the radio blaring a Koranic reading, volume as usual full on; by the time the second dock hooter goes, there is no question of any but the most determined being still asleep. Across Mnazi Mmoja there is a steady stream, three or four across, hurrying to the docks and the other employers of labour. Most of this stream is past by half past six, but then the other streams have begun, more house-boys, sweepers, or merely those with business the other side of town.

The Morogoro road as it crosses the Msimbazi creek is solid with pedestrians, cyclists and buses, the reverse of the evening rush. By the time the sun is visible the town is indistinguishable from any other time of day.

Crime

Casualness in sexual relations is only one aspect of an amorality which shows itself in other directions. Petty theft is common in any dock area in the world, and this is no exception; pilfering from cargoes and from lorries is too easy to be ignored, and a man who refrained would be considered odd by his fellows; one of the juvenile occupations, the collection of scrap, provides a good training for this, as the border-line between nails and iron sheets which have been thrown away and those which have just been left lying about is a fine one.

Crime figures are not high, and not noticeably increasing when the growth of population is taken into consideration. What crime there is is mainly in the areas surveyed and the victims African. There is a small core of professionals, and a larger fringe of those who merely take one of the many opportunities afforded by the Swahili house to get to know the movements and habits of a potential victim and take advantage of a moment of carelessness. To have been to prison is not a bar to society, nor is it uncommon to find the relatives of well-off and established persons in the dock.

---

[1] *Duka*: shop.

'In the Ilala Court a boy faced a charge of fighting and slightly wounding another boy, both aged 12 or so. The boy was sentenced to a fine of 10 Shs. or 7 days; the guardian was in court and explained that the boy's father who was dead had been the Sheikh of the neighbouring mosque, a highly respected man; the guardian, his uncle, gives the boy food and shelter. He refused to pay the fine, saying it would do the boy good to go to prison. An elder remonstrated, saying that in prison the boy would come into contact with bad hats and be spoiled, but the guardian was unmoved. The boy then came up on a second charge, of trading in coconuts without a licence: he defended himself on the ground that the coconuts he was selling came from his own plantation, left him by his father and harvested by permission of his uncle; at this point the uncle stepped in and said "it is lies", demolishing his defence; the audience murmured against the uncle for having given the boy away. The uncle agreed to pay the two fines rather than let the boy go to prison for 14 days. There was general approval.'

.　　.　　.　　.　　.

'In the British Legion Bar the other day an old man came in and sat down at a table where there were some town boys drinking coconut palm-wine. The old man took his basket and put some things in it; then he also put in it his money, six ten-shilling notes and some silver. When he had sat down he spoke politely to the young men, saying "good evening" and they answered him in the same way. The old man called the waiter and ordered two bottles of Coronation beer, for 2 Shs. 60 cents. When it came to paying he had to take the money out of his basket, and the young men realized that he kept money there. Well, they all sat and enjoyed their drinks and talked a lot. After about an hour some of the young men went out, leaving one behind with the old man. Soon afterwards the old man felt a call of nature and went out for about five minutes. The young man stealthily put a hand into the basket and drew out some of the money that was in it. When the old man returned from the lavatory he didn't worry about the basket but went on drinking and talking. When the young man saw that he had got what he wanted he went out, and the old man went on drinking alone, until he was satisfied, and then he too left.

'The people who were there disapproved of the young man taking the old man's money, but they said nothing, because "it was the old man's fault for showing there was money in his basket when he bought the beer".'

.   .   .   .   .

'There was an incident one night recently as I was going to a concert: just across the road, in Bagamoyo Street, in a dark patch I suddenly noticed a commotion and heard a man pitifully groaning. I thought people were playing a game or something. Two people had got hold of a third man. One had him by the neck under his armpit, and was twisting it to prevent him from shouting. The other was running his hands through the pockets of the man so held. For a second or so the man held made another painful groaning noise, and I saw the first man who held his victim twist him so hard that the man held was not able to raise an alarm. Then they left him and ran away through the dark street behind the houses.

'The man that was held flopped to the ground. It appeared as if for a second or two he was dazed and had lost consciousness. He got up and ran two or three steps, but fell down again, but managed to raise an alarm, by which time neighbours began to come out of their houses to see what was going on. By now the man was groaning under the lamp-post and I noticed that he was an Indian. A fellow Indian came out of his house and asked what was wrong. He spoke in what I thought was Hindustani, but what appeared to be incoherent speech. The other Indian took a bicycle and disappeared. When I made some inquiries as to what had happened, I was told that the two men were robbing the Indian, and to prevent him from raising an alarm they caught him by the neck which method is known by the Dar Africans as *kumtia kabali*. What surprised me was that one or two people passed by the very place where the two men were robbing the Indian, but did nothing and never took any notice whatsoever. Whether they were like myself who thought these three people were merely joking with one another I don't know.

'I left the scene before the askaris arrived.'

There is a common denominator to these three stories: the

R

neutralism of the bystander which prevents him identifying himself with law and order; the uncle was wrong to give the boy away and thus bring him to justice; the other men in the bar would have been wrong to call the old man's attention to the theft, or prevent it happening before their eyes; and the passers-by—and the recorder himself—were content to watch, interestedly enough, a robbery take place in one of the main streets of town without lending a hand to help the victim.

It is not suggested that crime is common: the figures of reported crime indicate that the incidence is at least lower than that in similar large towns of East Africa, and there is no evidence to suggest that the victims refrain from reporting crimes on any very large scale. But the fact remains that the instinct to help the victim and the forces of law and order is simply not there. This I believe to be an extension of a fundamental Bantu way of thinking, which appears time and again in magic formulae, where a misfortune or sickness is cast off from a man himself or his close relative and wished on to a stranger or a man of another hamlet: the unit to be protected is the man himself and his strict family, and thence his extended family; even to the tribe at large he has a loyalty only in certain circumstances; but towards the world at large it is every man for himself; there is no call for him to identify himself with the suburb in which he finds himself, or the members of the house in which he lodges, or even the girl he sleeps with; he does not automatically form loyalties to whatever unit he is in—only to that of his family: and he expects everyone else to do the same; it is every man for himself and each man responsible for his own protection.

If this is true, then indifference to crime (unless committed against oneself or family) is not a product of town life, though other factors in that life make it more serious; it is, however, in town that it becomes prominent, for it is there that so many people live surrounded by persons for whose protection they accept no responsibility; a shout or scream at night in an up-country hamlet will turn out all the neighbours, for they are all related and have a mutual loyalty: but in town a shout in one house at night is a signal only for a locking of doors.

The same feeling is apparent when it comes to the repayment of debts, or the payment of such dues as rents: there is no real feeling of obligation, only that one pays if one is forced to; whence the constant quarrels between landlord and tenants, and between creditors and debtors.

Again and again, on different subjects, crops up the phrase 'freedom from responsibility'; it is also a sense of freedom from supervision and from discipline; the decline of whatever discipline the tribe in town was once able to exert has been described; the discipline of a firm marriage tie has been shown to be more often than not successfully avoided by both the man and the woman, both of whom have broken away also from the restraints normally imposed on their behaviour by the family sponsors of a marriage; the independent status in town of so many women is reflected in a similar status of children.

In the rural village society the child, more than any other member of the community, is firmly kept in its appointed place: as soon as it is able it is introduced to the routine chores which are to be its lot; the boys go to herd the goats or cattle, the girls help with the washing-up, and later with the harder chores. When they are stronger both are brought in to assist with cultivation and made as soon as possible to contribute to the family food supply; boys are sent on errands, they fetch and carry, and though there appears to be ample time for play they themselves regard it as an eternal round of work.

From the countryside which surrounds Dar es Salaam many are lucky enough to be brought in on a visit, either when the father is doing a periodic spell of employment in town, or when he is going to see some relation. When the boy reaches town he is very often used by the parents for jobs outside the house: his mother may eke out their income by making rice-flour cakes for sale, and he will be sent out to peddle them; or she may have some other small trade, and he be put in charge on the veranda: in either case his bright eyes quickly perceive many of the delights of town life and he conceives a longing to stay and live in it himself. While peddling cakes he may be able to make a few pence himself, and if so he has started on a new level of independence of his parents.

More often the child has been into town and on return up-country has become discontented with the hard manual work and dullness of rural life: he may plead to go and stay with an uncle or aunt in town, and his parents may give him the fare;

they may in fact do so with the laudable intent to give him the better schooling available in town; or he may have heard of the monthly hundreds who are repatriated, and decides to rely on this for his return; he then comes to stay with this relative, who although he may call him his 'elder father' or 'younger father', has in practice a disciplinary authority, and an interest in exerting it, significantly less than that of the true father. Often the child, who must feed at the relative's expense, is regarded as a nuisance, and if he finds some way of getting an income the foster-parent is only too pleased; so the child gets work, which is easily obtained, as a servant to an Indian, Arab or African, where most often food is included, and the wage becomes pocket money; as such it is often a very considerable sum to the child, and having it in his pocket he is under no compulsion to return home to his foster-parent for meals, or at night; if he is told off, he may run away, and having the means to pay his own rent he may set up for himself, very likely sharing with another like him to reduce the rent. Nor is it only those living with foster-parents who escape parental discipline in this way and achieve an independent status at a very early age: often a child will do so though his parents are in Dar es Salaam, even with their encouragement. Some light on the number of children who grow up in this freedom from parental discipline is shed by figures obtained from the survey, which show that 38 per cent. of all children between the ages of 6 and 15 had no father in town, while 29 per cent. had neither parent. The proportions were as high as 45 per cent. and 34 per cent. in the central suburb of Kariakoo.

Figures were also obtained of the number of juveniles in paid employment; these are unreliable in that the survey excluded those resident in the commercial area and in the Burton Street and Oyster Bay areas, etc., where there are known to be many juveniles employed on the premises. Of those resident in the mainly African areas, however, 13 per cent. of males aged 6–16, say 1,000 boys, were in work in August 1956. Some nearby tribes, particularly the Zaramo, Rufiji, Luguru and Ndengereko, had a higher proportion. There was little difference between the suburbs, except that Ilala/Buguruni had rather more, and Temeke and the Kekos rather less, than their fair share. The jobs taken by juveniles were mainly domestic (40 per cent.), unskilled labour (22 per cent.) and office-boy jobs (14 per cent.) being also important. (This sample is suspected to include some who for tax reasons understated their age.)

Outside the main sample, a small sample of fifty children found playing with a tennis ball in Mnazi Mmoja was interviewed; its tribal composition was not far off that of the town as a whole, the bulk being Zaramo with a sprinkling of the other coastal and central line tribes, with a few from those more far-flung. Their ages were spread between 8 and 17, with some grouping between 10 and 15. The most noticeable thing about the group was that nearly three-quarters (72 per cent.) had no father in Dar es Salaam (in the case of 30 per cent. the father was dead). Despite this 30 per cent. spent their nights with their fathers, the discrepancy being accounted for by a few having fathers outside Dar es Salaam but within reach. 20 per cent. went to a brother's to sleep, 18 per cent. to a mother's, 18 per cent. to an uncle's, 4 per cent. to an aunt's, the remaining 10 per cent. to a variety of sister, sister-in-law, grandfather and grandmother, one being on his own; he and one other paid the whole or part of his own rent.

With the Mnazi Mmoja school not far away it is not surprising that this sample was comparatively well educated, only 20 per cent. having never been to school. Although 96 per cent. were Muslim only 6 attended a Koranic school. 44 per cent. were still at school, and an additional one was going to night school.

28 per cent. of them considered themselves 'in employment': 10 per cent. as houseboys, 6 per cent. as unskilled labourers, 6 per cent. selling fritters or cakes for their parents, the rest selling cashew nuts (for grandfather), cakes (for uncle) and one an apprentice carpenter.

22 per cent. had spent all their lives in Dar es Salaam, of the rest 18 per cent. had less than one year, the rest being well spread.

One-third gave as their reason for coming the availability of schooling (it is very easy to get into school in Dar es Salaam, as there are always vacant places, and another factor is that often a well-off resident will pay the fees for the son of a less well-off relative from the country: the son then goes to live with his benefactor). A quarter had come to get a job, a sixth to visit relatives, and a ninth came with their parents who were visiting. The others came for a holiday, or to see the town. In half the cases a relative, not a parent, had paid the fare, and in a ninth the child had paid for his own.

No less than four-fifths had both an uncle (or aunt) *and* a cousin in town and a quarter had grandparents.

Over half did not want to return home, and another fifth would like to return, 'but not yet'. When asked what they disliked about home the largest group gave the absence of paid work; another group said they 'liked the town life'. Four gave the absence of schools where they came from, while the rest painted a distressing picture of country life as too full of farm work, too quiet, too small, too many lions and too much witchcraft.

What they liked about Dar es Salaam, by contrast, was the prospect of a job (29 per cent.), the schools (20 per cent.), the fact that they were 'used to it', i.e. that they liked it (18 per cent.), the many sights and wonders, the bigness of things, the fun and liveliness of it, the football, cinema and dances, the freedom, the security from drought and famine, ending with the same little boy who enjoyed the absence of dangerous animals; nearly a third mentioned some aspect of the glamour of a big town.

The boys were then questioned about the jobs open to them: nearly half mentioned 'houseboy', far more than any other job; the next—but with only a quarter as many mentions—was newspaper-boy, then apprentice mechanic ('spanner-boy') in the railways; selling oranges, nuts, fritters, coconut-ice or sweet beer; collecting scrap, messenger, building labour, smith, and tennis-boy. Asked which was the best, even more mentioned houseboy first, with 'spanner-boy' second and paper-boy third. What then did they all intend to do when they grew up? A quarter aimed to be clerks, then mechanics, carpenters, houseboys, dispensers, drivers; and two wanted to be policemen (one specified sub-inspector) while telegraphy, farming, the Navy and the mosque each had their supporters. From this one may gather that opportunities and rewards favour the boy who becomes a houseboy or an apprentice on the railways, the superior glamour attaches to the clerk; with this in mind it is interesting to note that well over half of this sample could read and write.

Another means by which boys are set adrift in town is the many broken marriages: as explained before, the child of any liaison less than formal marriage is the property of the mother, who is most likely to marry again shortly. In the nature of things it often happens that the stepfather is not interested in the child of another and careless of what it does; similarly the children of formal marriages which have broken up go with the father, who again is likely to marry another wife with a similar danger that the stepmother will not bother about another's child. The extent to which this may happen may be gauged from the figures of divorce of couples who have already borne a child, as shown in the table below.

All tribes together		Of those divorced Children born before divorce	Maximum estimate
Sample	Divorce		
2,168	males 15%	43%	2,800 cases
1,558	females 36%	56%	6,260 cases

The 'maximum estimate' need of course not be anywhere near the true number of cases in which the child is liable to be neglected: in very many cases the child or children will have been dispatched to a relative up-country where it will be in no such danger; in many others it will be fortunate to find a step-parent who will give it at least as much supervision as it had before; many of the divorces recorded may have occurred up-country, and many of the children may never have come to town; the total figure of a maximum possibility of some 9,000 can, therefore, be taken to indicate only the potential size of the problem.

Another saving point is that the tribes most addicted to divorce: the Yao, Manyema and Ngindo among men and the Manyema, Nyasa, Yao and Ngindo among the women, are below the average when it comes to bearing children before the divorce takes place; to offset this is the thought that these are the tribes most settled in Dar es Salaam, the people who are setting the pattern for the future.

One reason why many parents are glad to see their children

go off to a domestic job at an early age is that as soon as a boy begins to grow up he is an embarrassment to his parents in their single room; in many houses one sees a bed set out in the passage, and often this is where a growing boy sleeps; sometimes if they can afford it he is hired another room in the courtyard; but economically speaking the ideal solution is for him to get a job with an Asian which will give him a free room. The same difficulty arises, of course, with girls, but it is more usually solved by sending them to a relative in the country.

The discipline which parents fail to give could be instilled in school, and in very many cases this is so; but so many of the coastal people of the older generation, who make up the bulk of the population, being themselves uneducated are not convinced yet of the necessity for their children to be educated. Many still have the feeling that modern education, being so closely connected with Mission activity, is a threat to Islam, and take a pride in sending their children, if they send them anywhere, to a Koranic school, where owing to the low wages and low standard of the teachers the discipline is very lax—it is often possible to see a class of children in a Koranic school playing and shouting, ostensibly under the supervision of one of the older boys, while the teacher is asleep in another room.

He can hardly be blamed for his lack of interest, for his livelihood depends on the fees, usually set at 1 Sh. a month from each child, and their collection regularly and in full is an uphill job. So in fact such teachers are often 'paid' only by the method of 'something on account' which can be got from an unwary parent; these criticisms do not apply to the better-run Koranic schools, but are true of most of the smaller ones, and one or two of the larger.

Even with the Government-run schools the periods when the children are in school do not by any means cover the whole day, since the schools run in 'streams' alternating between morning and afternoon periods, though an attempt is being made to start boys' clubs. For a good half of the day, therefore, most children are free to roam around, unless their parents are prepared to spend the time on their supervision. There are others who do not go to any sort of school and have the whole day to roam. The 5 per cent. survey (which is of course not a complete picture of Dar es Salaam) indicates that there were in August 1956 some 13,000 children, boys and girls together, aged between 6 and 15. If they are evenly distributed (which is only a guess) between these age-groups, there might be 6,500 children of an age to go to primary school. Available places in 1956 were 3,915, and those filled 2,861, or 72 per cent.; in 1957 the figures were 4,580 available places and 3,550 filled. In either case there would seem to be a considerable margin of children who do not go to school, which is not accounted for by the comparatively small number who go to Koranic school. A more accurate estimate should become available when the age-group breakdown of the August 1957 census is complete.

INTERLUDE
In the Ilala court

A young man of some 25 years was being charged with stealing a cloth from an Arab pedlar. The Arab, who spoke little Swahili and brought one with him who spoke it fluently, said that four young men came to him and made bids for various things, and when they had finished he found one cloth missing, and believed it was this man who took it. He caught hold of him, but he denied having it, and went inside a house saying 'come inside and get it', which the Arab feared to do, so he took instead the man's bicycle, and wheeled it to the police and made a complaint (he had to ask the way); when the case proceeded the three other men were called as witnesses but had by then disappeared; the bicycle was said by the man to belong to a police askari, a relation-in-law of his, but the police suspected it to be black market; finally they looked into the man's antecedents, and he admitted that he had once been up for brawling, and when he was then charged he was acquitted but convicted on another charge of having failed to pay tax, and imprisoned for three months; this statement was checked by the police who found that he had in fact three previous convictions, under two different names, in Dar es Salaam, in the Resident Magistrate's court, and at Bagamoyo. Accused pointed out that if he had no evidence to rebut the charge, neither had the Arab to confirm *his* statements. In the end it turned out the cycle was his after all.

Escape from responsibility and from the surveillance of authority, is one of the great attractions of town life. The payment of tax, which though only a matter of 20 Shs. per annum or 8d. in the £ on the lowest annual wage before the imposition of the minimum wage, is irksome—like any tax—is far more easily avoided in a town where there can be no possibility of keeping registers up to date; where it is estimated from a sample taken in this survey that a quarter of the younger people move house every three to four months; and where there is no pass or registration system or any restrictions or check on movement in or out of town. In such circumstances the only way to enforce the payment of tax, voluntary payment having failed to bring in a reasonable proportion, is by tax drives, a suburb at a time, wherein messengers, Jumbes, some police, and lately a sort of local special police formed from residents of the area block roads and ask all comers for evidence of payment. To the determined even these drives are not difficult to avoid, as they cannot be done all at once and any road has half a dozen detours. Where avoidance of tax becomes a game which all play, as is the avoidance of customs duty in most countries, there is encouraged an extension of the spiv mentality which is dormant in all of us. When to this is added the many restrictions in town—petty laws which have no backing in public opinion and which, therefore, it is fair game to break— there is built up that carelessness of petty crime which became apparent in England in the days of rationing. Every hawker should have a licence (and the number is restricted) but few except professional hawkers would consider taking one out: the casual pedlars of a few coconuts or oranges, of sweet beer or fish, seldom bother to comply with the law. There is a good deal of illicit drinking as a result of the few remaining restrictions; for the popular *pombe* or grain beer can be legally obtained only in one place, the Msimbazi *pombe* market, and nowhere else; as a result it is brewed in many other places, mainly just outside the Municipality, and sold clandestinely within (there appears to be no reason for the restriction other than that the Municipality, which wishes to turn the profits to be made from *pombe* to good account, has for long been intending to build its own additional *pombe* markets, but has not found the opportunity to do so); Western-style beer, spirits, and palm-wine (*tembo*) can be legally purchased from any licensed bar or retailer, but *moshi*, a particularly raw brand, is illegal, and so the places which sell it have to be sure of their customers, who must be introduced by a known contact, and the brew is drunk in secrecy—even if it is in fact a very open secret. There is also a fair sale of legal liquor but in unlicensed premises.

'People buy cases of beer or spirits from beer stores and sell them at 2 Shs. a bottle of beer or 7 Shs. 50 cents a half-bottle of spirits. These people run their business mainly after midnight when all the licensed bars are closed. When I asked why they were charging 2 Shs. for beer, which is the bar price, I was told that if these people were caught by the police they would have to pay a heavy fine, so they had to charge higher just in case they are caught. But if they are surprised the seller is always ready with the excuse that he was only throwing a party for his friends.

'Zachariah has a friend Abdallah, so he arranged with him to get a bottle of *moshi*. One evening we went to Abdallah's place and found a whisky bottle full of *moshi* It cost 6 Shs. I was told that a dealer buys it from outside the town at about 4 Shs. a bottle and resells it in town for 6 Shs. The seller sells this drink only to somebody he knows; so people who are not well known must contact one of his regular customers and ask him to get a bottle. There were three men with us, and a woman, and they were drinking it neat. Usually people drink it mixed with either beer or soda, though some Indians have it with Coca-Cola. While we were drinking an Indian came to the door and asked for a bottle: Abdallah went out and came back after half an hour to say that the stuff was sold out.'

Compared to the severe restrictions in other East African towns those in Dar es Salaam are not onerous, consisting merely of a prohibition on *moshi* and restrictions of selling hours: but none the less the restrictions have bred contraventions, as they must do in any society where they are not backed by public opinion, and the prevalence of such petty contraventions all contributes to the 'spiv' mentality.

Another restriction honoured in the breach is that on new building in the Village areas, such as Buguruni, Msasani and the Kekos; this dates back to the end of the period of great housing shortage during which so many of these villages had sprung up. In 1950 a register was made of all the then existing houses, whose building was then condoned on the condition that no further building took place. Each house was given a number, painted boldly on the door, to ensure that any new house was easily identified. But inspection was not frequent enough, or thorough enough, to stop building, and by the time a count was made by this survey, early in 1956, no less than 154 new houses had been built; fortunately these were roughly balanced by demolitions. Many ruses have been thought out to evade the restriction: some had duplicated existing numbers —which do not run in straight lines—others had invented some highly improbable ones; some had brought with them numbers from another village which had been demolished in the course of slum clearance; in another case a man had bought a numbered door from a disused hut, intending to build himself a new house into which it would be fitted, but meanwhile another man had rebuilt the hut on the same site and used the old number, and painted it on a new door. As there is no local village organization to sort out where and when a man may build, it remains in the hands of a distant department of the Municipality, and public opinion sees no reason why anybody who is willing to take the risk should not go ahead.

Pitches of 'find-the-lady' are also illegal though a feature of the everyday scene; at any strategic street corner where the men returning from work will pass these pitches are to be found: again the general view is that they do no harm and the law is ignored.

'Settled men'

Who should be forming the public opinion which is so conspicuously not on the side of enforcement of all these regulations?

In the country community opinion is formed by the consensus of elders (among whom are to be counted the Chiefs and others in authority); in early Dar es Salaam this must also have been the case, the elders of each tribal group setting the tone and being automatically consulted by both their juniors and the authorities. To a large extent it is so today, particularly in the more rural and village areas where the power of the elders is more or less intact. These elders who wield influence are not merely older than their fellows, they are also longer-resident. As has been shown, in such villages as Buguruni and Msasani the first settlers and their descendants still wield considerable influence, so that leaders cannot be selected from the village without their being consulted.

Whether long-resident or not, and whether young or old, a house-owner also has standing in the community; he knows where he is, and so do the authorities; he has some power over his tenants, if not of control, at any rate of letting or evicting; he has a steady income, and a secure future.

A man with many relations, junior to himself, is also a man of standing: if he has wisdom too, he is an important man; some define that difficult word 'importance' as being the state of having one's advice sought after.

Others have influence in their own spheres: the religious man among those disposed to respect the awe of religion; the bold man among the lot of those disposed to admire strength and daring; the successful man among those who regard success with admiration rather than malicious envy. The educated or the eloquent each in his own circle forms and guides opinion. Personality plays its universal yet unclassifiable part. Some come and others go. In the end opinion, the steady, underlying public opinion, or public morals, is formed and guided by those who are always there: the settled men.

Who are these 'settled men'?

The growth of the African population of Dar es Salaam though at a slowing rate, has been rapid:

		Average annual increase
Aug. 1947–Feb. 1952 (3½ years):	23,000	9,200
Feb. 1952–Aug. 1957 (5½ years):	19,000	5,530

The rate of further increase will depend on the continued growth of the port, trade and industry. Here it is well to remember that employment for the African population depends to a significant extent, not on the level of trade but on the active growth of the town, since much of the employment of Africans to date has been supplied by the construction industry.

Assuming, however, a further growth in the population, probably at a much reduced rate, what effects may be expected on the nature of that population as a whole? There are always some who stay and begin to form a nucleus who may be described as 'citizens of Dar es Salaam' rather than immigrants from such and such a District. As the town grows, so will the nucleus, by accumulation, even if it does not grow in proportion to the whole.

When we speak of a settled urban population we tend to think only of those who have no other home: those born and bred here, such as the Manyema and the Nubi, whose original homes in the Congo and the 'Sudan' now mean nothing to them, who never visit there to see relatives, or even remember the names of the original villages or the language which they used to speak. Others fall almost into the same class: some of the early Yao and Ngoni families who came in German times and settled here, and have no desire to return, though they still have their links with relatives, whom they receive on their visits to Dar es Salaam.

After them are a class who, though born and bred in Dar es Salaam, still retain strong links with home, visiting every so often, perhaps marrying a girl from the home village, educating a child of a relative here in Dar es Salaam, receiving presents of food and sending presents of clothes, sugar and tea. These may be of any tribe, but among those of whose members many were born and bred here, are the Yao, the Nyasa, and the coastal tribes, Zaramo, Ndengereko and Matumbi.

Others though not born here are of the same type of settled citizen, living here 'for life' and with no intention of moving permanently away. They too will probably bring up their children in Dar es Salaam: in very many cases they spent their own childhood here.

The last of the classes which may be roughly called 'settled' are the 'border-men', living in the rural fringes of the Municipality: most of these are of course Zaramo-born.

They do not move much, anchored as they generally are to a particular plot of cultivation; and though their numbers are continually being reinforced by the arrival behind them from the country of others like themselves there is also a stream of desertions, particularly from among their children, for whom the gravitational pull of the city life is not balanced by a strong desire to 'stay rural'.

The above four classes: the man who has no other home; the Dar es Salaam-born retaining strong links with his place of origin; the similar man from outside, with strong links with his old home, but no intention of permanently leaving Dar es

Salaam; and the border-man; are all settled in the sense that they intend to end their days here; the border-man, however, cannot truly be called urbanized, and to the extent that he or his children become urbanized they must drift into one of the other classes. Beyond them are those who, although they may spend very considerable periods of time in Dar es Salaam, never regard it as Home, nor expect to end their days in it: these are of four main kinds:

1. The career-man: he is a very different man from any of the preceding; he was born and brought up elsewhere, learned a trade, or attained to a grade of education sufficient to get him a steady job, and came to Dar es Salaam in search of the best market for his talents. He will stay here for the duration of his working life, either—as one class do—bringing his wife and children to live with him as a self-contained unit of the type that is supposed to be the ideal, and making periodic visits home on leave, ending with retirement and the cutting off of his ties with the town; or leaving them at home, keeping open his claim to land in his home country, perhaps tending some cash crops, and bringing up his children in the atmosphere of his home country.

2. A second type of less settled inhabitant of Dar es Salaam may be called the 'spender': he is the man who comes in order to get on to a cash economy, to get money in order to spend it then and there in town; he belongs mainly to the coastal tribes, and comes mainly from the south and near west; as he enjoys the cash life, with all its difficulties and frustrations, he comes back again and again, and may spend all his working life in Dar es Salaam, but with frequent spells at home; he too probably leaves his wife and children at home, tending the crops, knowing that it will not be long before he sees them again: indeed, they will probably visit him in town at fairly frequent intervals.

3. A second class of 'spender' does not fundamentally like the cash life, but being attracted to it like the former class he comes, does one or two tours of work in town, tires of it and does not return; to this class may be assigned those who never make good and, when the small savings they came with are gone, have to limp home.

4. Finally there are the least settled: the 'target-men' who

never wanted to live in a town, but needed something which the town alone could give, whether it was a skill to which he apprenticed himself, staying as many as ten years, or a sum of money to buy bridewealth, or a bicycle or a house.

To recognize the types is not difficult: to measure what proportion of the population falls into each is. Almost the only sample tested in which a majority admitted to liking the life in town was a sample of 50 children; their elders almost to a man denied any liking for the urban as opposed to the country life: yet here they are, in ever-increasing numbers. Similarly to attempt by a direct question to discover a man's intention to stay or to return home is usually to invite a meaningless answer, for so often he himself has no idea: one such answer, 'Until things get too much for me', is probably about as near as he can get. But there are a few concrete facts which bear on the matter: first is the plain one, whether he or she was born in Dar es Salaam: here the statistics show that a high proportion (though still just less than half) of those who live in the Rural areas of Dar es Salaam were born in Dar es Salaam; the figures also show how in each housing type the proportion of females born in Dar es Salaam is greater than that of the males; a table, below, shows how the areas of town vary in this respect, partly because of the greater or smaller proportion of Rural housing in them, but also because of the differing ages of the suburbs themselves:

	Percentage born in Dar es Salaam	
	Males	Females
Kariakoo/Kisutu	28	39
Ilala/Buguruni	23	31
Magomeni	17	31
Temeke	33	36
Kinondoni/Msasani	24	30

The low figure for Magomeni males is partly due to the inclusion in this area of a large number of 'career-men' housed in the 644 units of Quarters there; the high figures for Temeke, despite a similar inclusion of a (smaller) number of Quarters, are due both to a solid block of Rural housing from Kipawa to the Industrial Estate and along the river line to Mtoni; and to a high figure in the Swahili parts of Temeke: much of this is to be attributed to the engulfing by this recently town-planned area of the original fairly close rural settlement there, very many of whom took up the offer of a priority for a building plot in what is now the Swahili area; many of these are virtually unchanged from their former Rural status, their houses though on a surveyed plot being the same low-roofed, two-roomed rural huts, and their standby a bit of land nearby; though now classed as Swahili for housing, they are still 'border-men' at heart, settled but unurbanized.

From a tribal breakdown, it is clear that the Luguru and Pogoro provide few indeed of the classes that are born and bred in Dar es Salaam; but that does not mean that they are less settled: for it is the established custom of the Luguru, for instance, that a wife who becomes pregnant in Dar es Salaam is sent home to bear her child there: hence many of those 'born elsewhere' may have been in Morogoro District for little more than the time it took for their mothers to bear the child and prepare for the world again, and thereafter many of them may have been steady citizens of Dar es Salaam; in fact most Luguru would fall into the third class, that of persons retaining strong links with their village of origin, but otherwise permanent in town, except for being technically 'born elsewhere'.

The breakdown includes, in the Zaramo total, many of the 'border-men'. The Zaramo and others of the coastal tribes have also many of the second class, who were born and bred in town but still retain strong links with the country village from which their family originated.

Another point at which the 'settledness' of a man may be tested is the length of his residence in Dar es Salaam. As explained above residence may be continuous, as of the class of those who have no other home; or of those who have no other permanent home but make periodic short visits to the village of their origin; or those who go home on 'leave' every two or three years, or those who retire home for periodic rest periods before another bout of making and spending money, the period of residence is not continuous, and one must attempt to assess the frequency of their absences and their length. For the classes of border-men residence is likely to be continuous, their visits away being of a day or so only, to nearby friends,

s

since they have not really left their rural environs and, therefore, have no need to make distant visits; the target-men will normally have continuous residence during the period of their contract, but in a number of cases, where they have found the work to their liking, or the sum resulting requires to be increased, they go home for a short visit and return for another contract; similarly some of the apprentice type of target-men on 'passing out' go home for a visit to arrange their affairs and marry a wife, and then return to Dar es Salaam as career men.

Of all males, 57 per cent. were found to have resided, more or less continuously, for six or more years, the rest being spread fairly evenly over shorter periods. Certain suburbs showed rather higher figures, such as 60 per cent. in Ilala, which reflects the fact that both in the Swahili part and in Buguruni —particularly the latter—the Zaramo form a large proportion of the population (in Buguruni 68 per cent. compared with 40 per cent. in the areas surveyed as a whole); these Zaramo are part border-men and part settled people with strong links with outside but no present intention of moving out; the figure for Ilala would be higher still were it not counterbalanced by a low figure for the career-men of Ilala Quarters; for the figure— of those with six or more years' residence—for the Quarters was only 36 per cent. with that for Rural houses at the other extreme of 64 per cent.

Many of those who inhabit the Quarters, clerks and artisans, are in the career-man class, but the growth of Dar es Salaam has been so recent that many of them are still, as it were, in their first tour; the high figure for Rural again reflects the border-men living on the fringes of town.

A tribal breakdown shows which tribes are mainly composed of career men: the Pogoro and the Makonde (many of whom, however, are target men, working on contract on construction, or in the one sisal estate inside the Municipality). The Nyamwezi with the lowest proportion of all for long residence, and the rest spread evenly over all shorter lengths of residence show up as the type which comes for one or two tours and then returns—part target worker and part agriculturalist: for they very often take a plot a little outside town while the man goes to pick cloves or get a job in town, and they will work and cultivate until they have enough to return home. This is a pattern which one may see repeated in Zanzibar.

But as explained above residence by itself is a crude and misleading measurement of settledness: for it does not even measure continuity of residence; an attempt was, therefore, made to measure the breaks in continuity of residence, and their duration; two questions were asked: 'Did you in the course of the past three years spend a month or more out of Dar es Salaam?' (This question was of course put only to those with three years' residence or more.) And: 'Did you ever in all your residence in Dar es Salaam spend a year or more away?' The results varied quite considerably according to the suburb in which the sample lived (see table below).

	Visit away one month in last three years (per cent.)		Visit away one year ever (per cent.)	
	Male	Female	Male	Female
Overall mean	25	28	8	8
Kariakoo	24	29	7	8
Ilala	28	40	8	9
Magomeni	35	28	13	10
Temeke	25	25	8	9
Kinondoni/Msasani	26	26	13	7

The distinctive figure for Ilala, which can be traced to even more distinctive figures for 'Ilala Village', which is Buguruni, gives an opportunity for trying to combine more than one set of figures.

Buguruni thus has figures for visits of one month of 34 per cent. for males and 52 per cent. for females; it also has figures for residence which though closely conforming to the mean for males, shows a much greater spread for females over the periods of shorter residence; finally Buguruni is an area where 68 per cent. of the population is Zaramo. It does, therefore, appear that while the womenfolk pay extended visits home, probably for planting, harvest, and for childbirth, the men tend to stay on; and this confirms what is generally supposed. This pattern does not show up in the Zaramo figures as a whole.

The second question, 'Have you ever spent a year or more away?' is intended to isolate those who came as spenders, stuck it as long as they could, and then went away to recuperate, coming back much later for a second attempt; those who make such long visits away should not include career men (who would lose their jobs if they did so; except those who were transferred elsewhere for a tour) but might include some target men who came back for a second contract after having spent their gains from the first. It will be seen that they live mainly in Magomeni and in Kinondoni/Msasani: a closer look at these two areas shows that they live for the most part in the Swahili area of Magomeni, and also in the small village called Magomeni kwa Hanna, and in the Rural area of Kinondoni/Msasani; yet when the house-types table is consulted it is Village which has the highest figure, due again to Buguruni, with some help from Magomeni kwa Hanna. Turning then to the tribal breakdown, one finds Nyasa, Ndengereko and Mwera as the highest scorers, with Rufiji not far behind. The Nyasa are here odd company, for they are not on the whole spenders, but career men or target men; their appearance in this galley is perhaps due to the distance to their homes, which makes short visits there uneconomic; otherwise the figures go to confirm the picture drawn earlier of a coastal type of spender.

It is already clear that there can be no question of measuring accurately the degree of settledness of a particular person or group: all that can be done is to take soundings at certain points, hoping that they are critical points which will give a true indication of the outline in between. Another of these soundings is the figure for houses owned: but first it must be pointed out that to own a house does not necessarily denote wealth or even permanence; for on the Rural outskirts the houses are often little one- or two-roomed huts set in rice-fields, requiring no capital to build and acting hardly at all as an anchor to make a man stay. The big Swahili houses are certainly proof of a certain success in coping with life in town, and (although many do not live in them but appoint an agent while they retire to the country) they act as an anchor to keep most of the owners permanently in town, except for occasional visits to relatives in the country. In the Village areas the house may be of either type. Some of the older ones, much renewed, are owned by some of the most permanent inhabitants of Dar es Salaam, the Nubi, the Shirazi and the coconut-owning Zaramo; some on the other hand are shanties thrown up overnight by labouring immigrants in the immediate post-war period, which have changed hands many times since then. With these provisos then, the figures are as follows:

| | Percentage owning | | | |
	1 House	2 Houses	More	Nil
Mean	18	1	—	81
Kariakoo	8	1	—	90
Ilala	13	1	—	85
Magomeni	17	1	—	81
Temeke	37	2	1	60
Kin./Msasani	30	2	—	68

At first sight this table seems to suggest that there are more persons, liable to be permanently settled through the ownership of a house, in the new suburbs of Temeke and Kinondoni, and the Village of Msasani with its mixture of old fishing village and new shanty town.

But both Temeke and Kinondoni contain large areas of Rural houses (where three-quarters of heads of households owned the houses they lived in). In the Village areas too there is a high proportion of house-owners (nearly a quarter as opposed to an eighth in the Swahili areas). Nevertheless Temeke, with a third of its Swahili population housed in their own houses, has a very much higher proportion than the rest; in the new plots at Kinondoni the proportion is much lower, only a ninth. The tribal tables give the Manyema, Nyasa and Makonde as having the most house-owners in proportion, though of course the Zaramo own most absolutely.

Even the high figure for house-owners in the Swahili areas of Temeke must be looked at askance: for in this town-planned suburb it is not really a concentration of owner-occupiers that the figures show but a lack of tenants: all the houses except those of persons evicted from Gerezani and Makaburi were built for letting—the same big six-roomed affairs that one sees in central Kariakoo and other good letting areas—but the tenants have up to now just not been forthcoming; so the community of house-owners will, if the docks proceed far enough in their direction and the owners have their way, be filled out eventually to a proportion nearer the mean.

One further sounding may be made, by studying those persons who are aged over 45, for there are few who begin a career after that age. These older people are, as one might expect, from the classes which have no other home or who, though with links outside, are permanently settled in Dar es Salaam. Outstanding among them are the Manyema, who have no less than 31 per cent. of their men in this age-group (the mean of all tribes is 6·5 per cent.); next, with 16 per cent., come the Makonde (these are of course not the Makonde who are target men, but the other Makonde who are very old inhabitants—for this tribe has a clear-cut division between the two, usually made obvious by the facial markings which the target men display) followed by the Yao with 14 per cent. and the Ngindo with 11: the Ngindo are for the most part coastal spenders like the Rufiji and Ndengereko, but some families date back a long way (Ngindo were among the first slaves to be brought up by Seiyid Majid to clear the bush for his coconut plantations in Dar es Salaam).

Is it a sign of being settled to have one's wife and family in town? Many career men do not, though in other ways they are perhaps the more desirable elements in town, with their comparatively moral ways, steady mode of life and ambition to improve their standard of living. Many who do are young men from the south who have made enough on their first 'tour' to marry a girl and bring her up to town; but they have no intention of permanently settling in Dar es Salaam. For what they disclose, here are the figures of households comprising a man, his wife and children and perhaps a relative (households of a man and wife only are excluded since they include so many casual liaisons), see table opposite.

It is noticeable that the Manyema, who top the list of those with old people, and many of whom are known to have no other home, come only half-way down this list, slightly below the average; while the Makonde head it; the Yao are well down but the Ngindo are towards the top. There appears to be no connexion between the two lists. Once again Buguruni is responsible for the high Ilala figure, and at least part of the Village figure, for Buguruni rates at 48 per cent. Is there a clue here—that Buguruni, with its many two- and three-room houses and the absence of effective restrictions on adding a room when required, gives a chance to the family man to build a small house in a position central enough for working in the town? Are these the people likely to stay and bring up their children in Dar es Salaam? Yet there is no higher a proportion in Buguruni than elsewhere of people who own their own house. These families, like the families elsewhere in town, are mostly (71 per cent.) payers of rent; they are able to have two rooms no more often than those in other areas, even though the level of rents is lower.

Mean: 39 per cent.

By area (per cent.)		By house-type (per cent.)		By tribe (per cent.)	
Kariakoo	34	Swahili	37	Makonde	56
Ilala	44	Quarters	73	Nyasa	47
Magomeni	41	Village	43	Zaramo	46
Temeke	38	Rural	38	Ngindo	41
Kin/Msasani	39			Rufiji	39
				Nyamwezi	39
				Manyema	38
				Matumbi	34
				Ngoni	34
				Pogoro	33
				Ndengereko	32
				Yao	31
				'Others'	31
				Luguru	30
				Mwera	20

The dangers of attempting to measure to what extent people are settled in town are evident from the foregoing discussion; yet the only way in which it may be judged whether as time passes the core of the town is increasing is to put some numerical values, however crude, to what seem to be the main indicators of 'settledness', in order that a later survey may, using the same indicators, make a numerical comparison. The material with which this can be done is available.[1] A suggested set of formulae to describe the various classes has been outlined. Their crudeness is immediately apparent, and particularly the weakness of the ill-defined term 'wife' in such calculations; but

[1] In the statistical tables omitted from this edition.

it is hoped that the repetition of the same questions, with refinements, may shed in time some light on this vital question.

INTERLUDE

Some of the settled ones

An old-timer

He was born well before the Majimaji rebellion, in a time of African tribal warfare known as the Mafite war. He is a Muslim. In his youth he served as a cook to the Germans and he visited very many places including Mbeya, Iringa, Nyasaland and Rhodesia. He married eight times and got six children, all sons, all but two of whom are dead. Now he lives in his own house in Kariakoo with two wives. He himself was an only son.

This is his only house and one of the unimproved type with no modern facilities save a rusty iron roof which only adds to the untidiness. Apparently they cook inside, for the rafters are smoky. It was built a long time ago. Recently he has built a latrine and soakaway, the former with two doors, one for Gents and one for Ladies.

In the main house are five rooms, two of which he uses himself (one wife in each), the rest being let at 15 Shs. per month. All his tenants are Africans but he would prefer, if his house was of better type, to have Indians or Arabs as they pay higher rents. His tenants all pay their rent regularly. There is also a three-room courtyard hut, two rooms being occupied by tenants paying 10 Shs. each, the third room used as a kitchen.

He also has a plantation of coconuts, cashew and mangoes at Mbagala, just outside the Municipal boundary: a relative looks after it for him.

He says he has never been a Ward councillor nor would he like to be as he is afraid of being bewitched.

He is literate.

His income is about 100 Shs. per month. Some of this comes from the profits of one of his wives' trade, selling firewood, and some from his own trade, buying fish from the fishermen and selling it retail.

A landlady

She is a Luguru born in Morogoro. She came here when she was very young, with her mother, after the latter had been divorced by her father. She was their only child. Her father took another wife and had five children by that one, three boys and two girls: all are alive in Morogoro. Her parents are now dead. She herself married twice. Her first husband divorced her but her second died. She bore no child.

She is illiterate: when she was young she hated going to school and always escaped the teachers and made her way to various dances, of which she was very fond.

She inherited her house from her mother. It has never fallen down but she has put in improvements: she has cemented the floors, plastered the walls, and roofed it with kerosene tins since inheriting it. She does not remember the cost. It now has six rooms, four let to tenants at 25 Shs. each, one used by herself and one reserved for guests. Her tenants are all Lugurus, and she would not like to have Indians or Arabs, as they are not helpful in time of adversity. Her tenants do not pay very regularly but they are very faithful, and will always make sure of making up the debt at some time or another. They are all nice fellows except one who is a bit of a nuisance, especially when he is drunk. He is very fond of slamming the door and disturbing everyone's rest. He is all right when not drunk.

There is a nice courtyard hut with cement floor and tin roof with two rooms which are both occupied by relatives. There is one latrine and a kitchen which is used by all.

She has no trade or plantation. She usually goes to Morogoro during the harvesting time and gets food from there. She normally eats three meals a day, cooking them herself. Her only source of income is the rent: 100 Shs. per month.

A Yao

He is now middle-aged. He is a Yao and left Nyasaland in 1923 for Songea, where he went to school up to Standard 6. He learned a bit of English, and arrived in Dar es Salaam in 1928. Here he stayed with his aunt in Kisutu up to 1948.

First he worked as a clerk, then as telephone operator in the then 'European Hospital'; finally he became a linesman inspector in the Posts and Telegraphs. Now he runs his own trade, selling charcoal in Kariakoo and firewood in Temeke.

He married in 1947 and now has two boys and a girl. His father married five wives but he is the sole child of his mother. He doesn't remember how many children his father had as it is a long time ago and he has quite lost touch with his family.

The house has modern conveniences but is old-fashioned: the walls are low and the roof of flattened kerosene tins; there are six rooms, four of which he uses himself, and the others are let at 40 Shs. per month each to an Indian tenant. He likes him because he pays very regularly. He does not like Arabs who are very troublesome. He asks new tenants their salary before he lets a room.

He has three other houses, one at Magomeni, another in Kariakoo, and one in Kisutu. He has no fields. He keeps accounts.

He will always be in Dar es Salaam: his children are studying at the Jumuiyyat al Islamiya. There is a mosque built by his aunt and he goes there very frequently.

He has four meals a day.

A Zaramo

He built this house in Ilala himself, having saved enough from his trade, a casual seller of cooked cassava and cow's-foot soup (*makongoro*). He built it in 1950. He cannot say how much it cost, as he built it in stages. It is his only house in town. He uses two rooms for himself, his wife and their five children, and lets the remaining four at 20 Shs. per month. He prefers African tenants as Arabs and Indians he thinks are tricky and if one is not careful one may lose one's house. An African tenant is also easier to understand and more ready to help in times of distress.

His children will inherit the property. He will always be in Dar es Salaam. He came originally from Masaki to get a job, and worked as cook, laundryman, etc., until eventually he started up in his own business as a trader. He occasionally goes home to Masaki to cultivate for two or three months and comes back to town. He keeps up his trade of cooked cassava and soup.

He reckons to control his tenants, and does not mind if they are married or not. The only thing he is careful of is drunkards, whom he dislikes. He takes care that his tenants are in regular employment so that he can be sure of his rent. The only Christian he had he had to get rid of.

A strict landlord

He built the house himself, in Ilala, out of the savings he put away while working in a carpentry shop for a Greek. It cost about 4,000 Shs. He himself uses the courtyard rooms and lets three front rooms and a veranda to an Arab for 100 Shs. per month and the other three rooms to Africans at 25 Shs. per month each. He prefers an Arab or Indian as tenant as they pay their rent without difficulty.

He was elected to serve as a Ward Councillor but refused as he devotes most of his time to religion. He has three children and they will inherit the house. He will live always in Dar es Salaam, though he came from Kinondoni (he is a Makonde): he first came as an employee in the Usagara Company, and after the first war decided to remain here, doing odd jobs and eventually joining the Greek workshop. He has left this now, and is a cultivator, with two wives.

He thinks he can control his tenants: when a room falls vacant he asks applicants where they are from, where they work, whether they have paid tax and why they left their previous lodgings. Christians, he says, are very good tenants, but Arabs are not, apart from paying their rent regularly. They are not good Samaritans.

A retired fisherman

He came up here from Kilwa with his father, who was also a fisherman, and he liked it here and stayed. He sent for his aunt, who is his only relative. He also has five children, and they all live in three rooms in this house in Ilala, which he built in 1947 for 2,900 Shs. out of his savings from fishing. He lets the other three rooms at 20 Shs. per month.

He has never heard of Ward Councils. He does not fish now, and subsists on his rents and a little small trade. He likes to have as tenants people from his own part of the country.

A barmaid who made good

She is an Ngoni, born in Tabora. She went to primary school but left at Standard 3, though she can now read, and likes to scan *Mwangaza*. Her mother is still alive in Tabora, her father dead. She lives with an adopted child and a cousin in her house in Kariakoo, which she bought in 1945 for 1,200 Shs. After her two marriages she had no desire to marry again, and preferred to see something of the world; so she left Tabora and went to Ifakara where she had relatives. Finding no future there she came to Dar es Salaam and stayed with another relative while she worked as barmaid. Ultimately she left this and began to brew beer herself, thus saving enough money to buy this house. She has since put in a lot of improvements and it is now in fair shape. She uses all but two rooms for her little family and relatives, who live free, and she keeps one spare for guests. One of her tenants is an African and one a half-caste, and both pay 30 Shs. a month. They are quiet people and she likes them. The half-caste is out of work at the moment and is three months behind with the rent. She cannot evict him as she sympathizes with him and moreover when in work he used to be a regular payer.

She has also a field of cassava on the Bagamoyo road, which she visits regularly; brewing beer brings in her main source of income, but she says she does not save much as she has many dependants as well as improving the house. Even if she had plenty of money she would not think of opening a bank account because she says that in time of war most of the banks become bankrupt and one loses one's money.

Politics

It should be understood from the first that African Dar es Salaam is almost 100 per cent. a Tanganyika African National Union (TANU) town. The presence in it of the territorial headquarters—a rather broken-down Swahili house of mud and wattle, with peeling plaster and a little whitewash, divided inside into some seven small offices—and, much more important, the presence in Dar es Salaam for much of the time of the President, Mr. Nyerere, and the holding from time to time of mass meetings addressed by him, ensure that politics hold a most important place in men's minds. Earlier in this description the antidotes to loneliness were discussed, and the increasing or decreasing influence of tribal group, or tribe, family, village, house and club; but today all these are subordinate to the most binding force of all: nationalism. When the survey began, in February 1956, it was possible for a European to walk the back streets and talk with people, and to find that their greatest suspicion was that he might be a 'Government' man interested in the collection of tax, or a Municipal building inspector investigating illegal house-building; some thought he was part of the Criminal Investigation Department. But by 1957 there was only one thought—that he was a recruiter for the United Tanganyika Party (UTP). From the appearance of UTP as a serious opponent of TANU, and the widespread belief that it was endorsed by Government, the work of the survey in Dar es Salaam became progressively more difficult. By November 1957 the intensity of suspicion, ultimately of UTP, but through it of Government, all of whose officers were popularly supposed to be *ex officio* supporters of, and recruiters for, it, had so grown that when elders of several of the leading tribes were asked to answer questions on tribal custom, and the early history of Dar es Salaam, all but three made excuses; even elders of such tribes as the Chagga, whom a long effort was made to interview, through an assistant who was himself a Chagga, continued to make one excuse after another until the assistant saw that it was useless to press them further. When informants were paid, as some were, in many cases they refused to take the money, if there were witnesses, for fear that they were taking UTP money. When a photograph was to be taken, even by a member of the

Administration, people made excuses for fear—as they explained
—that the photograph might be hung up in UTP headquarters
to prove that they were members. During 1957 intense suspicion
of Government as being behind UTP was steadily growing.

An Assistant who was an African Officer of the Social
Development Department was interviewing some women:

'She answered the first two questions; but when I started
asking her more questions the other women became suspicious
and asked me whether I was a TANU member or UTP. I said
I was neither and they remained so suspicious that I did not
pursue the conversation.'

At the docks:

'I met another dock worker, a Zaramo. I tried to put some
questions to him, but he would not answer when he knew that
I was not a member of TANU.'

The elders of some villages used to be invited once a month
to take tea and discuss life in town: in Kinondoni these meetings
took place in the school; after the first one the head teacher
was approached and asked if I was a recruiter from UTP.
At Buguruni, after the first such meeting the local tea-shop
refused to sell the tea (they said it was 'spoiled') and the elders
sat dumb for fear of appearing to give any support to the
meeting, which all assumed to be UTP-inspired. In Kipawa I
was asked to write down my name and department, and the
piece of paper was then taken to Mr. John Rupia for clearing
with TANU.

Any African who was a supporter of UTP—and there were
very few in Dar es Salaam (the UTP has since been dissolved)—
would, it is true, have a lot to put up with: ostracism by all
Africans, abuse in the streets from small children, chalked
slogans on his house: but it would be self-deception to suppose
that it is fear of intimidation which makes all the African
population TANU. On the contrary TANU is the lodestone
to which are attracted many different types of men: the
traditional elders of the hamlets and the tribes, except those
few who are so committed to Government that they cannot
detach themselves; the house-owners and the long-residents—
the staid core of conservative society; the artisans and clerks,
the educated; and the drifting mass of unskilled and semi-
skilled who make up the bulk of the population. The last class

provide the hooligans who are as apt to political intimidation as they are to tax evasion, petty thieving or any other town nuisance: but they are only conforming to the norm, and they are neither more nor less loyal to TANU than the more reputable sections of society.

Many signs can be observed of the hold which TANU has on the Dar es Salaam population, even to the extent of restraining the hooligan element: the writer was in the crowd when Mr. Julius Nyerere made his entry on return from New York in 1957, and when they engulfed the car one or two in high spirits began to drum on the sides: at once one of the organizers appeared, apologized for the ill manners, and stood in front of the car directing the crowd to either side. When the hooligan fringe, calling themselves the Bantu, began to attack all Sheikhs (because one was a member of UTP) they were called to order and for a time disappeared from the scene. For a time TANU opposed the classes for women at the Arnautoglu Community Centre, hoping to organize something of the sort themselves, but when they reversed this policy and gave their backing to the Arnautoglu classes, they filled overnight.

It will be noticed that, while the tendency of the crowd, undirected, is to go off the rails, with intimidation, rudeness and hooliganism, the direction when it appears is on the side of correct behaviour: the top leaders of TANU in Dar es Salaam (where alone it comes under their direct eye—and even there to a perhaps limited extent) are desperately anxious to prove themselves on the side of the angels, able to control the mob, and to show themselves responsible and disciplined. This desire could be a potent instrument, not only for law and order (where there is the difficulty that the reins could not in any way be handed over, only their co-operation sought) but in the field of social and educational development; the schools are even now an eighth empty: it is believed that TANU could fill them. Their influence in women's adult education has already been shown. In other ways much assistance to Government could be given: were they not almost by definition opposed to Government.

It is helpful to any political party to be 'agin the Government'. Many of the things which any administration must do are unpopular, and he who opposes can reap an equivalent popularity. An opposition must gain by being attacked, both in solidarity of its followers and in a clearer definition of its own identity. Where there are unpopular things to be done, it will gain by being able to dissociate itself from them. Where there is misunderstanding of Government's aims, an opposition that is boycotted at all levels is relieved of the responsibility of helping to explain them. But where the strains inherent in the difficulties of town life, as described in this survey, remain to be resolved, the co-operation of a strong nationalist movement can be a most potent ally in the real and continuing struggle for better living.

INTERLUDE

In one of the main streets a photographer's shop carries in the window an epitome of the struggle within the modern African: a photograph of a member of a current association, dressed in a toga-like cloth, one shoulder bare, as symbol of his rejection of all things foreign and Western and his cleaving to the world of his ancestors; and in his lap—a brief-case, the accepted symbol today of organizing ability: that he could not reject.

APPENDIX A

FULL LIST OF TRIBES FOUND IN THE 1956 SURVEY
(In order of numerical importance)

1. Zaramo
2. Rufiji
3. Luguru
4. Ndengereko
5. Indian
6. Ngindo
7. Arab
8. Nyamwezi
9. Yao
10. Mwera
11. Matumbi
12. Ngoni
13. Pogoro
14. Nyasa
15. Manyema
16. Makonde
17. Hehe
18. Zigua
19. Mbunga
20. Kutu
21. Nyagatwa
22. Haya
23. Sukuma
24. Makua
25. Kami
26. Shirazi
27. Chagga
28. Wemba (Northern Rhodesia)
29. Mwere
30. Ganda
31. Iramba
32. Bondei
33. Luo
34. Nyakyusa
35. Sambaa

36. Sagara
37. Gogo
38. Kinga
39. Digo
40. Half-caste
41. Rangi
42. Sumbwa
43. Rundi
44. Fipa
45. Comorian
46. Bisa
47. Doe
48. Ndamba
49. Vidunda
50. Pare
51. Manda
52. Turu
53. Nubi
54. Tonga (Nyasa)
55. Rungu
56. Sangu
57. Tiriki (Kenya)
58. Gunya
59. Nyanza
60. Luhya
61. Bena
62. Somanga
63. Burungi
64. Ruanda
65. Nyamwanga
66. Segeju
67. Zulu
68. Tusi
69. Henga (Kenya)
70. Shasha

T

71. Kuria/Tende
72. Vira (Congo)
73. Maragoli (Kenya)
74. Wanji
75. Zita
76. Kamba (Kenya)
77. Machinga
78. Sudanese
79. Kimbu
80. Sandawe
81. Pimbwe
82. Tumbatu
83. Cheluzi
84. Coromanga
85. Holoholo
86. Kiki (Kenya)
87. Kerewe
88. Runga
89. Meru
90. Mambwe
91. Nguu
92. Ikalebwe (Congo)
93. Vinza
94. Pangwa
95. Safwa
96. Subi
97. Barawa
98. Teita
99. Bwani (Congo)
100. Kitosi (Kenya)

APPENDIX B

THE NON-AFRICANS

ALTHOUGH the survey was deliberately concentrated in the areas of Dar es Salaam which are mainly inhabited by Africans, it included such non-Africans as lived in those areas. Apart from a relatively small number of mixed blood (0·3 per cent. of the whole population surveyed), most of whom (94 per cent.) lived in Kariakoo, non-Africans were of two races, Indian and Arab. The Indians were confined entirely to Kariakoo; it was always the intention, when each new area was mapped out for low-standard dwellings, that it should be for Africans, free from the commercial competition of Indians and Arabs, in order to give the Africans a chance to launch into trade; this intention never got very far in Kariakoo, in which Indians have lived since the beginning (when what is now Mnazi Mmoja was a continuation of the Commercial Area, and was then cleared, some of the Indians it contained moving east and some west) and in the post-war period when housing of all kinds was very scarce many Indians rented African-owned houses in Kariakoo, and some gradually acquired the houses they lived in, or rebuilt them into the three- and four-story concrete constructions which can be seen now. The knowledge that they were living where they were not intended to live retarded this development, and it is only in recent years, when the Indian expansion into Kariakoo has ceased to be frowned on, that they have gone into the ownership of houses. This is still reflected in the figures, for only 2 per cent. of all Indian households in Kariakoo own a house. The same considerations did not affect Arabs, partly because 'they have always been here', and partly, particularly in the newly laid-out areas built from the Colonial Development and Welfare Fund (which assistance was in this case specifically allocated to Africans only), because for the purposes of the conveyancing of land and houses an Arab is included in the definition of a 'native'; as a result of this all shops in all the new areas are in the hands of Arabs (with whom Africans have been unable to compete), while not one is, overtly at least, in the hands of an Indian. Arabs lived almost all in Swahili houses, just over half of them in Kariakoo, a little under a quarter in Temeke and an eighth in Ilala.

An estimate of actual numbers may be obtained by reinflating the August 1956 5 per cent. sample figures, by multiplying by 20:

	August 1956	
	Indians	*Arabs*
Kariakoo	3,800	1,820
Ilala		440
Magomeni		100
Temeke		740
Kinondoni/Msasani		20
Total	3,800	3,120

It appears from the February 1952 census figures that in Kariakoo at least the Indian population has decreased while the Arabs have doubled in the past four and a half years.

	Indians	*Arabs*
February 1952	5,418	897
August 1956	3,800	1,820

The decrease in the numbers of Indians is due to a number of factors, but in the main to the building which has taken place in Upanga and the Sultan Street area of the Commercial Area, both of which were able to absorb large numbers. The decrease is mainly of adults, and of adult men in particular. The Goans, who in 1952 numbered 345 in Kariakoo, seem almost to have left entirely, for only one family turned up in the August 1956 survey, from which one may guess a total of 80 remaining in the area. As Goans have a decided preference for banking, other clerical, jazz band and chef jobs it may be surmised that they lived in the comparatively poor housing conditions of Kariakoo only for want of an alternative, and that now that alternative accommodation is fairly readily available (it is not difficult now to get a bungalow at Chang'ombe which is uncomfortably far out for many) they have moved out of Kariakoo.

The Indians of Kariakoo were nearly equally divided between Hindu and Ismaili Khoja (45 per cent. and 40 per cent. respectively), the balance being filled in with Cutchi Sunnis and Punjabi Muslims, and a few Ithnashari Khojas. The Goans were of course Christian.

The Arabs, being nearly all Hadhramis from the Eastern Aden Protectorate, were Sunnis (the only Arab Shi'as here are Kuweitis, a few of whom come down with the monsoon, but do not usually stay over like the others). There are also a few Omanis and Yemenis; many of the so-called Hadhramis (known locally as Shihiris from the coast town of Shihr) come from the Mahra coast bordering on Oman: it appears to be mainly these who have increased in the past four years, though an influx of Yemenis attempting to make their way to the motor-car factories of Coventry and Birmingham has recently become apparent.

The same questionnaire was used for the Indians and Arabs as for the Africans.

As between Hindus and Ismaili Khojas, more of the latter were born in Dar es Salaam, presumably of the adults, as there was little difference in the numbers of children. There were more than twice as many entirely uneducated Hindus as Ismailis, and the surprisingly high figure was found for Hindu males of 61 per cent. with no education whatsoever, whereas the Ismailis had only 26 per cent. in this category. This was confirmed by interviews, wherein many were encountered, particularly of the older generation, who could speak hardly a word of Swahili: the survey figure was of 21 per cent. of Hindu males literate in Swahili (Roman script) and 45 per cent. of Ismaili males. The figures were almost the same for literacy in English. In Gujerati there was a much smaller margin: 60 per cent. of Hindu men and 66 per cent. of Ismaili men were literate in this language, and a little over half that proportion, in both cases, of women. The Swahili newspapers were almost unread by Hindus, but a small number of Ismailis claimed to read them: both read the *Tanganyika Standard*, an English-language daily newspaper, much more frequently, and much the biggest group of Hindus (21 per cent.) read newspapers in their own language. The longer residence of the Ismaili families was again reflected in the figures for the presence in Dar es Salaam of parents, where they scored nearly twice as often as the Hindus, and also in the figures of individual residence, where 75 per cent. of Ismailis and only 62 per cent. of Hindus had been in Dar es Salaam for six years or more. The figure for Hindu females dropped to 28 per cent., compared to the Ismailis' 57 per cent.

There was little difference between the communities in the number of rent-paying tenants and house-owners, nor in the scale of rents paid, or the standard of accommodation, but a greater proportion of the Hindus were living in one room (here the sample was probably overbalanced by a roomful of no less than five Hindu bachelor barbers—none of whom incidentally appeared to speak any known language). The Ismaili community seemed to have a much larger share of the shop-keeping trade.

Of the 60 per cent. of the Indians who were not born in Dar es Salaam 14 per cent. were born in Zanzibar (with which several of the families have close financial links): others had been born, in descending numerical order, in Kahama, Kenya, Tabora, Kilwa, Bagamoyo, Tanga, Uganda, Moshi, Madagascar, Singida, Rufiji and Dodoma; but the biggest group of those not born in Dar es Salaam were those, 33 per cent., who were born in India.

Of the Arabs 43 per cent. claimed to have been born in Dar es

Salaam, but as illegal immigration is a live issue it is unlikely that all these were speaking the truth: many times in interviewing I was told 'I was born here, and my father before me', an instinctive reply, but after a little conversation it has appeared that they were born in the Aden Protectorate. 28 per cent. admitted to having been born in Arabia and the rest were divided among Zanzibar, Rufiji, Bagamoyo, Kenya (Mombasa and Lamu), Tabora, Kiserawe, Mafia and Lindi. A very large proportion, 60 per cent., of Arab women claimed to have been born in Dar es Salaam, and this reflects the shortage of women (one for every two men), few wives being brought here from Arabia. The normal custom is for the man to marry in Arabia and then go abroad to make his fortune, even it may be for twenty years without returning, or if he is successful he may make recurring visits home, taking with him any children whom he has begotten in this country; the 'Shihiri' does not usually enter into a marriage with an African woman, though he will often have a concubine. Those with African wives are nearly all the old Muscatis and Omanis, of the slave- and plantation-owning families, who settled finally in this country; the Shihiris, who came as porters and askaris, and latterly as traders, did not settle in the same way.

An interesting comparison is that of the means by which the sample 'first heard of the survey': no less than a quarter of the Arabs heard of it through the radio—or said they did, compared to 4 per cent. of the Indians. This is not necessarily true of course, but at least indicates the high proportion who had a radio (and, therefore, thought they ought to have heard the survey broadcast!). This confirms what is clear from observation, that every Arab shop has a radio: and most Arabs are based on a shop.

One of the surprises of this part of the survey was the very small numbers of both Arabs and Indians who owned a house: in the case of the Indians it must be partly due to the fact that this is the poorest section of the Indian community, and that it is only recently that they have felt safe in openly owning houses in an area formerly supposed to be reserved for Africans. In the case of the Arabs it is likely that the true figure is much reduced from an innate tendency to secrecy: for many houses pass from African into Arab hands by a gradual process, the Arab making an advance to finance improvements by the African owner, in return for a monthly reduction from the rent. He then lends money, or gives liberal credit in his shop, if the African is improvident or unbusinesslike, until the stage is reached when first the one or two rooms which the Arab occupies cease to yield rent, and then the whole house gradually passes into his hands. In such circumstances, although the Arab is careful to keep documentary proof of his ownership (and being a 'native' for the purpose he does not have to obtain, as an Indian does, Governor's permission for the transaction) he is usually reluctant to admit the fact to strangers. And in many other cases where the process is not complete he is correct in saying that the house still belongs to the African, although the mortgage is never likely to be paid off.

Very few fields were found to be owned by the Indians or Arabs, although most of the creek rice-fields are owned by Indians: most are owned by big property owners who live outside the areas surveyed; the same applies to the ownership of coconut plantations.

Many of the Arabs are young men or boys who are used to peddling cloths round the houses, on deferred-payment terms. The most usual system is for them to be given cloths which remain the property of the established shopkeeper, and to be fed and housed by him, and receive their rewards in a lump sum at the end of the agreed period. By so doing the young man is enabled to save up a capital sum to start up on his own; some receive assistance also from the Arab Association, but usually those who have attained to larger-scale operations. This goes some way to explain the extraordinarily rapid spread of the Arabs in the past few years, and the way in which they have taken over entirely the shopkeeping trade of all the new town-planned suburbs, where there are no overtly Indian shops and very few African indeed. They are not able to compete with the Indians in such areas as Kariakoo where they trade on equal terms, for the Indians besides having a greater business acumen have the advantage of being longer established in shops there and being able to take the steadier trade with smaller risks of bad debts; but in the peddling trade, the Arabs are supreme, despite the extreme difficulty of tracing their clients and the large number of bad debts which must ensue.

Competing with Africans the Arabs have won hands down: whereas the Arabs band together, as described above, to help the accumulation of new capital, an African shopkeeper is at the mercy of a horde of relations and friends, who expect credit (which is not easily recovered) and a share not only in the profits but in the capital stock; few are able to distinguish between what is clear profit (and which may, therefore, justifiably be spent) and what is required for the renewal of stock, and whereas the Arab grudges every cent which is spent on keeping himself alive instead of being ploughed back into the business, the African shopkeepers regard the shop, not as an end, but as a means of acquiring spending money.

When it comes to relations between the races, there is of course a wide variety of reactions, according to fortunate or unfortunate personal experience; many dislike 'the Arab' because, they say, he is hot-tempered, quarrelsome and overbearing; on the other hand there is a great deal of respect remaining, particularly in the older generation, for the older type of Arab, recalling the days when Arabs were the ruling caste. Similarly 'the Indian' is often said to be crafty, overbearing and contemptuous: yet by comparison with Arabs many find them more quietly behaved, though perhaps less accessible. Europeans most of all have the reputation of being too proud to see the earth beneath their feet: in all three cases the language barrier is a great divider. In some ways the European's love of segregating himself increases the feeling that he is over-proud, but on the other hand it tends to decrease the friction generated between African and both Indian and Arab whom he sees all day, in the areas surveyed, usually at a disadvantage. Half-castes usually take a position half-way between the two races from which they sprang, but again there is infinite variety.

APPENDIX C

RESURVEY OF MAGOMENI

A comparison of 1956 with 1959

THE original survey made in 1956/7, the statistical basis for which was collected mainly in August 1956, has been followed by what is intended to be a continuous series of re-surveys, suburb by suburb, so that comparative data may be obtained, after an interval of time, and trends revealed; the factual data will also by this method be kept up to date.

The first of these re-surveys was completed in 1959 in the suburb of Magomeni. Like the original survey, it used a 5 per cent systematic random sample, but a fresh sample was taken. The questionnaire used was the same, with a few amendments.

The suburb of Magomeni includes two large blocks of 'Swahili' type houses; a further large block of similar houses built since the 1956 survey; a smaller block of improved houses—based on the Swahili design but to an advanced standard, with the help of Government loans; a block of terraced Quarters built for the public by Government and rented through the Municipality; a small Village of houses built without a controlled layout on freehold land; and a scattered fringe of Rural houses interspersed with cultivation: all are within the Municipal boundaries, and all (except the Quarters which are owned by Government) are African-owned.

Magomeni is close to the centre of town and to places of employment; extensive building took place after 1956, mostly in the demarcated plots set aside for African building, but also in the still-rural area beyond the demarcation, where a number of houses were added to those already existing. As a result of all this building the population rose by half, from an estimated 14,340 in 1956 to 21,340 in 1959 (this estimate being made by multiplying the 5 per cent. sample by 20). This increased population is still well within the planned total for this 'neighbourhood' of 25,000.

The additional population has brought far more of a balance between the sexes, which in 1959 had almost equal numbers. This change, which may be an index of 'urbanization', or the adoption of a settled town life and an intention to remain there with one's wife and children, is reflected throughout the re-survey.

For instance the proportion of males born in Dar es Salaam, though still below that of females, rose perceptibly: by contrast that of females fell by a small margin. This pattern is repeated in the age-grouping, where the balance swung towards more children and fewer in the working-age groups—though here the picture was blurred by a change in the groups themselves, which are now designed to follow the school age-groups.

Incidentally by reinflating the sample it may be estimated that in 1959 Magomeni had 1,080 boys and 1,180 girls of primary school age; and 580 boys and 340 girls of middle school age, and that children of primary school age form just over 10 per cent. of the population: this compares with 720 school places in Magomeni itself (a number of Catholic children go across the way to Msimbazi); there is no middle school in the suburb, which feeds the middle schools elsewhere in the town.

As another index of 'urbanization' a new question was tried out; after a man's District of birth and tribe had been asked, he was then asked where was his 'real home' (in Swahili *kwenu hasa*); to this question a surprisingly large proportion, 11 per cent. of males and half as many females, gave Dar es Salaam; the proportion is surprising in that apart from the Manyema and Nubi who have lost all touch with their origins, and a few Zaramo whose ancestors were settled in or around Dar es Salaam, there is no tribe which can claim Dar es Salaam as its tribal territory.

Another somewhat surprising result was a fall in the proportion of Muslims, from four-fifths to two-thirds. This not due to a change in the religion of individuals, but in the attraction to Dar es Salaam of more educated persons and trained artisans, who tend to be Christians owing to the lead given in modern education by the Christian missions, and the suspicion with which that education was for long viewed by local Muslims. Another change was a small increase in the proportion who admitted to an ancestral religion—which is often hidden because its followers are looked on in town as unsophisticated.

The questions on education and literacy showed the expected steady progress, not so much in education beyond the first primary stage as in reducing from nearly a half to a quarter the proportion of males who had had no education whatever. Females still lagged well behind but showed a proportionate improvement. Literacy was defined at the lowest level as the ability to read or write a few words: here again there was a steady progress in Swahili (Roman script) among both males and females, but leaving vast scope still for the acquisition of literacy by nearly half the males and over three-quarters of females. An interesting sidelight is the increase in literacy in Swahili in the Arabic script (paralleled by the increase in those educated at Koranic schools) which is taught particularly on the coast and to those south of Dar es Salaam. Literacy in

English reached the respectable figure of 11 per cent. of males, but this time none were found literate in Arabic.

A further index of 'urbanization' is the question as to the where-abouts of the parents of the person questioned. This question showed a small but definite increase in the proportion whose parents (if still alive) were in Dar es Salaam, more particularly the parents of males, and fathers rather than mothers: this again goes to show a steady increase in the numbers who have chosen a settled family life in town.

This is supported by the table of years of residence in Dar es Salaam (ignoring periods away). As before there was a slight hump of newcomers—since the suburb is still expanding—but an even greater concentration, rising from half in 1956 to getting on for two-thirds in those resident for over five years.

Another series of questions was addressed only to the heads of 'households', defined as a single person or group which fends for itself—the head of a household being the one who either pays the rent or finds free accommodation for others in his 'household'. These heads of households (which of course include a number of single persons) were again predominantly male, though the pre-dominance was slightly reduced.

The ownership of houses in Dar es Salaam is another index of the extent to which a family settles in and sees its future in town: here there were conflicting changes, a slight increase in the pro-portion of males who owned houses but a big decrease in the proportion of females (the sample of female heads of households was, however, a small one). But the proportion of households which owned their own house remained low. This is hardly sur-prising as many of the better-off live in the rented Quarters, and the less well-off find it hard to obtain the capital for building. Moreover the better-educated, who have the larger salaries, are most often from other parts of the country, and if they have the intention to build a house, prefer to do so in their home areas.

Another change was the decrease in the proportion of households which paid rent. From four-fifths it dropped to two-thirds. Once again two-thirds of those who did not pay rent owned their own house, but there was a steep rise in the proportion living free with a relative (it should be remembered that these questions were answered only by head of households so that it excluded from the reckoning any of their dependants: thus it is a whole household which is given free accommodation by a relative). If this meant that those who have built new houses in Magomeni had found is best to accommodate their relatives, without payment, this may have good social results, provided that the converse economic result—that houses cease to be an economic investment—can be overcome.

The composition of the households themselves showed little change, though there was a slight swing towards the larger households of five or six persons. The single male or female remained— just—the biggest group, though now closely followed by the two-person household.

The question which sought to know the relationship to each other of the members of the household was changed between the survey and re-survey, so that no direct comparison can be made: all that can be said is that the single person, a man and his wife, or a man, his wife and a child, are by far the most common combinations: a somewhat unexpectedly large group was of persons outside the close relatives, but members of the same clan.

One of the surprises of the 1956 survey was that in every suburb and in every wage-group the 10–15 Shs. rent group was the largest. Despite the better type of house put up in Magomeni in the interval this rent is still twice as common as the next above (16–20 Shs.) and nearly eight times as common as the group above that (21–25 Shs.). A welcome trend was a decrease in the proportion paying the lowest rents (under 10 Shs.) which indicates a reduced use of the smaller courtyard rooms for renting.

Again much the most common accommodation is a single room, whether the household owns or rents its accommodation; but there has been a levelling-off, so that now little more than three-quarters of the households live in one room each, with a large increase in the proportion using two and three. This again is an indication that people are beginning to settle in with their families, and beginning to live on a permanent basis and, therefore, demand the two or three rooms which they customarily build for themselves in rural areas, instead of being content with temporary 'digs' in a single room. To some extent, however, it reflects the existence of a number of unfinished main houses, the family living temporarily in what will later become courtyard rooms.

A most encouraging trend, emphasized by the extent of the new building of 'Swahili' type houses, is the much higher proportion of houses of the better type. While the proportion of rooms with whitewashed walls went up by three-quarters, those with a cement floor had a spectacular increase, by more than three times; the smaller number with piped water increased proportionately, and there was a substantial increase in the proportion roofed with some non-inflammable material, usually corrugated iron. By contrast there was still no increase in the proportion with electricity, or those having a separate latrine. This is a fair indication of the priorities as seen by the African house-owners—and their tenants who now have some margin of choice. It indicates also how rents, while they have edged slightly upwards in the three years, are lower in real terms since far more amenities are provided. The decrease in the proportion of households renting the cheapest rooms shows that this increase in the amenities provided, even if the rent rises slightly, is in line with the tenants' demands, and reflects a general increase in material standards of living.

Another, though not very reliable, index of 'urbanization' is the number of people who, while living in the town, retain land under cultivation either on the town fringes or in a not-too-distant home area. The comparison shows a distinct drop in the proportion cultivating land within the Municipal boundaries, and also, among males, in those cultivating land elsewhere: by contrast there was a slight rise in the proportion of females cultivating elsewhere—and presumably coming to town between planting, weeding and harvest. This is practicable for those living on the Rufiji and in the Morogoro or Bagamoyo areas. The cultivation in Dar es Salaam was mainly done by the persons questioned themselves, but 14 per cent. employed persons outside their own family to do it for them. Even the up-country fields were in 5 per cent. of the cases cultivated by persons outside the family, but it is interesting to note that whereas a third had the up-country field cultivated by a member of the family, none cultivated so in the town. This could mean that fields in town are cultivated for themselves by individuals, perhaps by older people as their main source of income, and that the urban wife does not go out to cultivate.

Another index of 'urbanization' is the question designed to show the gaps in 'years of residence': do people go away to visit their areas of origin for long periods, or do they pay short visits, or have they cut themselves off entirely? Those who had paid a visit away of up to a month during the past three years were again about a third of males, but the proportion of females had risen considerably: this could perhaps be explained by the recent increase in the female population, particularly perhaps in those from Morogoro and the Southern Province who like to return home to bear children. Those who had paid a visit away of one year during their stay in Dar es Salaam, on the other hand, showed a decrease to under half: this decrease is probably in the group who like to do a spell in town followed by a fairly prolonged spell at home, before going to town once again, those termed the 'spenders' in the original survey.

Coming then to questions concerning employment, the first question, aimed to measure 'unemployment' (a term which in the African urban context requires close definition), is blurred owing to a change in the form of the question. It was found in the 1956 survey that few of those in casual employment could remember what jobs they had had during the preceding month; so the question was narrowed to employment during the preceding *day*. With the question so phrased, there was a small apparent rise in the proportion of males gainfully employed: but as the comparison is further blurred by a change in the age-groups, cutting out those aged 16 and 17, no great reliance can be placed on this increase.

In the somewhat arbitrary grouping into types of work there was an increase in the proportion of small traders and of clerks, at the expense of the 'skilled' (that is, roughly, the artisan group). An increase in small traders can usually be taken as a sign of increased under-employment, since hawking and peddling are the standard expedients of those unable to find paid employment.

This increase in small traders was spread among a number of small trades: compared with the rather small sample in 1956 there were some changes in relative popularity: for instance the most popular in 1956, tea-vendor, did not appear at all in the 1959 list; fish-sellers, second in 1956, had reached the top of the list and were now 2 per cent. of all workers; water-sellers (who take tins of water at 1 cent a tin from the public kiosks and sell it at the door for 15 cents a tin in the centre of the town or 10 cents further out) had jumped from obscurity to equal second place with fruit-sellers—a sign of increased sophistication and affluence on the part of householders who prefer to buy their water at the door at fifteen times the kiosk price a hundred yards away. Another disappearance from the lists was the charcoal-sellers, but they were replaced by the firewood-sellers, who like the coconut-sellers formed 1 per cent. of all workers.

A gap in 1956 was filled when a shop-owner and a transporter appeared for the first time, classed as 'large traders'.

Among the 'semi-skilled', who retained their 1956 proportion of all workers, the messengers (or office boys) once again headed the list by a long way, though they formed a smaller proportion of all workers. But second came some newcomers to the top of the list, the sanitary labourers, who tied with garden boys and constables (there is a Police post in the suburb). Turnboys (drivers' assistants) and foremen lost ground, and herdsmen gained—employed in the dairies on the rural fringes.

Clerks, who outnumbered shop assistants in their group by three to one, were (after the unskilled) the biggest single group of workers, at 7 per cent.

Of the 'skilled', whose proportion of all workers decreased between 1956 and 1959, the biggest decrease was among dockers: here there had been a change from mainly casual to mainly monthly labour (which is reflected in the tables for daily and monthly wages), with the result that the pool of dockers was much reduced; as Magomeni is a favourite suburb for dockers, and particularly for the type of casual docker who in 1956 averaged only 17 shifts a month, it has reflected this change. Another group to lose ground was the masons (reflecting the end of the building boom); trades which gained were the carpenters (who now head the list bracketed with dockers), smiths and electricians—mainly linesmen.

In 1956 the question designed to show how long a worker remained in the same job (and hence the possibilities for training and advancement) was misunderstood and yielded no good results. There is, therefore, no comparison in this table, but the 1959 results show a very even spread over the years, the largest group being those who had been in the job for between one and six months. 11 per cent. had been in the same job for over ten years, and nearly a third for over five years. The stabilizing of the labour force and the stabilizing of family life in town are of course interconnected, and future trends in this table will be important.

In tabling the places of work the main change encountered was a steep increase in the proportion who worked in Magomeni itself, presumably the small traders, since there are no large places of employment there apart from two dairies. Once again the bulk worked in the Commercial Area (what might be called, as in Zanzibar, the Stone Town); after Magomeni itself the third largest group worked in the industrial estate along the Pugu road and Chang'ombe. The laying-off of casual dockers was reflected in a decrease in those working at the docks. The increase in small traders, too, was reflected not only in the proportion of those working in Magomeni but in a new group of peripatetic workers. Decreases were shown in the group who worked 'elsewhere' (mainly Upanga but also in the Stirling Astaldi road camp), and in Kinondoni and Oyster Bay (domestic servants). These reflect a falling off in construction work, and the cutting down of domestic staffs as wages have risen.

The questions concerning actual and preferred paydays were repeated, but in an amplified form, with the result that comparison was not easy. There was a fall in the proportion of daily paid owing to the decrease in the number of casual dockers, who form the largest block in this group. The amplified question brought out that the biggest group was of those paid on a monthly basis but with a right to an advance at mid-month; these outnumbered by a small margin those paid on a monthly basis in one lump sum, who were the next largest group. The third considerable group was of those paid by a weekly advance (mostly an advance on a work-card, but also to some paid on a monthly basis). The amplified question on preference showed a surprising preference for having a full half of the wage at mid-month (and not, as was previously thought, an advance of rather less than half, leaving a margin for lump-sum purchases at the end of the month). The lesser mid-month advance was preferred by a smaller group than those preferring a weekly advance or a single monthly payment. It is noticeable that although half the wage at mid-month is by far the most popular method of receiving wages, very few indeed (only 1 per cent.) are actually being paid in this way at present.

Of the sample of workers half were paid on a monthly basis, the other half being divided almost equally between self-employed and daily paid. In the tables of wages, both daily paid and monthly paid showed a marked shift upwards between 1956 and 1959. Among the daily paid this shift was masked to some extent by the departure of the casual dockers, who were among the most highly paid of daily paid. Nearly three-quarters had been in this group, receiving 7 Shs. a shift in 1956. But now that most dockers are on a monthly basis the emphasis has moved to the unskilled labourer, and the rise in his wage is marked, the most common wage having risen from 2 Shs. to 4 Shs. a day; the 1956 figures were obtained before the imposition of a statutory minimum wage of 43 cents an hour, yet curiously enough it is the 1959 figures which show a higher proportion in the lowest wage-groups, with 5 per cent. still getting less than 2 Shs. a day. Some of these are clearly odd-job men who may unload only a single lorry in the day and are in fact paid by the job rather than by the day. The other noticeable change in the wages of the daily paid is the extension upwards, above 7 Shs. a day, with some receiving as much as 20 Shs. a day (these top wages were paid by an immigrant construction firm to artisans); altogether more than four times as many were in receipt of over 7 Shs. a day as in 1956.

Among the larger group of monthly paid the effect of the minimum wage is more easily visible; those receiving 75 Shs. a month or less were reduced to less than a quarter of their previous proportion. In this group too the marked shift upwards is to be seen both in the higher 'modal' wage—the most common group—which shifted from the 76–90 Shs. group to the 91–120 Shs. group; and in the extension upwards beyond 210 Shs., where twice as many earned wages in this range as before, up to an 'over 600 Shs.' group, and examples were found in every group including the highest.

As regards receipts other than cash, only a small proportion, mostly dockers and domestic servants, received free food, but a surprisingly large proportion, over a quarter, received free uniforms or working clothes.

The ownership of means of transport is an early indication of increasing affluence; however, no comparison is possible because the form of the question was changed to make it more precise. In 1959 workers were asked whether, on the day they were questioned, they owned cycles, mopeds, motor-cycles or cars (whereas in 1956 they were asked how they got to work at around payday, and around the 21st of the month, the times of highest and lowest liquidity). The figure of 15 per cent. cycle owners given in 1959 will be of greater interest when it can be compared with figures obtained in Magomeni in 1964. As yet only half of 1 per cent. owned a moped, and no owners of motor-cycles or cars were netted by the sample of 360 workers.

From work the questions passed on to more domestic matters, and recorded a small swing away from the use of kerosene for cooking, towards the almost universal firewood. This is to some extent a reflection of the decrease in the preponderance of single men and women, who often use a primus as being quicker and more convenient, though more expensive, than firewood.

Next the 1959 re-survey attacked once again the elusive question of 'marriage', within which term may come a number of definitions which are not easily separable. However, without inquiring too closely whether the 'marriage' was one celebrated with full religious or customary rite, or a casual union, or something between, the comparison shows, despite a difference in the age-groups, a definite decrease in the proportion of single persons, both male and female; however, this is accompanied by a small but discernible increase in the proportion of second and third marriages. It is possible, therefore, that the figures show only an increase in casual unions and a decrease in the proportion of persons who consider these not to be marriage. This is a question which can only be answered by far more lengthy inquiries than are possible in an enumerative survey of a large sample. But in 1959 a new question was introduced in an attempt to throw some light on it, by measuring the length of time during which such unions had been in force, and the answers show that the great majority of those 'married' had been living together for over a year—a period long enough to be more than a merely casual union. Another factor to be borne in mind is that frequent divorces and remarriages are characteristic of the coastal people in rural as well as urban communities; even so the apparent doubling of the proportion of females married three times or more is striking. This is repeated in the table of divorces, but this table shows that although divorce is still much more frequent among

U

females (indicating a resident force of wives who periodically change hands), there has been a most marked increase in the proportion of males divorced, who were tripled. One result of such numerous divorces is the disturbance to the upbringing of the children, and here it is noticeable that most of such broken marriages had already borne children. It is clear from these results that the instability of marriage in this coastal town remains an unsolved problem.

Finally the table showing the proportion of married women who had borne children was virtually unchanged; once again a quarter had borne no children; once again between half and two-thirds had borne no children in Dar es Salaam, and once again half had no children with them now in Dar es Salaam.

In sum this comparison at a three-year interval of time, of a suburb where new housing, owned and largely built by Africans mainly on traditional lines, has raised the population by half, shows a number of significant trends: higher standards of housing (induced not by controls and only partly by official loans) with little movement of rents; an evening-up of the disparity between the sexes—never as marked in Dar es Salaam as in some other large towns—and a move towards family living and a reduction in the disproportion of men of working age; but a contrary increase in the instability of marriage; a slow but steady raising of a low standard in education and literacy; reduced opportunity for employment in construction and in the docks; and a marked shift upward in wages.

It is a picture of general material progress, and the beginnings of an urban nucleus: but there is no sign of the solution of the moral and social problems arising from the unfamiliarity with town life of those, the majority, brought up in a traditional rural community.

APPENDIX D

SOME USEFUL SOURCES

Townsmen in the Making, by A. W. Southall and P. C. W. Gutkind (East African Studies No. 9, East African Institute of Social Research, Kampala, Uganda, 1957).

Some Problems of Social Survey in the Sudan, by G. M. Culwick.

Jinja Transformed, by C. and R. Sofer (East African Studies No. 4, East African Institute of Social Research, Kampala, Uganda, 1955).

East African Royal Commission, 1953–55, Cmd. 9475 (H.M. Stationery Office, 1955).

Report on the Census of the Non-African Population taken on the Night of 13th February 1952 (Government Printer, Dar es Salaam, Tanganyika, 1954).

Report on the Census of the African Population taken in August, 1957 (Government Printer, Dar es Salaam, Tanganyika).

Patterns of Income, Expenditure and Consumption of African Labourers in Dar es Salaam, 1948 (East African Statistical Department, Nairobi, Kenya).

Budget Survey, Dar es Salaam, 1957 (East African Statistical Department, unpublished).

Social Conditions of Dar es Salaam, 1931 and 1939, by E. C. Baker (unpublished).

'Nyakyusa Labour Migration', by P. H. Gulliver, in *Human Problems in British Central Africa* (Rhodes-Livingstone Journal, No. 21, 1957, Rhodes-Livingstone Institute, Lusaka, Northern Rhodesia).

Economics of Detribalisation in Northern Rhodesia, by G. Wilson (Rhodes-Livingstone Papers, Nos. 5 and 6, Rhodes-Livingstone Institute, Lusaka, Northern Rhodesia, 1941 and 1942).

Report on a Proposal to Establish an Institute of Social Research at Makerere and on Social Science Research in Uganda and Tanganyika, by W. E. H. Stanner (Colonial Office, 1949).

District Team Minutes (Dar es Salaam, Tanganyika, 1955, unpublished).

Political and Social Aspects of the Development of Municipal Government in Kenya with Special Reference to Nairobi, by M. Parker (Colonial Office, n.d.).

Enquiry into African Land Holdings near Dar es Salaam, 1929 by H. McCleery (District Office, Dar es Salaam).

U*

The Urban Social Survey in the Colonies, by L. Silberman (Report for Colonial Social Science Research Council, 1950).

Labour Conditions in East Africa, by G. St. J. Orde Browne (Colonial Office, H.M. Stationery Office, 1946).

'The Role of African Courts in Urban Communities of the Northern Rhodesian Copperbelt', by A. L. Epstein, in *Human Problems in British Central Africa* (Rhodes-Livingstone Journal, No. 13, Rhodes-Livingstone Institute, Lusaka, Northern Rhodesia, 1953).

'An Estimate of Fertility among Africans on the Copperbelt of Northern Rhodesia', by J. C. Mitchell, in *Human Problems in British Central Africa* (Rhodes-Livingstone Journal, No. 13, Rhodes-Livingstone Institute, Lusaka, Northern Rhodesia, 1953).

'British Divorce Law and Stability of Marriage, Northern Rhodesia', by A. L. Epstein, in *Human Problems in British Central Africa*, Journal No. 14, 1954.

Distribution of African Labour by Area of Origin, Northern Rhodesia (Rhodes Livingstone Papers).

Relational Patterns of Kampala, Uganda, by E. S. Munger, Review of, by J. C. Mitchell in *Rhodes-Livingstone Journal*, No. 15, 1954.

Two Studies of African Nutrition: an Urban and a Rural Community, by B. Preston Thomson (Rhodes-Livingstone Papers, No. 24, Rhodes-Livingstone Institute, Lusaka, Northern Rhodesia, 1954).

'Social Survey of the Old Town of Mombasa', by L. Silberman (*Journal of African Administration* vol. 2, 1950).

African Housing in Nairobi, by T. G. Askwith (Government Printer, Nairobi, Kenya).

Detribalisation, by M. J. B. Molohan (Government Printer, Dar es Salaam, Tanganyika, 1957).

Report of Committee on Employment of Juveniles, Kenya, 1938 (Government Printer, Nairobi, Kenya).

Minutes of Dar es Salaam Vagrancy Committee, 1957 (unpublished).

Housing of Africans in Urban Areas in Kenya, 1954 (Government Printer, Nairobi, Kenya).

Report on Employment and Wages in Kenya, 1954 (Government Printer, Nairobi, Kenya).

Earnings of African Labour in November, 1948, Kenya (Government Printer, Nairobi, Kenya).

The Psychology of Mau Mau, by Dr. J. C. Corothers, 1954 (Government Printer, Nairobi, Kenya).

Report of the Committee on Cost of Living, Nairobi, 1954 (Government Printer, Nairobi, Kenya).

Committee on Constitutional Development; Evidence and Memoranda, 1950 (unpublished: Office of Prime Minister, Dar es Salaam).

Native Courts Memoranda, 1955 (Government Printer, Dar es Salaam, Tanganyika).

Nairobi City Council Reorganisation, 1955 (unpublished).

Nairobi Ward Councils Constitution, 1955 (unpublished).

A Study of the Social Background of Young Children in Nairobi, Department of African Affairs (Government Printer, Nairobi, Kenya).

Notes on a Visit to Elisabethville and Ndola, by C. C. Harris (unpublished).

Royal Commission, 1953–1955—Observations by Tanganyika Government (Government Printer, Dar es Salaam, Tanganyika).

Rooiyard: A Sociological Survey of an Urban Native Slum Yard, by E. Hellman (Rhodes-Livingstone Papers, No. 13, Rhodes-Livingstone Institute, Lusaka, Northern Rhodesia, 1948).

African Life in an Urban Area (Bulawayo), by B. W. Gussman (Parts 1 and 2) (Federation of African Welfare Societies, Bulawayo, Southern Rhodesia, 1952).

Bantu Bureaucracy, by L. A. Fallers (Heffers, Cambridge, for East African Institute of Social Research, 1956).

Economic Development and Tribal Change, edited by A. I. Richards (Heffers, Cambridge, for East African Institute of Social Research, 1955).

Hadhramaut, by W. H. Ingrams (Col. 123, H.M. Stationery Office, 1937).

'Dar es Salaam under the Sultans of Zanzibar', by Sir John Gray (*Tanganyika Notes and Records* No. 33, July 1952).

'The Joking Relationship (utani) in Tanganyika', by R. E. Moreau (*Tanganyika Notes and Records*, No. 12, 1941).

'Joking Relationships in Central Africa', by P. H. Gulliver (Letter in *Man*, November 1957).

Report of the Census of the Non-Native Population taken on the Night of 25th February 1948 (Government Printer, Dar es Salaam, Tanganyika, 1953).

African Population of Tanganyika Territory: Geographical and Tribal Studies (source, East African Population Census 1948) (East African Statistical Department, Nairobi, Kenya, 1950).

Census of the Native Population of Tanganyika Territory, 1931 (Government Printer, Dar es Salaam, Tanganyika, 1932).

Annual Reports: Departments of Town Planning, Development, Treatment of Offenders, Public Relations (Tanganyika Government Department Reports, Government Printer, Dar es Salaam): Departments of Probation Service, City Council (Kenya, Government Printer, Nairobi).

INDEX

Abercorn, 129
Acacia Avenue, 113, 186
Aden Protectorate, 278
Administration, 9; in Swahili houses, 166; general, 183–91
African Housing in Nairobi, by T. G. Askwith, 292
African Life in an Urban Area (Bulawayo), by B. W. Gussman, 293
African Population of Tanganyika Territory: Geographical and Tribal Studies, 293
Africans, increasing population of, 1, 88, 152; reasons for coming, 1–2, 23–31, 104–5; loneliness of, 1; frustration of, 4, 105–9; hunger of, 4, 115–16; as houseowners, 9, 153, 154–5, 167–8, 178; in Municipal Council, 9, 183–191; as object of survey, 17–18; in Swahili houses, 78, 176; fellow feeling of, 102; as shopowners, 126, 279; prospects of, 130; in trade, 136–7; using pawnshops, 144; in Kariakoo, 172
African Urban Housing Loans Fund, 156
Akida, 183
Akida Askara, and offspring, 99–100
Ali Magurumbasi, elder of Ngoni, 45, 46, 63, 97–8
amorality, in marital relations, 12; in criminal sector, 15; among children, 15; general, 209–10, 236–7, 239
Annual Reports, various, 293
Arab Association, 279
Arabia, 78, 278
Arab Street, 47
Arabic language 48, 80, 217; script, 77, 282
Arabs, controlling radio, 10, 199; Hadhrami, 20, 276; in Interlude, 191–200; Omani, 20, 199; numbers of, 21, 275–80; migrant, 35; as protectors of Manyema and Sudanese tribes, 48; in Swahili houses, 77–80, 176; loans from, 85; in Mikorosheni, 96; rich, 106; clothes of, 110–12; in trade, 136–7, 142, 279; using pawnshops, 144; in Kariakoo, 171, 172, 279; in Buguruni, 179–83; Islam among, 213–14; prostitutes among, 232, 233; owning houses, 278–9; reputation of, 280

Arab 'tribe', in Appendix A, 273
Arnautoglu Community Centre, 269–270
artisans, education of, 6; wages of, 119, 140; in Quarters, 174, 176, 258; owning houses, 179; in Magomeni resurvey, 286
Asians, overcrowding among, 8; as shopowners, 126; in Kariakoo, 172; in Interlude, 191–3
Askari statue, 47, 168
askaris, British and German, 37; Sudanese, 47, 48; Shihiri, 99; German, 49, 98; 164
Askwith, T. G., author of *African Housing in Nairobi*, 292
Asmani Kumra, 35
Asmani Singasinga, a Mwera, 65
Associations, tribal, 39–57
Azania Front, 186, 238

Bagamoyo, loss of population in, 1, 22; Hindu traders from, 21; *utani* in, 33; outlet to sea diverted from, 34; Doe of, 40; old part of, 41; Ngoni in, 45; landlord of Swahili house from, 76; Digo from, 90; fish from, 135; Islam in, 211; 277, 278, 285
Bagamoyo Street, 47, 168, 205, 240
Baker, E. C., author of *Social Conditions of Dar es Salaam, 1931 and 1939*, 291
Bakari Salum, Imam, 49
Baluchi, 99
Bantu Bureaucracy, by L. A. Fallers, 293
Bantu, Conservatism, 12, 215; magic beliefs, 15, 241; converts to Islam, 213; Christian leaders against, 216
bao, 101, 197, 269
Baragumu, 197
Barawa tribe, in Appendix A, 274
baraza, 71, 75, 199
barua, 223
'baswezi', 94
Bembe tribe, 34
Bena tribe, 36, 37; in Appendix A, 273
Binti Madenge, of Buguruni, 66
Bisa tribe, 80; in Appendix A, 273
'Boma', the, 48, 186, 193
Bondei tribe, 35, 36, 37, 41; in Appendix A, 273
Bori dance, 48
bride-price, 12, 13
bride-wealth, 223–7